ANGEL OF THE GHETTO

ONE MAN'S TRIUMPH OVER HEARTBREAKING TRAGEDY

SAM SOLASZ

WITH JUDY KATZ

"In the face of suffering, one has no
right to turn away, not to see."

—Elie Wiesel (1928-2016), survivor, author, Nobel laureate.

ANGEL OF THE GHETTO
One Man's Triumph Over Heartbreaking Tragedy

SAM SOLASZ with Judy Katz

Published by New Voices Press
315 West 70th Street, Suite 6C
New York, NY 10023
212-580-8833

For permission to reprint material from this book please contact Judy Katz at judy@katzcreativebooksandmedia.com or call 212-580-8833.

Library of Congress Cataloguing-in-Publication Data
ANGEL OF THE GHETTO
One Man's Triumph Over Heartbreaking Tragedy
SAM SOLASZ with Judy Katz
Published by New Voices Press
ISBN: 978-0-9883591-3-0

1. Holocaust. 2. History-Jewish. 3. World War Two. 4. Founding of Israel.
5. Immigration. 6. Biographies and Memoirs. 7. Entrepreneurship.

Cover and Interior design by Tony Iatridis
Creative input and research by Ramona Flood
Line editing by Bonnie Egan
Editorial assistance by Layla Baez
Back cover headshot photographed by TJ Jeong
Solasz family at Sam and Rose's 60th Anniversary 6/24/17. Photo by TJ Jeong

This book is dedicated...

To my wonderful wife Rose.
To Diane and her husband Matt.
To Scott and his wife Flor.
To Mark and his wife Corie.
To all of our beloved grandchildren.

And, last but not least, I am telling my story for
my lost family, and for the millions of brave souls
who lost their lives to the Nazi murderers.

Sam Solasz
Queens, New York
January 2018

TABLE OF CONTENTS

Foreword: An Ordinary House on a Quiet Street 1

1. The Sky Turned Firebomb Red 5

2. Forced From Home 15

3. A Barrel and a Tire 27

4. The Angel of the Ghetto 37

5. The Underground, Spies, and The Bialystok Uprising 51

6. The Treblinka Death Train 61

7. The Polish Farmhouse 69

8. A Bittersweet Liberation 79

9. Return to Knyszyn and Hunting Landmines 89

10. Life in the DP Camp 107

Photos 119

11. Helping Palestine to Become Israel 131

12. A Long Journey to a New Life 147

13. A Rocky Ride to a Very Big Voyage 165

14. Finding Solid Footing in My New Country 177

15. Attaining the American Dream 189

16. The Rise of Master Purveyors 207

17. Poland: A Complicated Homecoming 225

Author's Afterword 241

Acknowledgements 243

Foreword

An Ordinary House on a Quiet Street:
Home to a Special Man and his Family

Picture this: a modest ranch on a corner lot, an unassuming house, like many others in the close-knit, largely Jewish community of Hollis Hills in Queens, New York. Inside this house is where Sam Solasz and his wife Rose raised their three wonderful children, Diane, Scott and Mark, who have all become exceptional individuals, now with families of their own, and who possess fine character, love of family, love of community, honor of their heritage, respect Jewish tradition and are dedicated to Jewish culture and education.

Sam came to America with nothing but ten dollars in his pocket and his butchering skills. Through his hard work and honorable work ethic Sam built an extremely successful business, *Master Purveyors*. And with his sons Mark and Scott by his side, they have put the company at the top by supplying the best restaurants with the best meats. *Top Quality* has always been Sam's hallmark and the key to his success.

Sam is not a flashy man. He lives rather simply. After gaining business success, he and Rose could have moved their family to a grander house, anywhere they wished. However, they chose to remain in Hollis Hills to continue raising their family, and became an integral part of the community. For many years Sam served on the Board of Directors of our synagogue, the *Hollis Hills Jewish Center (now Hollis Hills Bayside Jewish Center)* and he and Rose were honored as *Couple Of The Year*. Many years later, bringing us to recent years, their son Mark Solasz was honored at our synagogue with an *Award for Continuing Education* (the apple does not fall far from the tree). Sam and his sons work 80 hours a

1

week. At 89 Sam is still going strong. The Solasz men do not get much sleep as they start their workday in the middle of the night, but they work together, have each other's backs and have a magical spirit!

Let me go back in time to help explain why I am in awe of Sam Solasz and how he is a great inspiration to me and to so many. As a youth, Sam witnessed and experienced the evil and frightening rise of the Nazi party and then the Nazi rule. Yet his unimaginable strength and courage allowed him to survive, while his entire family perished. Over the years I have had the privilege of hearing Sam's story as we sat together and talked for so many hours over time, and I found myself captivated by his every word. I knew how difficult it was for him to talk about it. What he went through was unthinkable. You see, Sam is not only a member of my synagogue but he is also my dear friend, and I was honored that he shared his life's story with me. It also fascinated me to observe Sam when he meets up with someone who likewise came from Poland, perhaps his same town or a nearby town. He is immediately drawn to them and they start to talk and remember.

Sam was not in a death camp, but he came dangerously close. As a boy Sam lived in a small, mostly Jewish, Polish town. His father, a butcher by profession, was a popular and outgoing jack-of-all-trades. Sam was the second youngest of 11 children. He was ultimately the only member of his family who did not perish in the Treblinka extermination camp, nor shot to death and buried in the Babi Yar massacre, as were his two sisters.

Growing up in Knyszyn (KIN-UH-SHEN) in the northeastern corner of Poland, young Sam saw how vicious people could become. As he grew into his teenage years, he witnessed hatred, inhumanity and betrayal, not only by the Nazis, which came later, but at first it was the betrayal of neighbors and friends who came to support the Third Reich. As he soon realized, even those he had trusted and considered his friends had succumbed to a dark side and turned on him, his family and his people. To Sam it seemed that almost everyone around him had given in to a common insanity.

Just as he lived through the intense rise of anti-Semitism in his hometown and surrounding towns, he also lived through the creation of the ghetto in the nearby city of Bialystok, and then experienced the historic three-day Uprising in the Bialystok Ghetto and its tragic, blood-soaked end. It was in the Bialystok Ghetto that Sam Solasz came to be known as "The Angel of the Ghetto." His bravery and determination took over as he would sneak in and out of the Bialystok Ghetto multiple times each day, for years, risking his life to find food and anything else that might help.

This is just one part of Sam's remarkable story. He ultimately jumped from the speeding cattle car train that was transporting him to Treblinka, running 20 miles an hour with unimaginable courage. Sam was able to save himself from the Treblinka extermination camp and survive.

Sam found his way to America with nothing but the 10 dollars in his pocket. That was money the ever-resourceful Sam earned cutting meat aboard the army ship that brought him to New York as a displaced person and a true survivor, seeking a new beginning. He and Rose met in 1957 while ice-skating at Madison Square Garden and with Rose, Sam found a new start, a beautiful family and a beautiful life.

Sam Solasz wants to share his story with all of us and with the world. And while it is not really possible to put ourselves in Sam's shoes and fully comprehend the depths of what he experienced, reading this book will allow us to feel and bear witness to his story. This book is about Sam's journey. He is a survivor, he is a good man, a loving husband, father and grandfather and he is my friend.

Come meet Sam, in an ordinary house on a quiet street, in a country where he found freedom and a beautiful life. Sam's story is one you will never forget.

Sol Zim

Sol Zim, Cantor at the Hollis Hills Bayside Jewish Center, has been a close friend to Sam and Rose Solasz for the past 50 years. Zim is a world-renowned Master Cantor, Composer, Songwriter, Recording Artist, Concert Performer, Educator/Professor and Lecturer.

"I don't believe that the big men, the politicians and the capitalists alone are guilty of the war. Oh, no, the little man is just as keen, otherwise the people of the world would have risen in revolt long ago! There is an urge and rage in people to destroy, to kill, to murder, and until all mankind, without exception, undergoes a great change, wars will be waged, everything that has been built up, cultivated and grown, will be destroyed and disfigured, after which mankind will have to begin all over again."

—*Anne Frank (1929-1945), globally beloved Holocaust diarist.*

1

The Sky Turned Firebomb Red
Evil Burns in Broad Daylight

Time can ease painful memories but it can never totally heal the cell-deep trauma. I have lots of memories from my boyhood in Poland, some good, and many others living nightmares. For many years I have resisted telling my entire story, because I did not want to reactivate those disturbing shadows and ghosts. And, why impose them on others? Mainly, I didn't want to reexamine the horrors one human can inflict on another, or how entire nations can descend into savagery. But now, with the final pages of my life turning quickly, I must write down what I experienced and bear witness to what must never be forgotten. I must add my voice to the historical record in support of the millions who perished needlessly, only to feed the megalomania of the few.

My early childhood was spent in a little town called Knyszyn in northeastern Poland, about 16 miles from the much larger city of Bialystok, and was largely peaceful. I was the 11th child in the Solasz family. My father was married twice, and we were seven brothers and four sisters. When the youngest child, a boy, died in infancy, I became the youngest by default. My given name was Moishe. Later I would also take the name Schlomo, my dead baby brother's name, to escape the Gestapo officers who were searching for me under my original name, which is Morris in English.

My grandfathers were both religious leaders. My parents, though not overly religious, observed the Jewish traditions. They were devoted to each other and taught us to be proud that we were Jews. As you can imagine, with such a large family, my parents were always busy, so there wasn't much time for casual chitchat—very different from today. As a kid I sometimes accompanied my father to his work. He was a skilled butcher and worked mainly in nearby Bialystok. I was excited to go with him because I loved the bustling airs, the crowds, the horses and wagons, the city smells and sounds. Very early on I was attracted to city life, exploring every nook and cranny. Today my wife Rose says I have an unusual memory. It's true. For some reason, every street I've ever been to, the dates I visited those streets, as well as everything that happened there, remain etched in my mind. That sort of recall is definitely a mixed blessing. There are many things I wish I *could* forget.

My father was a hard-working man, and back home my mother was constantly cooking and cleaning. She also enjoyed doing things outside the home. When she had a free moment she attended plays at the Yiddish theater or spent social time with other ladies in our town. I often think of my mother in the kitchen preserving cabbage and cucumbers with salt, as women did then, or making brisket. I can almost smell those special aromas. When I was on my best behavior she'd cook sweet noodle kugel and potato latkes for me. That was always a special treat, because she knew how much I loved them. Sometimes the youngest kid gets special privileges.

I went to *Chabad*—religious school—from age nine to eleven, but then the war broke out, and there was no more school. In fact, I only had two years of formal school—but still I made my way in life. In my free time I played with my brothers, sisters, and the neighborhood kids—including Christian kids. I also used to carve toys out of wood. My strongest memories of my childhood were the Jewish holidays. They were special times our family spent together. When we walked to Shul I'd tease my slightly older sister and pull her hair, which I thought was funny. On Yom Kippur, after we broke the fast, all the kids would race over to our neighbor's house, where we knew we would be offered warm ginger cakes to eat. That was always a special treat somewhere.

When I was growing up, Knyszyn was a prosperous place. World War I was behind us and World War II was not yet on the horizon. The grown-ups undoubtedly knew of the Weimar Republic and the growing power of Hitler, but we kids were in our cocoons. Our town was also a very Jewish place. Poland had always had the biggest Jewish population in Europe, and our culture was deep.

In fact, the town had five kosher restaurants and two kosher food stores. I would hang out with my friends at the bakeries and the carbonated water shop—all Jewish-owned. Jews owned three mills, a leather goods shop, and a gas station. The richest man in town was Jewish. I don't know how he made his money, but he had the biggest house in town and people said he was very rich. That was the reality of our town. As far as I could tell, my father was well liked and respected by all our neighbors, including the Christians, or so it seemed to me as a boy.

At the same time, although Jews carried on their daily lives, buying staples at the market, baking challah, celebrating the big and small things in life, I can't honestly tell you that Knyszyn was an untroubled place during the thirties. A strong thread of anti-Semitism ran through the Polish people. In the summer, Polish boys, who were mostly Catholic, came out of their churches and taunted us Jews as "Christ killers" and threw rocks at our houses and into our shuls. This was even before the Nazis institutionalized hatred, which then gave the anti-Semites a free pass to torment us.

They say that the youngest child in the family is the most charming and a born salesman. Well, I was the kid on the block who got along with everybody—even the Christian kids. This was from 1937 to 1939, when I was between nine and ten years old. In those days there were fights and occasional skirmishes on the corner, mostly by teenage boys acting up, nothing serious. In 1939, the Nazis invaded western Poland and the Soviets occupied eastern Poland, supposedly to protect us from Nazi invasion. Unknown to us, the Nazis had made a secret pact with the Soviets that divided the country in two. By the late 1930s, however, attacks on Jews escalated in the Soviet Union and became more tolerated in Soviet occupied Poland as well. Formerly bitter enemies, the secret Hitler-Stalin Pact must have made anti-Semitic prejudices more "reasonable" to the Soviets and to many Polish Christians who were jealous of Jewish success in business.

In 1939, when I was 11, my family moved from Knyszyn to Bialystok, for many reasons, but they told us it was because my father had a shop in the city. I was excited that we were going to live in the big city, and hardly gave a thought to leaving Knyszyn. My parents rented a serviceable two-room apartment that had one bedroom and a kitchen. It was very tight quarters but we managed. At the time Bialystok was a prosperous, heavily Jewish city with numerous cultural and welfare organizations, two Jewish newspapers, five Jewish high schools and a Jewish trade school, along with a Jewish-owned weaving factory, two Yeshivas and a large 50,000-book library named after the famed Yiddish writer Sholem Aleichem. As a curious kid from a provincial town it was all new to me. I had been a frequent visitor to the city, but living there was as different as visiting Manhattan and actually *living* there.

Some days I'd meet my friend Haskell Greenstein by the *Ratusz*, the Polish word for the old Town Hall with a tall clock tower, and we'd eat Bialystoker pretzels—which many years later became the famous bialys we all know today. On other days we'd walk by the gardens of the grand Branicki Palace, on the banks of the Biala River. The palace was surrounded by many acres of gardens, a grand residence built by a Polish nobleman who wanted to be king. Knyszyn had nothing like this, and the city was much more exciting to me. My mother used to say I had wide eyes because I was so curious about everything. I had big ideas even then. Later, as it happened, Haskell and his two brothers were in the ghetto with me. But that comes later.

From my earliest days I was an observer. I slowly began to sense a change in the air. Something was coming, but I didn't know what. In the meantime, full of energy and life, my buddies and I would run through the Bialavest Pushcha forest, so green and fresh and filled with towering Norway spruce trees. There we searched for animals and treasures, or played games of hide-and-seek. It was great for a bunch of active boys who lived in cramped houses and flats. A railroad line ran between the town and the forest. The railroad tracks used to go from Russia to Warsaw. We thought nothing of it at the time.

The dislike of the Poles for us Jews was often impossible to mistake around the Bialystok town square. That many of the stores and haberdasheries on the square were owned or managed by Jews only heightened tensions. One day, on Lag B'Omer—a light-hearted Jewish holiday that falls in the spring—Jewish high school kids were playing in a street band and were amusing the crowd. Suddenly, out of nowhere, a group of angry Poles attacked those helpless kids. Bottles were thrown at the young musicians and there was name-calling and fist fights. It felt like a vicious gang war. Even before that, serious skirmish rumors were rampant of sneak attacks on Jews in nearby towns. Naturally these were serious and deeply troubling incidents to my parents and the other adults, but we kids were largely kept in the dark. It was a time when young people were not thought of as equal to adults in any way.

Passover, *Pesach*, is always a special holiday—and even today a favorite of my kids and grandkids—so not even these nasty incidents could stop us from observing Passover. Before sunset on the first night of *Pesach* we had to come home, scrub the *schmutz* off our hands and faces, comb our hair, and put on the good clothes we normally wore for Shabbat. Then, in a group, we'd walk to my cousin's house. There the smallest kids played for hours under the big Seder table while the adults droned on during the never-ending Seder ritual.

A portion of the Torah that is read at every Seder tells the story of four brothers: one wise, one wicked, one simple, and one who does not know how to ask a question. This story was my favorite part of the Seder. According to my siblings I was the wicked one, probably because I was strong and clever. My brother Schmuel was six years older than me. He was the wise one. He was a university student and also a singer with a wonderful voice. Dovid was the schlimazel, the one who did not know how to ask a question. He would try to hide the matzo—a fun part of our Seder celebration—and right away our brothers and sisters would find the matzo, which always made Dovid mad.

As I said earlier, Moishe was the name I was given at birth. In 1941, when I was 13 going on 14, and confined with everyone else to the Bialystok Ghetto, I took my dead brother's name, Schlomo, which in English later became Sam. I thought it was smart to take on a new identity since there were rumors that the Nazis were hunting me down in the ghetto as Moishe because of my secret missions. In the ghetto nobody but my family knew my real name, and they protected me by calling me Schlomo. However, to most people I soon became known simply as the "Malach," which is the Hebrew word for angel. But let me not get ahead of myself.

In those days, Bialystok had become a major political football between Germany and the Soviet Union, and because of the secret pact, the city was occupied by the Russians. Back then the city had about 120,000 citizens, half of whom were Jews. When the Russians came we were all worried about what was going to happen. Then, in 1941, the Nazis violated their agreement. Hitler had engineered the pact with the Soviet Union to ensure that only his army could invade Poland, unopposed by another major power.

As Hitler saw it, Poland was a prize. Poland has wonderfully rich soil for farming. With its ports on the Baltic Sea it was also important geographically in giving Hitler access to Northern Europe and Great Britain by sea. Hitler had designs on conquering the entire continent as well as the British Isles, so in Hitler's mind Poland was a major component to his success.

By 1941, the long fingers of war were reaching into Jewish homes in Soviet-occupied Poland. On every Jewish household's front door Poles drew a Star of David with a big white chalk, making it clear that Jews lived inside. On the doors of Christian homes they drew crosses. Our Polish neighbors were more than happy to identify us and put us in harm's way. Of course we tried to erase it, but they just kept coming back to draw more stars.

By June 27, 1941 we no longer had to worry about people simply branding our doors. That was small potatoes. Things had gotten far more treacherous. On that beautiful June day, the Nazis entered the city—and not quietly. Nazi troops from Police Battalion 309 marched into the town square, which was right by the Great Synagogue of Bialystok. They pounded on doors of all the nearby homes that were marked with the Star of David and brutally yanked the residents out into the street. Parents, children, cousins and neighbors were herded out of their houses and pushed against the walls of buildings. Once all the Jews were out in the open the Nazis started shooting; they were both bloodthirsty and crazed. Of course, we didn't yet know about the Third Reich's larger plans, aiming to kill each and every Jew—not only in our town, but also in the whole of Europe. We only knew that the people of Bialystok were being terrorized.

On that day—one I still visualize with my eyes closed and in my dreams—the Nazis directed hundreds of poor souls into the Bialystok shul. Some worshippers were already at evening services in that big Synagogue on Suraska Street. It was the largest shul in Poland, and set in the very heart of the Jewish community. It was about two blocks from the Town Hall with its big clock. The Nazis wanted to fill up the shul, so they began pushing more and more Jews into our sacred place. The Nazis wanted to make sure that our house of worship was bursting to capacity with Jews—people they would sneeringly call *Juden*.

When they were sure no more people could be squeezed into the temple, the Nazis locked the doors and tossed deadly firebombs through open windows and into the shul's vast interior. Pop, pop, pop! You could hear each firebomb burst, and the screams of the captives within. I was standing half a block away with a crowd of gawking Gentiles. With my blue eyes and red hair, I blended in. I will never forget the blood-curdling cries and shrieks of agony as one by one those trapped innocents so painfully and horrifically succumbed to the flames. To make it even more worse for me, right then I had no idea if any of my family or friends was among those crying out.

Some of the Poles openly cheered as the flames leapt up, but I could see expressions of horror on some of our Polish neighbors' faces, yet

11

they kept quiet. In truth we were all terrified and powerless. There were spies everywhere. For those who were sympathizers, it wasn't safe to support their Jewish neighbors suffering such an unimaginable fate.

A short while later I was relieved to learn that no one in my family was a victim of this atrocity, but my mother had frantically combed the neighborhood to make sure we were all accounted for. My sisters and brothers were all in hiding during the worst of the inferno and street murders. Luckily we did all come home that night.

Not content with destroying our temple with an estimated 2,000 trapped inside, the Nazis also systematically shot innocent Jews right in the street—mostly men, and in front of their wives and children, who were cowering nearby. Not even satisfied with shooting Jews like sitting ducks, they also threw firebombs into homes, burning down nearby houses. Soon the entire square was the scene of countless ghastly horrors. When I looked up, I saw that the sky above the city was the color of blood. It could be seen for miles around. It was the reddest and most chilling color I have ever seen. I can never forget it, no matter how much I try.

I watched the burning of the synagogue, paralyzed with disbelief at what I could see, hear, and smell. The stench was incredible. The Great Synagogue burned for many hours, and was still burning the next morning. Only then did Commander Friedle, the Gestapo officer in charge of the ghetto, issue an order to extinguish the smoldering embers of the fire. And who do you think they ordered to clean up the debris, ashes and charred bodies? It was the Jewish men who survived! The acts I witnessed, the pain, the inhumanity of it was beyond understanding. Even now, to my mind, there are not enough tears in the world to dampen those flames.

My family's house was four blocks away from the destroyed temple, so fortunately we all escaped that particular fate. Much later I learned some of what was actually happening *inside* the inferno. Many people, after suffering in the suffocating smoke, slashed the wrists of friends, and then their own, to shorten their agony. One young man, not yet overcome by the smoke and gasses, knocked out several panes of glass and climbed up to a window, cursing the Nazis. They shot him, and he fell to the ground, dead. Several old men, knowing they were about to die, began singing a Hebrew lament, "*Shema Yisrael, Adonai Elohey*—." Then the singing stopped, those brave singers silenced forever. Terrified wails and hysterical cries for *Mam* or *Tate* (mother or father) emanated from children being burned to death inside the temple's thick walls.

Meanwhile, outside, German soldiers continued their taunting and kills in many other neighborhoods. I could hear bloodcurdling screams from a few streets away. No wonder I still have nightmares. And this was only the first of the horrors.

At the age when Jewish boys have their bar mitzvahs, I did not. Instead of studying the Torah, I was listening to guns pick off old rabbis and frail doctors, firebombs exploding in a house of worship, terrified children seeking comfort from their mothers, innocents being murdered inside the House of God. At the time the Nazis occupied the city, Bialystok had about 65,000 Jews. Over the course of the next month the Nazis not only destroyed the synagogue but also systematically murdered a total of 5,000 Jewish people. Their sole "crime" was their religious birthright.

The temple burning also destroyed a symbol dear to us Jews. Sadly, that great domed edifice was never rebuilt. And, almost immediately after the Germans brought the temple down, they undertook building the Bialystok Ghetto. We knew that there was a ghetto in Warsaw, by far the largest in Poland, and in other cities such as Lodz and Krakow. Altogether there were over a thousand ghettos in German-occupied territory. At the time we didn't really grasp what a ghetto was, or have any idea what living in the ghetto would be like.

Once the Germans started building the ghetto, it didn't take them long. They'd had quite a bit of practice. They simply carved out a run-down section of the city, bisected by the Biala River, and moved out any locals who were not Jews. Then they surrounded the whole area with high fences, topped with barbed wire. They installed gates in certain places, and guardhouses, then shoved in every Jew they could find. It was unbelievable how fast they worked, but then, I suppose, they had the whip hand of the Führer at their backs. Once inside the ghetto, the Jews, all densely crowded together, were conscripted into forced labor, working in factories and plants that the Nazis had taken over for their war effort.

As I said earlier, in Bialystok, as in cities, towns, and villages throughout Poland, most of the Gentiles worked for the Jews. Jews were the core of the business community and had built the factories and shops, employing many Gentiles. Still, on Sundays these same Poles, who knew we observed the Sabbath, would go to church, then get drunk and show their hatred for the Jews by breaking windows in Jewish homes. Maybe it was jealousy. Maybe they were thinking: "Why is this Jew living better than me, and making money when I'm not?" I can't explain their behavior—I can only condemn it. There is no excuse.

In the 1930s most Gentiles in Poland worked on farms, while the vast majority of Jews worked in non-farming occupations—as shopkeepers, small business owners, artisans and traders. A number of Jews were also trained as lawyers and doctors. So, yes, they were better educated than most Gentiles. Between the wars Polish Jews made up the largest Jewish population in Europe. Only in America, a much larger country, were there more Jews. Probably the main reason for Poland becoming the largest site for the Nazi extermination program and for the largest concentration of death and labor camps is because that's where most Jews lived.

In June 1941 the war started in earnest, with Germany attacking the Soviet Union, their former allies. That same month was when they firebombed the Great Temple. The horrors had only just begun.

2

Forced From Home
Bearing Witness to Unspeakable Acts

As I mentioned earlier, World War II robbed me of a Bar Mitzvah—the ceremony meant to celebrate a boy's passage into manhood. But my passage into manhood had begun long before I reached the age of thirteen, since I was pushed over the threshold of adulthood by the cruelty and hardship I witnessed every day.

The burning of the temple was such an atrocity that it was hard to believe the Nazis could top this vilest of deeds. They managed—and it didn't take them long. One day after the flames engulfed our Bialystok synagogue another depraved act of mass murder, almost beyond imagining, took place. Fearing that the strong-minded Jewish men who remained would take reprisals against the police or Ordnungspolizei, the Germans determined to preempt any possible retaliatory action. Commonly known as *Orpo*, this was the uniformed police force in Nazi Germany between 1936 and 1945. To prevent any such reprisals, the Nazis rounded up about five hundred of the youngest and strongest Jewish men in Bialystok, along with some fit and able older men. Then the cold-blooded Nazis murdered these sturdy men in the most unthinkable way.

We were all still in shock from the temple burning and were huddled in our house, trying to keep a low profile for obvious reasons. Sitting in the kitchen, I could hear my parents whispering in the other room. Their whispers always meant that something was up. Although I tried hard to eavesdrop, I couldn't hear a word they were saying. While this was happening inside, I could suddenly hear a big commotion outside. People were crying out and sounds of scuffling came from the street. I crept to the window and peeked through the shutters.

My parents ended their conversation and came into the front room to see what was going on.

"Moishe," my mother said very quietly. "What is it?"

I turned and looked at her seriously. "I think more arrests are taking place."

"What?" said my father, "What more could those *mamzers* do?"

"I don't know, Tate," I said with a shrug, "But I heard Nathan Levitski's voice. He was screaming something in Yiddish. They forced him to get into a truck with a swastika on the side."

"Oh, *meyn Gat*," exclaimed my mother as my father hushed her.

I looked out the window again. Crouching low so I could see a battalion of Orpo police combing the streets, I heard another neighbor's voice cry out and signaled my parents to be quiet.

"*Ach! Ach! Halt! Juden*," an Orpo cop ordered. He had his rifle pointed at someone. His captive's back was to me, and my vantage point wasn't that good, but I knew that deep voice. It was Yoni Horvitz, my brother's friend. Yoni was a very tall, broad shouldered guy who had been an amateur boxer back in Knyszyn. Then I heard a loud thud. The cop had hit Yoni in the back with the butt of his rifle. In seconds Yoni was pushed into a truck that was over-burdened with men. A door slammed and the truck hurtled out of the neighborhood.

"What do you suppose is happening?" my mother said in a voice filled with fear.

"Nothing good," I said.

"Moishe," grumbled my father, "Get away from that window. Those terrible people are gone."

But they'll be back, I thought to myself.

The next day we learned what happened to Yoni, Nathan and the others. Our neighbor Reb Moshman came to our door, almost out of breath. Once he was safe inside our little house he said to my father, "You know what happened to my boy Zevi and many others?" The old man was in tears, his eyes already red from crying. I knew he didn't want me to hear the ugly news, but I wasn't leaving and he was bursting with it. His news was beyond shocking.

Not content with administering beatings or intimidation through other violent means, which were ghastly enough, the corrupt, soulless Nazis had taken our vital Jewish men, all in the prime of life, and buried them alive! Once they'd dragged enough men out of hiding, they'd driven them to a field a mile or two out of Bialystok in a German Army convoy. There, in yet another instance of depravity, these living, breathing, energetic men from our community were forced to dig a large pit themselves. Then, when the pit was deep enough, they were made to lie down inside as the pit was filled in. It is still hard to even think of this.

Once the Jews were lying in this deep pit, the Germans and their Polish chimps kept shoveling, laughing gleefully at the slow, ugly deaths taking place at their feet.

Bit by bit, as the pit filled up, the dirt stopped up their captive's mouths and nostrils, until the weight of the soil constricted their lungs. As a result they died slow, painful deaths by asphyxiation, endless and agonizing. That was the way the sadistic Nazis liked it. I later learned that the same terrible torture was used by Nazis in Jewish towns throughout Poland, including in one town twenty-eight miles from Bialystok where 2,800 people were buried alive!

While the Germans were monsters, reveling in the pain of the Jews, in some ways the Poles were even worse. Just as the Poles had helped the German soldiers fill in the pit, they also demonstrated time and again that they were eager to vent their animosity toward their Jewish neighbors to prove their loyalty to the Reich. They may have done some of it out of fear, but of course it was mainly cowardice. It was as if they felt justified committing vicious acts of anti-Semitism to appease the Occupiers. The full extent of Polish participation in the massacres of the Jewish population during World War II is well documented. You can see why it's impossible for me to forgive or trust *any* Poles, even today. Yes, the Germans were merciless. But the Poles, who actually knew us as human beings, and neighbors, and in some cases as employers who provided them with livelihoods, were relentless in their hatred. And that personal connection somehow made it worse.

Reb Moshman finished telling his heartbreaking story, and my father offered him some table wine to help calm his nerves. The old man, near tears again, declined and left in a hurry to return to his distraught wife. Just as we heard from Moshman, the news of this mass murder spread quickly through the neighborhood. Buried alive! It was unthinkable. My dad was a stern man who didn't easily show his emotions, but he was clearly deeply affected by the old man's story. Meanwhile my mother was shaking with fear for her own sons.

Later that day my friend Haskell Greenstein's father came to speak with my father. What went on between them I cannot be sure, but whatever my father said to Mr. Greenstein really set him off. A chubby, amiable man—the town comedian—he began to argue with my dad, which was not his usual way. While they were talking inside, two other men were standing outside by our open kitchen window. I didn't know their names but I knew they were my father's cronies. These four friends often came together for quiet games of cards. They kept this hush-hush since some in the Orthodox world frowned on card playing, especially if gambling was involved. Today they were here for a bit of a gossip, I supposed.

Both of the two men outside were tall, thin, and dressed in black. One, I later learned, was a physician named Nemitov. The other, Glitstein, was the head of one of Bialystok's two yeshivas, and a prominent man in town. I remembered Glitstein because he always called me *royt kop,* and would tousle my red hair. After a while these two came inside and I saw these four guys whispering. This told me something was up. My mother caught me spying and chased me away, but I'd already noticed that they were all pale and more worried-looking than usual. I had no doubt they were exchanging more bad news.

Later I found out what that was. It seemed that only a few days before, Reb Glitstein had witnessed another horrible act of blasphemy. Unbelievably, the Nazis had sheared the long beard off an elderly Orthodox rabbi and forced the frail, pious old man to sing and dance, making him perform like a trained monkey. They mocked and humiliated the aged rabbi for their amusement. And then, not content with this degradation, smashed his face against the ground, with other Jews forced to watch and applaud. I can only imagine how this affected the Jews made to witness this heinous act—not to mention the elderly rabbi himself.

We Jews had been witnessing a lot of dreadful assaults, but for a time these events had been intermittent, with no apparent pattern. What I later learned is that a week before the temple burned SS Lieutenant Colonel Adolf Eichmann—a principal organizer of the Holocaust—had promised Herr Hitler that in three years time he would destroy the entire Jewish race. This would be no small task, since there were an estimated nine million Jews in Europe before the war. He nearly accomplished that pledge, systematically eradicating two-thirds of all European Jews before he was done.

As I began paying attention with more mature eyes, I noticed the quickening pace of these anti-Semitic acts. It was like watching a gathering storm. And the blood red skies over Bialystok I saw when the temple burned seemed to herald the end of our world. Like an invisible blanket sweeping over us, the Germans had begun their dehumanization of us, as, act by act, they stripped us of our civil and legal rights. By that time Germans had already ordered registration of all Jews, and "*Jude*" was stamped on our identity cards, which everyone had to carry. If the Orpo stopped you for any reason and you didn't have your ID card it meant big trouble. Restriction after restriction was implemented. Can you believe that Jews were forbidden to walk on the sidewalks? We had to walk in the gutters, and also couldn't use buses or trollies. Before the end of 1941 all Jews in German-occupied Poland except the children had to wear badges on their clothing depicting a yellow Star of David: one in front, on the right side, and one in back on the left shoulder. Although they spared the children this ignominy, they certainly didn't spare them the gas chamber.

19

Maybe it was my inborn resilience, but to my teenage way of thinking I wasn't able to fathom what was to come. Needless to say, my family and I knew some of those poor guys who were buried alive. I still shudder to think of dying in such an awful way. In addition to Yoni, Nathan and poor old Reb Moshman's boy, our neighbors Asher, Isak and Yankel also lost their lives in that pit of death. That was enough for my parents. The following day they announced to us kids that they were moving us back to Knyszyn, deeming it safer than our life in the big city. My siblings seemed fine with moving back to our hometown. I was a different story. I begged to stay put.

A few days later my parents left Bialystok with my siblings. After much pleading and persuasion I was permitted to move in with my father's stepsister, Aunt Hafka, who lived in town with her large flock of kids—four boys and three girls. It was also the only way for me to stay in the city in a way that my parents would allow.

Following the terrible events of June 1941, the summer kept getting worse. During July and August 1941, the Nazis orchestrated the creation of the Bialystok Ghetto. By August 1941 the ghetto was fully established. This city-within-a-city was sealed off so that the Germans could isolate us even more from everyday life. The area where the Jews were allowed to live was roughly bordered by Lipowa, Poleska and Sienkiewicza Streets. Although people were given so-called "living" quarters, two to three families were squashed into tiny cell-like rooms where they were all in essence prison inmates. As soon as the ghetto was established Aunt Hafka and her brood—along with me, of course—were forced to move into the ghetto. Once inside, those who were able-bodied were forced to work for the Germans in textile, clothing, shoe and chemical factories, and even forced to make uniforms for the German army.

Next to the enclosed houses the Germans erected high fences with three feet of razor-sharp barbed wire on top to prevent anyone from climbing in or out of the ghetto. Leaving nothing to chance, the gates were also guarded by armed *gendarmes*. This meant that Jews were effectively cut off from the main streets of the city, degrading our status even further. Even on these streets one side was for Jews and the other side was for Christians—the "Aryan" side. And if any Jews did try to escape, Germans would snuff them out, leaving their bodies lying in the street as a warning to others.

The Nazis mandated that a *Judenrat,* or Jewish Council, govern each ghetto, since Gestapo members worked in buildings outside the ghetto, and weren't around all the time. Based on German orders, a *Judenrat* was established in Bialystok at the end of June or July 1941. Rabbi Gedaliah Rosenmann was appointed chairman. His deputy chairman, Ephraim Barash, was actually in charge, and served as liaison to the German leaders. Members of the *Judenrat* consisted of men who were Jewish leaders before the Occupation. These Jews, appointed by Christians, were unarmed. Their main job was to ensure that things inside the ghetto ran efficiently. They were also charged with quelling any attempts at revolts, which the Germans feared. Judenrat officers did not kill other Jews, but some were terrible while others were kind. Barash, for example, despite knowing about the construction of the ghetto, the transports to the camps, and the awful machinations of the Germans, seemed to have convinced himself that if those in our particular ghetto were efficient and productive, we Bialystok Jews would be too valuable for the Nazis to kill. He was, of course, completely and dangerously wrong.

While some members of the *Judenrat* sincerely strove to alleviate the suffering of their neighbors, many on the Jewish Council played right into the hands of the Nazis in order to ensure their own survival. It was dreadful to witness our own people turning against us. In fact, the Germans deliberately created a dynamic to turn Jew against Jew. I soon learned that people could shift their loyalties as quickly as the wind. I certainly had my eyes opened to all this at a young age, and in a deeply disturbing way.

The ghetto, with its makeshift walls and ugly barbed wire, was the first thing you saw when you came into Bialystok. About 65,000

Jews—every Jew in the city—now inhabited this *de facto* prison. Jews who once had standing in Bialystok now lived in these awful conditions. Now these Jews and all others were treated like animals, quarantined behind fences, living in cramped spaces, forced to work for German industry. Food supplies were severely restricted, but even if you somehow still had money you could not go "outside" to spend it on food or other necessities. Jews were forbidden to leave the ghettos on pain of death, and any Gentiles that dared to try to help Jews in any way would be subject to death as well. Few of them were willing to take the risk. It was a living nightmare. This was an area of need where I would eventually play a major role.

As Jews were forced from their homes and into squalid ghetto conditions, many of their fine homes were left vacant. Thanks to a lottery, many lucky Gentiles were given possession of the Jews' comfortable homes. These Poles felt as if they'd struck gold—and they had. You'd see entire Polish families carrying trunks and suitcases, kids' toys and family pets, laughing excitedly as they took over fully furnished Jewish houses. The best part for them was that these homes were free, their occupancy sanctioned by the town hall on Kosciuszko Square.

Because my parents had returned to Knyszyn they were spared the ignominy of the ghetto for some time. Towns like Knyszyn were left alone—for the time being. I stayed in Bialystok, living in the ghetto with my aunt and her brood, but I would sneak back to Knyszyn from time to time. I was in Knyszyn with my family when our time together ended abruptly on the night of November 2, 1942.

That was the night the mayor of Bialystok issued a proclamation. The Germans had a new order for the Jews from our town, along with those of six other mostly Jewish towns situated around Bialystok. On that day every Jewish farmer, rancher and store owner was ordered to convene in the town square. This was announced at two o'clock in the morning. Jews who had contributed so greatly to the Polish economy, culture and lifestyle now had only until 9 AM the next morning to gather their belongings and show up for their uncertain fates. Men, women, and children were allowed to carry ten kilos each of belongings, which is about 20 pounds. Gestapo guards with snarling dogs would make sure the Jews didn't carry more than the ten kilos permitted.

My family and I were among those soon-to-be-evicted villagers. Despite everything that had happened, when the news came a tremor of disbelief went through our family. We gathered in the kitchen, coming together for support. My father was sitting at the kitchen table, silently sipping his coffee with chicory, barely eating Mother's raspberry strudel. Silence was not his usual way, but now, in shock, he had no words.

"Saul," my mother said to my father, "finish your strudel. Who knows when we will eat again."

"Who knows what happens next to any of us?" my brother Dovid blurted out.

"Hush, Dovid," my mother urged, obvious strain in her voice, and a familiar look that said "Please do not upset the others."

The rest of us were talking amongst ourselves, mostly speculating about what we feared might happen. Some of my siblings were clearly despondent. A couple of my sisters were busily filling their little satchels and suitcases. I knew they were frightened, and imagining the worst. My heart broke for them.

"We just need to get on with business." My mother, the soul of our family, was trying to put on a brave front for all of us.

"Esther," said my father in a warning tone. She returned a resigned smile. There was so much unsaid in that silent exchange between them. I can still see the faraway look in her blue eyes as she tidied up the kitchen, as she had done every day and night, as if things were normal. Then, being a mother first and foremost, she directed each of us to put on as many of our warm clothes as we could manage, so that we had layers of garments, for insurance. Her dazed expression let me know her mind was elsewhere. I observed it all, which perhaps helped me stay cool and unemotional. I was always trying to figure out a way around bad situations, how to get by, the best way to survive. Even so, I had no idea what fate would have in store for us when morning came.

After the endless night, our family exchanged nervous hugs and kisses before we trudged out into watery daylight. Snow was falling lightly, coating the skeletal tree branches and brushing roofs and tops of nearby hills. The sky was a sad gray as glistening flecks of damp snow wafted down, blanketing our town with its white purity. The scene around us appeared deceptively clean and pure. But we knew too well it was a moment in time orchestrated by pure evil. The Germans and our fellow Poles were always at the ready to do us harm.

Maybe the snow wasn't snow at all. One young sister, the most sensitive child of us all, said it was God's frozen tears falling down on us. As I stood in the snow that awful day I thought back on what one rabbi, also standing in the snow, had said: *"We didn't cry alone, that God cried with us and for us."* He then quoted Isaiah 63:9. *"In all their affliction, He was afflicted, and the angel of his presence saved them; in His love and in His pity He redeemed them; He lifted them up and carried them all the days of old."*

For me this was gibberish. I didn't believe a word of it. With all this happening around us, God wasn't weeping. He wasn't lifting us up out of this nightmare. God was not carrying us or our heavy belongings to safety that cold November morning.

Eventually we were forced to board horse-drawn wagons, with no idea where we were being taken. My sister Dina's raggedy cloth doll fell out of the wagon, tumbling into the deepening layers of snow. We hadn't moved yet, so I jumped down, picked it up and handed it back to her. That's when I realized I didn't have my gloves. They weren't inside my pockets where I usually left them—one pocket had a hole in it from stuffing too many little items in it. There was no going back now. At that moment I somehow knew I'd never go home again.

Meanwhile, all around me, the Jewish townspeople trudged through the snow, dragging their personal belongings, before being loaded onto wagons and sleds.

It took five long hours from Knyszyn, over bumpy roads, to get to Ten Pulke, the Polish Army Camp that was our destination. It was on the outskirts of the city, just two miles from Bialystok. There we were, Jews from seven of the smaller towns, in this God-forsaken camp. There was no food and little water, so leaders from the Bialystok Ghetto brought in small rations of food. Russian prisoners of war would also come in driving tractor trailers, to bring us daily rations of drinking water.

This, as it turned out, was a way station before they put us in a train to Treblinka. Warehoused in the army camp, we slept on dirt floors, packed together like sardines in cold, damp conditions. We were always hungry, always thirsty, and, worst of all, always fearful of what would happen next. Mothers and grandmothers tried to reassure the younger kids that things would be okay. But we teenagers, half way between childhood and adulthood, saw our precarious position more clearly.

I would remain in that army camp for only 17 days, but that time marked the end of the Solasz family as a unit—and certainly the end of my childhood as I'd known it.

"The question shouldn't be 'Why are you, a Christian, here in a death camp, condemned for trying to save Jews?' The real question is 'Why aren't all the Christians here?'"

—Joel C. Rosenberg (born April 17, 1967),
American communications strategist,
founder of The Joshua Fund,
and an Evangelical Christian.
Quote is from The Auschwitz Escape.

3

A Barrel and a Tire
Ten Pulke and After

By the time we got to our mysterious destination—the Polish army camp Ten Pulke—we were all hungry, thirsty and disoriented. Of course, that's what the Nazis wanted—Polish Jews defenseless and afraid. When the wagons came to a stop, a stern Gestapo officer wielding a rifle ordered us to get out of the crude wagons. I held back, letting my parents and my brothers and sisters climb out first. When it was finally my turn, I jumped to the ground and looked around with deep concern. It was still snowing and there was nothing but mud and slush beneath my feet.

I heard my mother whisper frantically to my father, in Yiddish of course, "Oh Saul. What does this mean?" I believe she knew what lay ahead, at least on some level, but didn't want to acknowledge the awful truth. My father just shrugged, which was often his way. He just put a finger up to his mouth to warn Mam and all of us to be quiet.

Curiously, I looked around. All I could see inside Ten Pulke was a vast expanse of old barracks, makeshift huts and drab buildings. These large camps, which once housed the Polish Army, were deserted during the Occupation when the Polish Army scattered. Some Polish soldiers joined Allied forces and fought in other theaters in Europe, and some soldiers became Polish resistance fighters, leaving these camps empty. Once these large crude military instillations were empty, the German's answer was to fill them with Jews.

Before we could collapse completely from hunger we were given small bowls of porridge and a single slice of bread. Then we were put through an induction. We had to give our names, ages, and the names of our towns. The Nazis were nothing if not thorough. This process took some time since there were hundreds of us from Knyszyn and hundreds more from the other towns. During this time I was careful to look around, trying to spot any weaknesses in the setup that might serve me later on.

It was almost dark by time we were marched to an old barracks, where we would sleep on wooden cots. On the way there all of us—and especially the younger women—suffered rough treatment at the hands of the Germans. My neighbor from Knyszyn, Batya Asher, who was about sixteen at the time, was jeered at and subjected to nasty suggestions by some of the German soldiers. This particularly rankled me because Batya was a pretty girl and I was a bit "sweet" on her at the time, as they used to say. But I knew I couldn't stand up to the Germans or I would be killed in a second. The Germans weren't supposed to harass us, but when their superior officers weren't around they would try to get away with anything they could.

Ten Pulke, meaning ten regiments, was in the middle of nowhere, separating us from the world outside and any real possibility of escape. This was by design. It was right by the railroad tracks where long lines of dilapidated railroad cars, only fit for livestock, would be waiting to transport us when the time came. The location of the camp was ideally placed for getting the newly corralled denizens of the camp to Treblinka and other hellholes. So practical, those Nazis!

The Knyszyn people tried to stick together. I was in an old barracks with my family and some of our neighbors. Even if we didn't know some people very well in Knyszyn, we quickly became close to them in this camp, because we needed each other for support.

Even though the camp was only on the far outskirts of Bialystok, where I had been many times, it seemed so strange. I had to pinch myself to remember that it was just another day—November 2, 1942. But really it was not just another day. As I would soon come to understand, no day in the future would be "just another day." Not for me.

Beginning in 1939, during the occupation of Poland, the Third Reich built all kinds of camps. Eventually there would be hundreds of camps in Nazi-occupied Poland, and throughout Europe. The camp system was well planned and formed the backbone of the Reich's economy of war and subjugation through terror. Beside the horrors of the extermination and concentration camps, the evil system didn't stop there. There were also forced labor camps, prisoner of war camps, and places like Ten Pulke—former army camps that were being used to house Jewish men, women and children. The core of the German design was to weaken the Jew's sense of self-esteem and independence, for we were crowded together like animals.

At Ten Pulke whole families, many large like ours, as I said, were crammed into cold, dusty barracks once used to house Polish soldiers. You can't imagine how Spartan it was, and there was precious little food or water. We Solasz kids had come from a home where Mam was always cooking, and where father brought home wonderful cuts of meat. Now we did not know where our next bit of food was coming from or if it would even be edible. We tried hard not to complain because we knew it upset our parents, and also it angered the German guards to hear our grousing. Luckily we spoke in Polish or Yiddish, languages they couldn't understand, which drove them crazy.

One day I was outside, hanging out with Haskell and Jakob, a couple of friends from our town, when a guard asked us who we were and where we were from. He spoke German, which most of us understood. His tone was angry and demanding.

I spoke up for the group and rattled in Polish, "May I help you, soldier?"

He looked at me perplexed, "What are your names, you Jews?" he demanded in a guttural Germanic voice.

"We are Polish youth. May we help you, sir?" Haskell spoke in the Polish dialect of the Bialystok region. He looked up politely with an ingenuous smile on his face.

Clearly the German didn't understand him, but didn't want to look stupid. "*Raus hier, sie Juden!*" He told us to go away. We were only too happy to oblige. Quickly we went about our business with innocent expressions on our faces, pretending we didn't understand his consternation, but we understood it only too well.

It is amazing now to think that there were 35,000 people—the population of a small city—in that terrible camp. Life there was tedious as well as harsh. There was nothing to do all day but worry about our survival. It was a little easier for the younger kids, who were kept busy singing and playing games, or playing with a few crude toys. Of course they didn't understand how perilous their situation was. Yet, you could still see the dread in their eyes and watch as they suddenly dashed to their mothers at the sound of a loud noise or sudden movement. Everyone was on edge. Even the littlest tykes seemed to sense the great anxiety of the adults, and that things were not as they should be in this place.

Shortly after we got to the camp, Isaac Greenspan, who was about seven years old and had lived down the street from us, was playing ball with his little brother Avram. Avram kicked the ball and it rolled toward a huge guard patrolling the perimeter of the camp. The ball hit his ankle and, like lightning, he punctured the ball with a sharp knife and threw it over the fence. As he did he spit out some angry words in German to the poor little boys. "That will teach you, *farflukta!*" Avram and his little brother didn't know that they'd been called "snot nose" by an enemy killer. All they knew was that they had lost the only toy they had brought from home. In tears, they ran to find their mother. Painful stories like that happened every day.

Despite our imposed isolation, news from the outside world trickled in, and we heard that life was difficult for Jewish children in the Bialystok Ghetto. Schools were closed to Jewish children, and all those young students had taken to the streets. Instead of getting an education many were trying to help their families by selling cigarettes and shoelaces on the black market, or anything else they could sell, just to survive.

I was among the older boys at the camp, along with my two best friends, Jakob and Haskell. To fill the time and break the monotony we would gather by a rotted tree stump near the edge of the camp and draw pictures in the dirt with a stick. Once in a while we'd play with the marbles Jakob had smuggled into the camp, or make a game of tossing rocks. When we thought we were out of earshot of the ever-present guards we would exchange news and speculate in whispers about the uncertain future and our options. With the optimism of youth and the naiveté of teenagers we batted around all kinds of ideas and plans, most of them too dangerous to try. We would take hope from anywhere. Haskell had heard rumors of a revolt stirring among the Jews in the Bialystok Ghetto. We talked about smuggling weapons in, and listened for any news we could gather about a revolt we hoped would happen. Information was fragmented, so it was hard to know where the truth lay.

The biggest news that filtered in was that the Warsaw Jewish Fighting Organization, a resistance group formed in the Warsaw Ghetto, had just sent one of their top guys, Mordechai Tenenbaum, an anti-Fascist who'd led the resistance against the Germans in the Warsaw Ghetto, to the Bialystok Ghetto to organize a resistance movement and direct secret activities to fight back against our German captors. That was all we knew about Tenenbaum at the moment.

On the very day we entered the Polish Army Camp, my father's friend, Lev Sternberg, who had been a successful businessman, whispered disconcerting news to my father. There was an ugly rumor that the Nazi command levied an enormous tax of five million rubles on all Jews who were in the Bialystok Ghetto—meaning our friends, relatives and neighbors. The Judenrat was said to be charged with making sure that each Jew paid his share of this onerous tax. How was that even possible, I wondered, when we were stripped of our homes and livelihoods? At the same time, the Nazis ordered teams of guards, soldiers and Polish locals to shrink the ghetto even more by removing several streets from the designated ghetto area, further tightening their noose around the Jewish population.

Rumors did not go to waste in the camp. We had a sort of grapevine that kept circulating bits of news. My friend Haskell had a cousin from another town housed on the other side of the camp. Haskell's cousin seemed to be plugged into ghetto news. One day, as we idly sat by our favorite tree stump, Haskell told us that, besides the growing Bialystok resistance movement, there was another shocking development that our parents had kept from us. It was reported that the first deportations from Bialystok to Auschwitz, Birkenau and Treblinka had already begun. He heard that while some Jews had been murdered in their hometowns, others were being sent to the death camps, which at first masqueraded as labor camps.

Clearly the extermination apparatus was already in motion, but no one had any idea what that really meant. Naturally this left a blanket of dread over our fellow Jews in the Bialystok Ghetto and all of us who had been left to rot in this God-forsaken army camp. Teenage boys like me wrestled with what we should do. We were frustrated because we were trapped, far away from the action, feeling powerless.

During those chilly November days and nights in the camp we were living from one moment to the next, never knowing what the next hour would bring. Our days consisted of eating meager rations, essentially breadcrumbs, drinking dirty water, and witnessing disturbing scenes such as when an elderly woman, with sad eyes and a face creased by age, collapsed from starvation. No guard stirred to help her or called for help until a Polish woman cried out in thickly accented German. "She is dead! Can't you see that?" Soon some emergency workers came to roughly remove the body. There was no dignity, no care. Things were so tense that even reading the smuggled-in newspapers kept us going, though the news was consistently terrifying.

The hard-eyed Gestapo guards seemed to be everywhere. Why did Jewish butchers like my father and other professional men still bother to argue with each other about things that seemed so trivial? Now, of all times, it was not wise to kibbitz and bicker. In fact, it made the hair on the back of my neck stand up when little spats erupted among us Jews, as they often did out of boredom. It was hard not to shiver from fear. The ever-present guards could be set off by the tiniest breach of the camp's harsh rules. If we were outside and a little boy started running around and making noise, as little boys do, you'd pray that somebody in his family would make him stop. You never knew what would trigger the menacing Nazi brutes. Some guards acted as though they were just doing a normal job. But many others, egged on by vicious Poles or their fellow Nazis, would take sadistic pleasure in harassing and torturing us.

One day a friend of my mother's named Yetta was murmuring about a terrible thing that had just happened to Yetta's cousin. I was seated near my mother and happened to hear the awful story. Yetta's cousin had a three-week-old baby, born just before she came to the camp. The infant was colicky and crying all the time. Nothing the mother did could quiet the child. Finally a German guard, fed-up with all the crying, tore the baby right out of the mother's arms and threw it against the wall. "Now that brat won't bother anyone," the guard spat out in German. The mother shrieked in horror and ran to the lifeless baby—so brutally silenced. As she rushed to her infant the Nazi bully shot her too. She collapsed and died on top of her bloodied baby. I watched as Mam's eyes filled with tears at the story, and her friend tried to get her to muffle her sobs. *What have we done,* I wondered, *to be punished so savagely?*

Bits of help came to us from here and there. Jewish leaders from the Bialystok Ghetto were sending parcels of food to Ten Pulke for small-town people like us, but it was very little for so many. A daily ration of water was delivered by Russian POWs, who drove huge German tractors to the camp. There were enormous barrels filled with water on the back of the tractors. Each of us had a tin cup for our piddling portions of water. The water didn't go very far. There were just too many of us. City people got their water from wells, but in Ten Pulke there were only the wells used to water the horses. We weren't as good as horses. In the eyes of the Germans, we were lower than low.

The arrival of the water tractor was a signal event every day, but on November 19, 1942, exactly seventeen days after I'd arrived at the camp, an event occurred that changed my life forever. By then we all knew the water tractor routine. As soon as the vehicle parked and the driver turned off the motor we Jews formed a line to get water. After the guys siphoned off the water and emptied the barrels, the driver of the tractor, a Russian POW, along with a German guard, went into the checkpoint booth to sign papers to prove they had done their jobs. Everything had to be well-documented and accounted for in the army camps, ghettos and even concentration camps. I watched them as they went inside. I knew they'd be a while.

It was a cold day and my hands were freezing. My eyes were glued on the big green tractor. I had no particular plan. I knew we Jews had no way out of the army camp. If someone tried to escape they were shot on the spot. Just then I spied an 11-year-old kid from my town who I knew only as Jonah. Jonah, a very cheeky kid, came out of nowhere and clambered onto the tractor. He had mere seconds to pull off his daring stunt. My jaw dropped as I saw him race toward the tractor, jump on the back, and scramble into an empty barrel. He lowered himself into the barrel until only the top of his head showed, then he disappeared. Nobody else noticed what he had done. The driver and the guard were still occupied in the booth.

No time to waste! My heart raced as I glanced around. No guards in sight. I didn't think about it for another second. I just moved toward the tractor quickly, but not too quickly. Everyone else had moved away with their water cups. I wanted to ensure that I wasn't noticed and shot at. You never knew who, among your fellow inmates, would rat you out for an extra crust of bread. Luckily I was strong and agile. In a flash I hoisted myself up on the back of the tractor. I climbed into one of the giant tires that were there, and curled my body inside. My heart pounded in my chest. There hadn't been time to think. The kid had shown me a path to escape and I took it. I waited inside the tire in the idling tractor for what might have been five minutes, but it seemed like an eternity. Fear makes time move slowly. Within a few minutes I heard the tractor's door slam shut and felt the powerful diesel engine come back to life. Pretty soon there was a bounce and rumble as the tractor's big wheels slowly began to grind on the rutted road.

As the vehicle started to move, I screwed up my courage and peeked out of the tire for one last look at the camp. I feared my red hair might give me away, but I had on a dark cap so I chanced it anyway. In that split second I spied my father and my uncle. By chance they were standing near the barbed wire fence, close to the entrance of the camp.

I gave them a small wave. I believe my father saw me, but if he did he couldn't respond. What he thought of my escape, I would never know, because those seventeen days in Ten Pulke were the last days I spent with my family. My hair-breadth escape, which saved my life, also robbed me of the chance to say goodbye.

"Everything can be taken from a man but one thing: the last of the human freedoms to choose one's attitude in any given set of circumstances, to choose one's own way."

— *Viktor Frankl (1905-1997), author, neurologist, psychiatrist, Holocaust Survivor.*

4

The Angel of the Ghetto

I crouched inside the huge tire on the back of the truck, in a short journey that seemed to last forever. After a while I could feel the rhythm of the truck slow and knew it must be entering the outskirts of the city. Soon, with a shudder, the truck ground to a halt. In that instant, the kid and I both jumped off the back, running for our lives to seek some shelter where we would not be detected.

When I got my bearings, I saw that we were near the entrance of the Bialystok Ghetto. By then it was dusk—the time of day when a large number of Jews had gotten off work and were returning to the ghetto. Many of their day jobs involved doing all the dirty work for the *Krauts*—literally. They were forced to clean the streets outside the ghetto, scrub toilets, and take care of sanitation for the Germans and Poles. Now they were going back to the ghetto for the evening.

Quickly Jonah and I lined up behind the straggling workers and snuck into the ghetto. We didn't dare look at each other for fear of giving ourselves away. As far as I know, no one else has ever escaped from this army camp and lived to tell about it. Somehow we had managed it. As we passed though those gates, my heart was thumping loudly. I was both relieved and anxious to be inside those walls again. Suddenly I felt a sharp tap on my shoulder. A ghetto cop was staring me in the face, towering over me. Jonah was in the same pickle. His arm had been grabbed by another ghetto cop. That cop was short and heavy.

"*Komm, Jungs,*" the first cop said roughly, his German heavily accented with Polish. In seconds we'd been pulled away from the crowd and were being marched to another area.

I was almost sick with fear, sure we had been discovered as camp escapees. But before I knew it we were escorted into a shower room and told to undress. Then, without saying a word, the cops scrubbed us down with brushes and foul-smelling soap. Next they deloused us, which stung our skin. When they were finished they gave each of us a new set of clothes. This was something of a ghetto luxury, since we had only been allotted one set of clothes. Then the cops offered us a most welcome meal. It wasn't much but we were starving, so even the small portion of bread and watery soup made a difference. By then I'd relaxed. We are alive, and out of Ten Pulke! Clearly we weren't in trouble—at least not now.

When the cops were all done, they gave us a wink and a knowing nod. In that instant I realized that we hadn't fooled them. I guess because of our youth we stood out in the line of older teens and grown men, and they knew we had slipped into the ghetto. These Jewish men had been assigned to be policemen by the *Judenrat*, though they may have been barbers or schoolmasters outside the ghetto. They were among those who manned five police stations within the ghetto to oversee all the Jews who were living there—if you can call it living—all 65,000 souls crammed together in inhuman conditions.

As soon as the policemen had finished with us, I was quick to tell them that I had relatives in the ghetto. This information gave me credibility. They were happy to help me locate my aunt, while they assigned the kid to another family. I have no idea what happened to him, because I never saw him again. I hope he survived!

Not surprisingly, my aunt's house was jam-packed with her kids and an assortment of others of all ages. My aunt was doing her best, but after a few days the crowded conditions and constant noise began to bring me down. I knew I needed space and freedom to roam about in order to keep my mind clear—which for me was paramount for survival.

Though I was glad to get into the ghetto after fleeing harsh conditions in the army camp, the conditions within the ghetto were also extremely harsh. Often fifty people were forced into a three-room apartment, sleeping on bunks. A curtain separated people sleeping, so it looked like a hospital ward. Only one bathroom was available to serve those approximately fifty people. Sometimes there was no bathroom at all. The foul conditions were beyond description.

By the time I was back in the ghetto I was 14 years old, and like many young teens I thought I was immortal and bulletproof. Despite all the evidence to the contrary I never doubted I would survive. I saw everything that was going on, the cruelty and suffering, and knew I had to keep my wits about me—which meant keeping my spirits up and not succumbing to the melancholy all around me. I also wanted to find other like-minded people with whom I could plot some actions. I knew they were out there.

Thinking about what to do next, and trying to not think about my family, all still in Ten Pulke, I decided that my best bet was to work as a courier and go in and out of the ghetto to trade for needed goods. To begin this new phase I went in search of Peter K. Peter lived on the other side of the ghetto. I had known him slightly before. He was older, about forty, and ran a black market ring of couriers who brought goods into and out of the ghetto, at serious risk of life and limb. Peter had a good thing going. He told me he paid couriers ten marks for every run, which meant taking goods out of the ghetto and trading them for other needed items that could be obtained outside the ghetto.

Becoming a courier seemed like a good fit for me. I needed to make money fast, to stave off my own starvation, and to help my aunt and the others as much as I could. I figured I could easily do a minimum of three or four trips a day, which would bring me thirty or forty marks per day. That was a lot of money then for impoverished Jews stuck in a ghetto.

Peter was quick to take me on. He knew I was smart, resourceful and energetic. I also had a plan. I already knew several ways to get in and out of the ghetto without going through the gates, because that would get you arrested, beaten or even shot dead. I knew that if I could get in and out of the ghetto walls and fences and travel the 16 miles to and from my hometown and other nearby towns I could make this arrangement work.

I began to work for Peter by making my way back to Knyszyn and forming an immediate connection with a number of Christians who lived in and around my former neighborhood, as well as with Poles who lived in nearby towns. I bargained with them with the gold coins, gold rings and watches, and even gold-filled teeth Peter had given me. In return I was able to bring ham, bread, butter and other foods back to the Bialystok Ghetto. I also brought back warm clothing and occasional medicines. It was the first of many trips.

I had posed as a Polish kid before, and was lucky that it worked. Because of my red hair I was able to pass for a Christian. To look even more authentic I wore a medal with the image of the Blessed Mother around my neck. I won the medal in a card game when I gambled a bit with a Christian who I was doing business with. I knew it would come in handy, and sure enough it fooled the Nazis as well as the Poles. The minute I stepped outside the ghetto I opened my shirts to make sure the medal was in plain sight. It turned out to be life-saving, though at one point it became a threat to my survival—a story I will tell you later.

Ghetto life was challenging every minute of every day. The Nazis kept us in a constant state of fear and humiliation. In those terrible times Jews, as I said, had to walk in the middle of the street with the horse-drawn carriages and the few cars. However, while wearing the Virgin Mary medal I could walk anywhere I wanted. One day, just to be cheeky, I walked straight up to two German guards and asked directions, as if I was a stranger in town. I tried to appear relaxed, though I always had goose bumps when I spoke to the Gestapo. One look at the medal—not to mention my red hair and blue eyes—and the Germans and Poles never questioned me. Not then, anyway.

Whatever fantasies I had about my family surviving and returning to the ghetto were soon dashed. The way I learned what had become of the rest of my family was this: one day I asked a Polish man who delivered food to the ghetto if he had any news of the detainees in the Polish army camp, since I knew that he also delivered food there. He did not know I had been in the army camp or that my family was there, so he bluntly told me the unvarnished truth: there were no more food deliveries. Recently the Nazis had loaded everyone from the army camp onto a train bound for Treblinka, its passengers headed to certain death.

I was shocked beyond belief, and shook all over at the news. I was a tough kid, but afterwards, when I thought no one was around, I cried for a long time, and for many years after.

I can only imagine what went on in the minds of my parents when they learned they were going to a transit camp. Along with their outright lies the Nazis had built a simulated train station for all to see when they arrived at Treblinka, complete with a clock tower and ticket counter. All of it was, of course, deception. They even used a famous Polish-Jewish violinist and composer, Arthur Gold, along with his orchestra, to play music welcoming Jews to the camp. Unbelievable—the deceit and cruelty, on top of the horror of the murders themselves. It still makes my skin crawl.

Years later I realized that I was actually lucky to learn the fate of my loved ones right away and not have to wait decades for the truth, as so many people did. Nonetheless it was incredibly painful to know— within a short time of my arriving back in the ghetto—that I was now truly and completely on my own.

Any chance of a typical childhood or the comfort of my parent's home was now gone forever, and that was painful to accept. I had to grow up fast, and I did. During the earlier bombings in Bialystok my mom used to take a big dress and make a tent with it to cover the smaller kids so they would think the bombs could not hurt them. She made it a game, of course, but it helped in the moment. Now, with the certainty that my own family was gone, I wanted to do something to help others. I knew that my risky courier activities, bringing in food and other desperately needed items, would bring a measure of comfort to my fellow Jews trapped in the ghetto.

41

After a few runs for Peter, I had realized I was taking all the risks and he was making all the money. He offered me a better deal, but I decided that I could do much better on my own. That's when I became the Malach. I was happy to be known that way. It gave me anonymity.

In the almost two years that I lived in the Bialystok Ghetto I continued to act as a courier. To help me I gathered a few boys around my age and trained them on how to do the job right, and my plan was very effective. I would be the outside guy to make the trades. They would get the goods and bring the requested items back to the customers. Eventually the people in the ghetto knew me only as "the Malach." A Malach is angel or messenger in Hebrew. It's a variation of Malachi from the Old Testament. I don't know how much of an "angel" I was, but I can tell you I learned a lot of lessons they don't teach at the Harvard Business School. Those lessons were priceless in later years, in America. But that is another story I will tell you in the chapters ahead.

When people needed me, they would just ask for "the Malach" and someone would find me. Of course, even with the Virgin Mary medal what I was doing was very dangerous. I went in and out of the ghetto through secret openings—holes in the fences mainly. I was a born risk-taker. I'd take the gold or money given to me or my inside guys and trade those valuables for food, clothing or even arms that were available on the outside. Then I'd smuggle the stuff inside by getting it to my inside guys. By identifying myself only as Malach I was somewhat protected. The name also made me feel good about what I was doing.

Understandingly, Jews in the ghetto were starved for news, so I also brought newspapers in every day, which wasn't easy. People coveted papers because they were cut off from the outside world and eager for any information—looking for glimmers of hope, or at the least distraction. I saw to it that newspapers were available to anyone who wanted them. To obtain the papers I had a deal with Russian prisoners of war who worked for the local printers. The printers put out three propaganda-filled newspapers a day, one in German, one in Russian, and one in Polish. I'd get the latest Russian newspapers at 5

AM on the button. I used to pick them up a block away from the printing plant. They'd set aside two hundred papers for me in one shot, but I'd only take fifty or seventy at a time. By this time the three or four guys who were my helpers were all very good at what we were doing. A couple of these boys would also sell some of these newspapers in the ghetto while I was gathering more papers, along with food and other precious goods.

Armed German sentries patrolled outside the ghetto fence, so to get in or out you had to time everything carefully to avoid being spotted. I had several different secret holes in the fences that I used to leave or re-enter the ghetto, including a few places known only to me. I was careful not to use the same place every day because I didn't want to arouse suspicion. One day I'd go through this hole, the next day through that, another time over there, still another time through a basement. I varied my routine constantly to lower my risk of being caught.

To pay the printers I'd bring them a variety of items—cigarettes, clothing and gold, or whatever I could scrounge up. It was a real barter economy. If someone wanted a newspaper or food, he had to pay for it in the ghetto. Jews that were displaced from their homes were allowed to bring in ten kilos of their goods into the ghetto, but most managed to bring much more. People hid valuables such as watches and other jewelry wherever they could, and later traded them for survival. We operated an enterprise that was much more than a black market. People were so desperate that they used to pull the gold fillings out of their teeth—or the entire tooth itself—to sell for food. It was horrible, but I couldn't dwell on it. In all this turmoil I served as the middleman, the best way I knew how to. Typically, I would go out and back into the ghetto five or six times a day. I didn't think of myself as a businessman then—it was all part of the dangerous game of survival.

The ghetto was in effect a city within a city, with a building that served as a *de facto* City Hall, a Mayor appointed by the Germans, and a ghetto police force. If the Germans wanted something they approached the Mayor, who was appointed by the Jews themselves. The

Mayor was put in this position if he was a man of substance who had perhaps once owned a factory or run a big business. There were plenty of *machers* in the ghetto, I can tell you. In this City-Hall-type building, there were offices for bookkeeping and various bureaucratic functions.

The ghetto complex covered about twenty to twenty-five streets. Every five blocks or so there was another police station. Jewish policemen wore bands on their sleeves, but, again, carried no firearms. Understandably, Jewish men wanted to become policemen because they were given extra rations of food and could better provide for their families.

Somehow I remained confident that I would survive this terrible period. I just focused on doing what I had to do at the moment and refused to dwell on negative thoughts and fears. Even today it is a mystery where I found this confidence. I attribute part of my survival to the fact that I was a listener, not a teller. As the youngest, I also had a special relationship with my father. Whenever he talked, I listened. In fact, whatever my father did, I did. As the youngest son perhaps he favored me a bit. My father never said *no* to me. During my childhood, if he wanted a pear from the pear tree in the garden, he would grab two pears and give the other one to me. Growing up in Knyszyn, I'd listen carefully to his and other adult's conversations and learn from them.

I've also always been a careful observer. That ability served me well as I navigated the ghetto. I'd watch to see what people were doing and decide whether they were right or wrong, then figure out how to do it better. Even as a young kid I'd go with a neighbor and watch him working in his field. I'd watch how he'd plow, how he'd milk the cows. I'd notice what he was doing wrong or how he could do something better. When my sister milked one of our cows I'd stand by with a little broom to chase off the flies. That way the cow didn't swing her tail and spill the milk. That is just a small example of what I picked up from listening to and observing others.

The local Nazi bosses were keen on persuading the bloodless Reich bosses in Berlin to spare the Jews in the Bialystok Ghetto from the death camps. It wasn't out of the goodness of their hearts. The Jews were very good workers. These criminals wanted to keep the Jewish prisoners working as long as possible so they could continue to exploit us. What permeated most of the chatter in those days was the mistaken belief that hard work and cooperation would spare us the same fate that we heard had befallen Jews in other ghettos. Some of us resisted that pie-in-the-sky idea and took action by secretly forming a counter-insurgency to shape our own destiny. It was that underground movement, headed up by the resistance organizer Mordechai Tenenbaum, that I'd first heard about in the Polish army camp. At that same time, trains were delivering more and more of their human cargo to the Treblinka, Majdanek and Auschwitz death camps in Poland. Those hiding in the forest were trying to form an Underground, while young people like me in the ghetto were battling complacency and acceptance of our fate in any way we could. We were focusing on how to sabotage German efforts to annihilate us.

In the ghetto there were some days that were business as usual, but you never knew what was going to happen. One day the Germans announced that they needed fifty people to go outside the ghetto to sweep the streets, and posted a list of people to do it. If you wanted someone to substitute for you, you paid them about ten marks for the day. Payment was due when the person returned from work, and not before. My brother's friend Israel hired me to substitute for him. Returning from a day of backbreaking work, I went in search of Izzy to ask for the payment he had promised. Clearly he didn't have the money, even though I'd put in a long, hard day working in his place. I think he was a bit embarrassed. "Here," he finally said, reaching into his shirt. Reluctantly, he handed me a bottle of homemade vodka. I didn't really want the alcohol, but I knew that I could use it as barter, so I took it and slipped it into my inner pocket. Most of the men and boys in the ghetto wore two pairs of pants; the first pair of pants had a pocket inside, to hide contraband. The system was very handy for sneaking things into the ghetto.

I tucked the bottle of vodka in my inside pair of pants. When I walked into the ghetto, a German guard's dog sniffed me all over and smelled the vodka. This big, menacing German Shepard began growling and scratching at my foot. The German said, "*Was hast du da, Junge?*" I knew he'd asked what I was hiding, but I pretended that I didn't understand. I shrugged and gave him a quizzical smile. He wasn't having that. When I didn't reply he ordered me to raise my hands.

Brusquely, he told me to stand against the wall. There was no mistaking his intention. I stood there while he opened my belt. My first pair of pants, the outer pair dropped to the ground. He quickly found the bottle of vodka in the second pair of pants.

He knew I wasn't old enough to drink alcohol. I'd barely ever had a glass of wine or beer. But the German forced me to guzzle the whole bottle while his dog kept me pinned in place. I drank this vile-tasting stuff until my throat burned. When the bottle was finally empty he pulled the dog off me and made me get up and walk. I walked ten feet, fell, and started throwing up horrible green vomit.

I felt I was about to pass out when a couple of guys who were nearby rushed me to the ghetto clinic. I hardly knew what was happening while the medics pumped my stomach. Then the doctor gave me some liquid in a glass. I was still very weak and woozy. The doctor told me to hold my nose as he poured the contents of the glass into my mouth. He said, "This will cure you." I drank it and stood up like nothing happened. Turned out it was vodka! He had used a little vodka in order to get my system to settle down. What he gave me cured me immediately, though I did later vomit up that extra vodka.

That was nothing compared to what happened the next time Germans caught me—and with more than vodka—which I will relate a bit later on.

Despite our forced incarceration, life for me settled into a sort of routine, until a couple of months later when Peter, the black marketer I used to work with, introduced me to a Christian woman who worked for the Germans. This woman was crazy for money. Her husband worked for the German authorities doing menial jobs—shining boots and feeding horses. She was clearly the smart one of the pair. If I had gold or diamonds, she'd exchange them for arms or anything else I needed. I used to give her Russian coins, similar to an American dollar coin but thicker, called Hasural—"hogs" in English. They were worth ten rubles in gold. I even gave her gold caps from teeth—all kinds of stuff. In exchange she managed to bring me Russian guns or bullets to smuggle into the ghetto to arm the Underground. She was very well connected, for sure.

I always thought of her as Frieda, though she would never give me her true name. She would also never come into the ghetto. She'd come close to the fence and leave the merchandise on the ground outside. I'd pass her payment through the fence. Sometimes I'd give her the gold in advance because people trusted me, and I told them to trust her.

One day somebody who had observed her activities squealed on her. From then on the Germans were on the lookout for her. I didn't know anything about that. Inevitably two Germans and one Polish policeman caught her as she came close to the ghetto. That day I was on the way to meet her to pick up a package. Suddenly the three policemen appeared. They apprehended her and demanded to know who her contact person was. They promised to let her go if she identified that person. Unaware of what was going on, I was walking toward her. Too fast for me to react she pointed straight at me, ratting me out. She lied and told them she was only delivering food to me, so they let her go. But once they apprehended me it was another story.

They grabbed hold of me, searched me, took the gold and everything else of value I had on me. Then they dragged me to the Gestapo. I was still wearing the Virgin Mary medal, so they didn't think I was a Jew. Nonetheless, they pressured me to confess who I worked for and tell them who was receiving the contraband food. The Gestapo intimidated me like nobody else and I was extremely scared. Trying to compose myself I said, "If you show me the people I will recognize them, but I don't know their names." Getting nothing out of me, they took off my shirt and gave me twenty-five cold, hard, excruciatingly painful lashes on my bare skin with a long leather whip.

I was in severe pain, and when they let me sink to the floor I thought the punishment was over. But about two hours later they whipped me again with that same lash, and kept at it until I passed out. When I began to come to, they had me take off my pants, put a wet bag on my naked butt, and beat me with a different leather whip—one that had metal tips. I had never known such pain. My body puffed up like a balloon. The German captors beat me three times in that one day. I think I received about seventy-five lashes. They were trying to force me to spill everything I knew. I kept my mouth shut and didn't tell them anything. Then they threw me against a wall. Still, I gave them nothing.

In almost unbearable pain, I was left in the yard along with eight Russian paratroopers who'd been captured. Terrified, we sat together in a courtyard outside the ghetto for about six hours. I had no idea what was going on. I did speak some Russian, but we were not allowed to talk to each other. The hours seemed endless. Once night came the Nazis put us all on an open freight truck. They chained and cuffed the Russians together, but they didn't cuff me—probably because they didn't have enough cuffs. A big ugly German ordered me to get in the front of the truck. I couldn't argue. There was a three-wheeled Gestapo motorcycle hitched to the front, and another motorcycle hitched to the back of the truck.

The truck began to move and when the truck turned, there was a loud noise of metal clinking against metal. The Germans looked to the back of the truck to check on the rear motorcycle. When I noticed that they were distracted I quickly jumped off the moving truck.

One of the Germans saw me jump and started shooting at me, but I moved too fast, despite my wounds. The truck kept moving and I soon escaped. I dashed to my friend Haskell's house, where his mother Ethel applied cold compresses to my open wounds. I stayed in his house for two long weeks, until I began to heal. The Germans were searching for me, but thankfully didn't look in the ghetto. Because of my Virgin

Mary medal they still didn't know I was Jewish. Once I had finally recovered from those wounds I returned to my usual four to six forays a day outside the ghetto.

The woman who had traded goods with me was then in her late fifties. She had sharp eyes, a sharp nose, and an expression like stone. After she turned me in I never saw her again. A year and a half later, when the war ended and I was liberated I went looking for her. I am not ashamed to tell you that I was hell bent on avenging myself on that good-for-nothing monster who had ratted me out and caused me so much trouble. I went to her house, but nobody knew where she was. I can only guess that when the Russians came to Bialystok to rout out the Germans she probably figured that I, or possibly someone else she double-crossed, would come looking for her. She would have been right. Fortunately for her, I never found her.

Perhaps that was also fortunate for me. I didn't need that stain on my soul, but I can never understand or forgive her actions, or the actions of so many other inhuman monsters. But that is why I am telling you my story.

"Some people like the Jews, and some do not. But no thoughtful man can deny the fact that they are, beyond any question, the most formidable and most remarkable race which has appeared in the world."

—*Sir Winston S. Churchill (1874 – 1965), British statesman, army officer and author. Prime Minister of the United Kingdom 1940 -1945 and 1951-1955.*

5

The Underground, Spies, and the Bialystok Uprising

By 1943, along with my usual "black market" activities, I was also making a lot of courier runs for the ghetto's Underground. The higher-ups were willing to give me anything I wanted because they knew how useful I was. I was fortunate: I didn't need anything. I had more food and clothing than others in the ghetto, and tried my best to help whoever and however I could, even if they had nothing to trade.

At the time I was smuggling in guns, explosives and other weapons that I got on the outside from collaborators—or just greedy Poles who could offer guns for gold. I was also sneaking messages in, along with general supplies, to help support the Underground Movement in as many ways as I could.

Soon I heard through the ghetto grapevine that the Germans knew about my activities and were hot on my trail. I got a real break because they were still searching for me as Moishe, so I was able to elude them. I took some pleasure in knowing I was outsmarting those nasty *mamzers*.

As the winter of 1943 set in, the war was grinding on and we continued to witness some awful events. When a man named Paul Chorowski left the ghetto one day to find food he ran into trouble. On his way back with whatever meager rations he could find, the Nazis saw him and fired shots in his direction. Though he was clearly in imminent danger he did not actually get shot. This means they were only trying to scare him, because, trust me, the Gestapo were expert marksmen. While Chorowski was sneaking back into the ghetto, I noticed several Gesta-

51

po officers coming right toward me. The Gestapo was sure I was Polish because of that Virgin Mary medal I wore around my neck. When they stopped in front of me they simply asked me "Where did the Jew go?" I told them that he had turned left. Of course, he had run to the right, in the opposite direction. We Polish Jews did almost everything we could do to cause consternation to the Germans.

Despite all this, I was almost never afraid. I suppose it was the optimism of youth, but I was a bit cocky too. Despite the horrible circumstances, I had a feeling of invincibility. My attitude was that no bullet can touch me. "How can a little bullet kill a person?" This was always in my head, even though I saw people killed by bullets all the time. I just never believed a bullet could kill *me*. I'm convinced that this instinct for survival protected me—maybe partly because I walked around with a confident air. Or maybe I was just one of the lucky ones. I remain certain that this illogical self-assurance and my mid-teens bravado was a blessing that helped keep me alive.

Needless to say, the Germans had spies throughout the ghetto. It was one thing knowing there was surveillance, and another thing never knowing whom you could trust. A lot of people knew that someone— the someone being me—was bringing in food, but they didn't know who it was. One day I was carrying a lot of stuff that I was going to give to the other boys on the inside when I saw that two Germans were waiting right by one of my secret passages. I tried to go underneath the fence in a nearby spot. As I was attempting this one of the Germans reached over to grab me. I didn't want to give away the secret place, so I began to climb on top of the fence. He ordered me to come down. I wouldn't do it and kept climbing, so to make me come down he stabbed me with a bayonet. I was hurt but I still did not jump down. Instead, I made it to the top and jumped over the ten-foot fence. He couldn't chase me over such a high fence so he started shooting. Fortunately his bullets did not hit me—and this was a real attempt to kill, not just to scare, as with some of the incidents I witnessed.

As soon as the German guard realized I was gone and he turned around to terrorize someone else, I marched straight to the ghetto clinic because he had cut me very badly. In the clinic they put three steel clamps in my knee to heal the deep wound. I still have the scar on my left knee to remind me of that day. Of course the Germans got the merchandise. Luckily it was just a ham, which was ironic—Jews eating ham. But all dietary laws broke down during the war. Our bodies are built for survival, and in a crisis our instincts to stay alive kick in. The Holocaust was way beyond a mere crisis.

One of the things the Underground partisans had to worry about were spies, some of whom were Jewish—luckily not many. They were taken from small towns and planted in the ghetto by the Germans. There was a town called Riginoi on the German-Polish border. The Gestapo hired two Jewish brothers and their sister, the Yukofski family, from that town to do some of their dirty work. These Jews ratting out other Jews were the worst kind of traitors, despised by all of us. The family was ordered to live in the Bialystok Ghetto alongside the rest of us. The minute they went outside the ghetto they'd go straight to the Gestapo with their reports of what was going on inside.

I knew for sure that the Yukofskis were spies. I told some people who were part of the Underground about these three adult siblings, and warned them to keep an eye out, that these turncoats were up to no good. Eventually we would find justice. Sure enough, one Sunday, a huge collective cry went up. Somehow people had learned that the Germans fully intended to kill everybody in the ghetto. Two Jewish men from the Underground saw the Yukofskis as they came back into the ghetto, took aim, fired their guns, and wounded them. They brought one of the brothers to the ghetto hospital for treatment. Two days later, while this brother sat in the sun on a hospital balcony reading a book, some ghetto guy in a mask climbed up the outside of the building and put three bullets in the traitor's head. That finished him off. That was in May 1943, a few months before the Bialystok Uprising. The other brother and their sister were later killed by the Germans because they didn't need them anymore.

Every day fifteen or twenty men left the ghetto to work in a factory where they made oil out of tiny sunflower seeds. Each morning they'd climb up on a truck that waited outside the gate, and travel three miles to the factory where the tiny seeds were pressed into oil. These men had the very messy job of crushing the tiny sunflower seeds to extract the oil. They worked all day with a shovel, while their bare feet would sink into the pulpy mush from the crushed seeds. Since their pants had cuffs, a few small seeds hopped in their cuffs. One day seven of these men were returning from work when the head of the Gestapo, Chief Friedle, stopped them and made them turn down their pant cuffs. A few seeds fell out.

For this offence, considered theft, the Germans kept them in the Jewish police jail for a day or two because of these "stolen" seeds. Then Chief Friedle took some matches and declared, "All the people that can fit into this little open square should come and watch now." The Germans had already prepared nooses in the square. They blindfolded all seven of the Jewish workers. Chief Friedle then took out four matches and broke them in half. The blindfolded men had to pick a match like it was a lottery—but a lottery of death.

A father and his two sons picked the smaller match ends. The German soldiers placed the father and sons on a truck, and, as they stood up on the bench, the Germans hung them. The Jews in the ghetto had to stand and watch this chilling scene. The thought made my blood run cold. The other guys who'd been found with the seeds received twenty-five lashes apiece, which, although a severe punishment was certainly preferable to death.

Ironically, ten years later the Polish government captured Friedle and hung him in that same square, where he remained hanging for five days.

By the winter of 1943, the Nazi death machine was in high gear. Tens of thousands of Jews were being shipped to Treblinka and the other camps each week, and the shipments of human souls just kept going at a rapid pace. This inevitable date with death befell most, but there were occasional exceptions. One such exception was the Brejinski family, who somehow managed to get to a small town outside Bialystok.

The Brejinskis consisted of a father, a daughter, and two sons— Ruth, their wife and mother, had been killed by a bomb in 1939. Once the family reached the small town they paid a lot of money to a wealthy Polish farmer by the name of Stanley Ojiyeski. Stanley, a devout Christian, was waiting for the Brejinskis with a sled when they finally arrived in his town. He took in the entire family, and a few more Jews, at great risk to himself and his own family. He hid the Brejinskis, and the others, in a ditch on his farm for almost two years. In gratitude, Mr. Brejinski promised Stanley that when the war ended all their property would go to him.

Stanley Ojiyeski went to church every Sunday, and was a teetotaler. He owned many acres of land. To feed the Jews he slaughtered pigs and cows and made many other sacrifices to help them stay alive. By time the war was over the Brejinski family had been living in the ditch on Stanley's farm for twenty-two months. When they were finally able to come out of hiding they were almost blind because they'd spent those two years in the dark. Still, they were so grateful to Stanley that they gave him many generous gifts.

Then the Brejinskis heard that bandits were roaming the countryside near Stanley's farm. Their aim was to kill any Jews that had avoided the extermination camps. To protect their Christian friend and themselves, all the Jews who had been on the farm moved back to Bialystok. Meanwhile, the bandits discovered that Stanley's brave actions had saved ten Jews. In reprisal they set his belongings on fire and demanded that he surrender everything he was given by the Jews he hid. Mr. Ojiyeski claimed that the Jews had only given him deeds to their property, denying that they had given him any gold. He did have the gold, but it was all he had left.

These marauders made him strip his pants off, and burned the flesh on his buttocks with hot metal tools found on his farm. The following day Stanley went to the local police, who took him into Bialystok, where Jewish doctors performed surgery to repair the severe damage caused by his third-degree burns. Surgeons took skin from different parts of his body and grafted it onto his backside. The pain was excruciating, and he was at high risk for infection. Fortunately, he recovered. Soon after he was sponsored by HIAS, the Hebrew Immigration Aid Society, which made it possible for him and his family to immigrate to the United States.

As a sidebar, I had known Stanley in Poland, and had a great deal of respect for him. When he got here my uncle Harry got him an apartment, and I gave him a job. He worked for me for five years, until he died. I think it's heartwarming that this man, a hero who bravely saved Jewish lives, and then was horribly tortured for his kindness and bravery, was ultimately saved by American Jews. But of course all this happened later on.

Back then, in the ghetto, I was holding to a fairly steady routine of going out up to six times a day to trade for necessities that the other boys took from me to smuggle in to those who had traded for those items. Then came the morning of February 5th, 1943. At dawn, as the sun was about to come up that unforgettable winter day, the Nazis stormed the ghetto. It was a Sunday and most people were still fast asleep. Suddenly a huge commotion erupted in the square, shots were fired into the air, and there was much hysteria. Women and children were screaming and crying, as they scurried about trying to find places to hide. It was clear that, finally, one of the death camp roundups we had heard about going on elsewhere had come in earnest to the Bialystok Ghetto.

In the chaos some people hid in the big cemetery inside the ghetto. The Germans never went into the cemetery, not in daytime or in nighttime. I don't know why. Instead, they sent in huge Ukrainian and Polish policemen to round-up the men, women and children who took cover in the cemetery. These Poles and Ukrainians served the Reich. Their specific job was to seek out hiding Jews, as if it was some kind of deadly hide-and-seek game.

Soon they were corralling a large number of men, women and children to transport them to concentration camps. It was heartbreaking to hear the sobs and screams of the defenseless as they were grabbed by brutal soldiers or taken at gunpoint. Altogether that day they took about 10,000 souls to the death camps.

For me, this chaos was my cue to attempt yet another escape. I was nimble and hightailed it through a section of barbed wire fence, my heart pounding like a drum. As fast as my feet could carry me, I made my way to the house of a Christian friend, one who lived outside the ghetto. I stayed there for a few days until I thought it was safe to go back. During that time I didn't dare even stick my nose out his door.

Once the round-up had ended and I thought the coast was clear, I returned to the ghetto and resumed my "Malach" activities. That routine continued for the next six months. Then, on the evening of August 15, 1943, Ephraim Barash, who headed the *Judenrat*, was summoned to Gestapo headquarters. Abruptly he was informed that the next morning there would be a mass deportation from the Bialystok Ghetto—in other words the ghetto was going to be emptied out. Supposedly the remaining Jews would be transported to work in Lublin—another big city in Poland where there was also a ghetto. Of course, this was another big lie—and it was the news that finally triggered the Ghetto Uprising. The Uprising had been simmering beneath the surface for many months, with arms being gathered long before that. To throw us off the scent of what was really happening, the Nazis told the Jews that they could take twelve pounds of possessions and tools to Lublin. Barash, meanwhile, had failed to inform the Underground of what was happening, even though he secretly supported the movement. Maybe he was paralyzed into inaction because he was in shock. In any case, the ghetto's final liquidation was beginning.

Members of the Underground were now continually taking turns to keep watch over the Germans. They would occasionally spot suspicious activity. However, it wasn't until 4 AM on August 16, 1943 that, literally, all hell broke loose. That morning the Underground watchmen and women spied German soldiers with submachine guns, three tanks, and several armored vehicles coming into the area. The menace was clear.

While thousands of Jews obediently followed the directions of Barash and the German's directives and packed to move, members of the Underground—of which I considered myself a small part—convened a hasty meeting. In truth we had been taken by surprise thanks to Barash's lack of planning, and had little time to prepare a counterstrike. We hoped to be victorious, or at least help as many Jews as possible escape into the nearby forest. That was always our last option at times like these. The deep, dark, cold and inhospitable forests of Poland did save lives. Of course, not that many lives—but some was better than none.

Bang! Pow! Rat-a-tat! The noise was tremendous as this well-armed, well-trained, well-manned and ruthless military taskforce came rumbling through the ghetto's makeshift gates. They came from all directions, surrounding us ghetto captives. The minute I heard the commotion I knew what was happening. My job was to supply various sorts of arms, which I'd hidden in secret spots throughout the area. I had caches in many hiding places, and they were well concealed. As the dawn cracked that day, I was scurrying everywhere, surrounded by my trusted couriers, all of us acting to quickly supply Underground fighters with the ammunition sorely needed to fuel our rag-tag resistance. My little group of inside couriers and I were moving as fast as our feet could carry us to distribute our stock of weapons.

Quickly, our fighters took strategic positions all over the ghetto. That part was well-planned. For the most part they were stationed at high positions, which gave each fighter a better chance of sniping from above and taking some Germans out. Others were shooting or throwing grenades from basement windows, to kill or injure our attackers.

Everyone in the Underground participated in the fray. One Underground fighter, a Russian girl who had been in the Russian Army from 1939 to 1941, was lying in wait on one of the balconies of a house facing the square. When the Russians lost to the Germans, she had somehow managed to steal a machine gun. As soon as this brave young woman saw the first tank emerge through the early morning fog she started shooting at the entire parade of tanks.

Ping! Ping! Ping! The bullets cut through the air with an ear-splitting noise. Many people stood with her on that balcony, while those in nearby windows launched hand grenades toward the ghetto fence. As Germans shot at the Jews, the Jewish people shot back. But of course it was a completely uneven battle.

Some Russian Jews threw grenades onto a German tank, and when the grenades detonated the tank was destroyed. Several Ukrainian soldiers who served in the German army, armed and walking behind the tanks, were injured or killed when the tank exploded. I think the Germans were very surprised that we had staged an ambush. But still, we were badly out-manned. As we attacked the tanks, Russian soldiers, along with a contingent of Polish soldiers who, like the Ukrainians, were also serving in the German Army, swarmed into the square.

It's hard to estimate the exact number of those who took part in the Uprising, but I can tell you that there were fewer than five hundred Jewish insurgents taking part. Nevertheless, they fought hard and were very brave.

Besides being outnumbered we were also out-armed. Despite my best efforts, and those of others, we only had about 25 rifles, 100 pistols, and a few machine guns, plus the grenades I dug out of the basement and hurled into the street. Several dozen Molotov cocktails were also used as makeshift grenades. Most of these weapons were ones I had smuggled in, trading the Russians and Poles for whatever goods I could, including clothes, shoes, bedding, and gold jewelry. I also did my part in the fighting, despite my brother Schmuel and his girlfriend—who were hiding in the street—urging me to hide too, saying "Stop, or you will get caught!" We kept on attacking the overwhelming German forces, but the Underground lost many of its brave members on that first day alone.

It was tragedy on top of tragedy. After running out of ammunition the commanders of the insurgency committed suicide in their bunkers.

Another seventy-two fighters, who were hiding in bunkers, were captured, lined up against a wall, and shot by the attacking army.

During the Uprising about one-hundred-fifty fighters managed to escape into the forest, where they ultimately joined other guerilla groups. Those were the lucky ones: others were shot in the back as they fled into the forests. Still other Jewish fighters were taken to a field two miles away and shot dead, their corpses left to rot in the mud.

In all, approximately 3,500 people were killed during the Uprising. This included many Germans, as well as Ukrainian and Polish soldiers and police, but that was cold consolation. The Uprising never had a real chance for success. Still, we had dug our heels in. We preferred fighting, no matter what the cost, rather than meeting a bleak and hopeless death in the concentration camps.

When the Uprising ended, the deportations to concentration and extermination camps proceeded. It was August 17, 1943. Out of the almost 65,000 Jews who lived in Bialystok before World War II, only several hundred or even less survived the Holocaust. The fact that I survived the Uprising was in itself a miracle. But by Wednesday, August 19th the Germans caught me. Along with thousands of others of my *landsmen* and women, I was put in a cattle car headed for what seemed to be certain death. But then, when the train slowed down from about 60 to about 40 miles an hour, I made an instant decision that changed everything.

6

The Treblinka Death Train
A Split Second Decision

I didn't think about it then, as I continued to struggle for survival from day to day, but my adolescence had become a series of life-and-death misadventures and escapes. Perhaps the most dramatic moment happened when I was 15. It was a moment when I once again avoided the grip of death, in what was undoubtedly my most daring exploit. How I pulled off the experience I am about to relate surprises me even to this day, and I am just past my 89th birthday.

Throughout 1942 or '43, the Nazis had been little by little emptying the Bialystok Ghetto of its inhabitants. People you would see every day suddenly disappeared, and these disappearances began to add up in large numbers. There were lots of rumors, all whispered, about the true whereabouts of these doomed souls. We all knew that their destination was not a happy one. The Treblinka or Majdanek extermination camps were the terrible fates of these hapless Jews.

During the week of February 5th-12th 1943, the Nazis methodically removed between 10,000 to 12,000 Jews from the Bialystok Ghetto, forcing them into cattle cars bound for Treblinka. Once locked into the cattle cars, these terrified individuals of all ages were taken directly to the death camps and immediately or eventually gassed to death—as the world now knows. At the time, however, nothing was certain. A mist of unreality clouded every day, and frankly nothing was made clearer by the endless speculation of the ghetto grapevine.

Those of us who were still in the ghetto knew about the cattle cars passing by, but could not see them, as the train tracks were about two miles away. Treblinka itself was about 62 miles from Bialystok. We knew that these cars were originally used to transport livestock, and had a little window in each car so that the cattle could breathe. In these same cars that now transported humans for slaughter, these windows had barbed wire coverings. We also heard that local Poles standing on the train station platforms would often ask, with false innocence, "I wonder where those trains are going?" But they knew. And soon we all knew.

As things ramped up, there were some Jews who managed to escape from the ghetto into the Aryan side of the city and find refuge in the homes of Poles. These rare saviors came to be known as "righteous Poles," because they took great risks to shelter Jews, who were otherwise destined for certain death. Some Jews survived thanks to these Christian Poles, but unfortunately their numbers were few. Alas, the vast majority of souls trapped in the ghetto were doomed to die horrible deaths.

This accursed place called Treblinka was an open secret. Jews who were able to get outside the ghetto for work—or for missions like I did—knew what was coming. We were the ones willing to take a risk to escape the deadly train transports because we knew it led to a place that was worse than nowhere. Some of us hid in the cemetery, knowing that the Germans never searched there. Maybe they were superstitious or spooked. I'll never know, but their reason was unimportant. We took refuge in any place that would protect us when we were being hunted down or being dragged to our deaths.

At the time I hadn't hatched a survival plan, and nobody really could. I lived like a feral animal, listening and observing, existing from moment to moment, always on the alert. Someone in the ghetto once asked me if I had a feeling of invincibility. He knew I had been beaten badly by the Nazis more than once, and managed to survive. At those times, the Nazis said they intended to beat me to death. I didn't think about being invincible. I just refused to allow myself to be killed. When they said they would kill me, I said to myself "No, you won't," and I stuck to the word "No." This way I kept my sanity, especially after they beat me twice for going in and out of the ghetto to trade goods—although they still didn't know I was Jewish and against all odds let me go. Here I was again, saying no to the Nazis, and trying to find a way out through the cemetery.

With some Nazi guards on my heels, I escaped through a hole in the cemetery fence and gave a sigh of relief. I thought I had made it by a whisker once more. Nope! Suddenly I felt the heavy knock of a gun butt on my shoulder. Someone strong grabbed me by the collar. I had been caught. He spat out the word, *Jude*, as he grabbed me and shook me very hard.

People have since asked me why, when I still had the St. Mary medallion around my neck, I hid it beneath my shirts instead of claiming to be a Polish youth. As dire as things looked right then, I believed with all my heart that I would find a way to escape, and that the medallion would help save my life again as it had before. I instinctively knew this was not the time to "flash" it. There would be too many questions. I would have to bide my time.

When he grabbed me I was very angry and scared, but I had learned to pretend to be unfazed. That was the only way to deal with these brutes, my best chance. So I looked him straight in the eye to prove to him that I wasn't afraid—but I was plenty afraid, believe me. This German *soldat* pulled me along and pushed me into a crowd in a nearby field, where dozens of us were waiting to be herded toward the cattle cars that would soon rattle along those nearby tracks. We were closely guarded. One wrong move and I was dead. I had finally been given my one way ticket to hell. There were many numbers of extermination camps in Poland. They were all heinous, but Treblinka was the worst of the worst.

This trip to Treblinka appeared inevitable, but I was still looking for any chance of freedom, no matter how slim. That's why I was always on the alert, listening to snippets of gossip, looking this way and that, inside the ghetto and on the outside. While I waited in the field with those thousands of others, I saw a guard beating an older woman as her husband looked on helplessly. I watched the drawn faces of families as they huddled together for comfort. Nearby, an Orthodox Rabbi prayed in the moving crowd, his lips trembling and eyes closed. I had no time for God. I couldn't believe there *was* a God who just looked on as all of this happened to the Jewish people. Samuel Willenberg, the last survivor of Treblinka's death camp, who died in February 2016, had said, "God must have been on holiday. I looked for Him, but there was only a beautiful Polish sky."

How much the Bialystok Jews knew as they were ordered to board the Treblinka train is hard to say. Too many stories had already circulated. Some denied what was taking place before their eyes, clinging to their faith. Others had followed Ephraim Barash, and like him had lived in the false hope that our ghetto would not meet the same fate as the other ghettos, thanks to our "usefulness" to the Nazis. These Jews had now become angry and bitter. Still others believed that civilized men in an educated society couldn't act this way. I'm sure others were too exhausted, demoralized, anxious and fearful to think about anything. Just surviving in the ghetto was a full-time occupation.

We stood in that field for hours, in the heat and damp weather, waiting for our turn to be herded into the cars, just like cattle. It is hard to believe, but as we were being put on board, I saw that people were selling bottles of water outside the trains. Desperately thirsty, but with no money, and already stepping onto the train, I took off my boots, intending to give the woman my boots in exchange for the water. However, as soon as I reached for the bottle of water the train started moving, jerking along the tracks. I grabbed for the bottle but it was out of reach, and there was no time to put my boots back on again. I tied the boots around my neck. I had no idea how significant that small gesture would soon become.

They had stuffed more of us into the already packed cars, and we had been yelled at, pushed and prodded until they could not shoehorn in another human body. About one-hundred-fifty people were crammed inside each cattle car, so tightly that nobody could move. Inside it was boiling hot and the air was fetid. I tried to station myself close to an air vent, but the car filled up too fast. Some people fainted, and some of the weaker ones perished. I later learned that Jews already at Treblinka were tasked with pulling dead bodies out of the cattle cars. Then they emptied cars so the trains could return to transport more people to their deaths, as the murderous transit machines continued.

As it happened, my older brother Schmuel and his girlfriend were in the same car that I was. I gave him a knowing look. I knew we were in big trouble, and there were so many things we wanted to say to each other. But with a hundred people squeezed between us it was impossible to talk. I've always wondered what we might have said otherwise.

From the outskirts of Bialystok, the train traversed about a mile deep into the forest toward the death camp. With no bathroom on board, people urinated and soiled their clothes. The odor of human waste was awful, but we didn't talk about the smell. In fact we barely noticed the stench, because we could only smell fear. All those around me—myself included—were terrified. I knew that if I wanted to live I needed to keep focused. In my mind I kept repeating the same word, "No, no, no."

As soon as the door to the car was slammed shut and the train began to move, a man near me pulled out a pair of wire cutters and began snipping the wire that covered the little window in the car. As the train approached a station it slowed down from about sixty miles an hour to about forty miles per hour. That wasn't a full stop, but to me this made a plunge for freedom more doable. I began climbing out. Some other people helped by hoisting me up and pushing me out. Suddenly, others grabbed my legs to pull me back in. They were fearful that if they let me go, and the Germans discovered my escape, they would kill all the Jews left inside. There was no talking to these people so I ignored them. My chance for freedom was quickly slipping away and I was not one to ever turn back.

It was my only opportunity and these people didn't see that, but I knew that some others were quietly cheering me on. Before I climbed out the window I turned to my brother and yelled, "*Tance! Tance!*" which means "Jump, jump," in Yiddish. I hoped he'd seize the moment and also take this chance to escape, but he either didn't hear me or didn't have the nerve. Then I used my foot to kick open the latch on the cattle car door. Once the door was open I jumped, rolled in a somersault out of the car and kept running, and that was the last I saw of him. Later I learned that he had died in Treblinka, as did most of my large family.

Others, however, did jump after me once I'd opened the door. Polish and Ukrainian guards, heavily armed, were positioned on the roofs of the train cars, and when the train had slowed and people tried to get out, the shooting started. In the next car over a woman threw her eleven-month-old baby out the window, wrapped in a pillowcase, and then the mother jumped. When she landed on the hard ground, an older German guard came up to her. He had a growling German Shepherd by his side. To her surprise he quietly asked her, "Do you have healthy bones?" "Yes, yes," she said, her adrenalin pumping. He told her to pick up her baby and run—and, of course, she did.

Meanwhile the guards on the roofs and the police on the ground were shooting. I could hear their guns and feel the breeze shift as bullets whizzed past my head. Still I kept saying to myself "No, no I will not die." When I jumped from the train I fell very hard but quickly rose to my feet. Once I stood up, I ran like the wind, even though I had no shoes on, and my boots were still tied around my neck. Behind me guards kept shooting, trying to take me down. A bullet grazed my arm, going through all three shirts I had on. Wearing multiple shirts may have helped save my life!

The brutal Nazis caught and killed everyone who tried to escape the cattle car except for the woman with the baby and me. The heroic mother and her baby survived with partisans they joined in the forest. They eventually wound up in Israel. Her baby daughter is still alive, still living in Israel today.

Between the railroad and the forest lay a field where farmers grew corn and wheat. As I raced across those farmland fields, I kept glancing around to see if I was being followed. As luck would have it, I soon saw that two Christian Poles were chasing me. Worse yet, they were gaining on me. I was running through the hay field, making progress toward the nearby forest. It was the only place to hide. Then I spotted these guys, about two hundred meters behind me. They had been cutting hay in the fields and still had their machetes in hand—great big scythes that they used to mow down the hay. They were field workers, and obviously wanted to turn me in to the Germans for a reward, steal my clothes, or both.

I was trying to outrun them while figuring out my next move. Acting on impulse—I could only act in the moment—I untied the laces on my boots and hurled them toward the men, figuring that at the very least it would buy time. As soon as I tossed the heavy boots toward these two guys from around my neck they stopped running and grabbed the boots. My boots were very worn, but times were so tough that these two thugs began fighting over my old boots. Once they paused, they began tangling with each other over the boots and forgot about me.

I took off again and raced toward the forest. To what I did not know. Running as fast as I could, it felt like I was going a hundred miles an hour on pure adrenaline—shoeless yet determined. At the time I didn't feel scared—action like that leaves no time for emotion. Even though I felt like a hunted animal running for my life, I was relieved to be out of that cattle car. When I threw the boots, I did feel a momentary surge of fear. My heart pounded like a drum until I was clear of all of the guards, field hands and assorted pursuers, real and imagined.

The Knyszyn Forest lay about 500 yards away from the railroad tracks. Fortunately it didn't take me long to disappear into the shelter of the dense summer trees, and I moved forward into the unknown.

As day turned into night I stopped running, deep in the forest, I smiled to myself when I realized that a pair of old brown boots had saved my life. Later some other things would save my life—my red hair and blue eyes, my ability to speak clear Polish, and, once again, the religious medallion I still wore around my neck.

Soon I noticed other people who were hiding deep inside the woods. I deliberately avoided them. I felt it would be a mistake to join up with others at the moment, sensing that it would only lead to trouble. Much later I learned that these people were Russians, Poles and Jewish partisans, all hiding from the Germans. I decided I'd be safer in the fields, and changed my course. It proved a judicious decision.

7

The Polish Farmhouse

After the Polish farmhands stopped chasing me to fight over my boots on that boiling hot day in mid-August 1943, I continued running like a bat out of hell, but once it was fully dark I decided to leave the forest. I crept back to the fields where local farmers raised their crops. I was young—only 17—and, despite the physical abuse I suffered in the ghetto, I was still strong.

Of course, in retrospect, my desperate need to survive gave this "Malach" wings. As I raced through the fields, farmers were bringing their animals in for the night. One farmer yelled out in Polish "What's wrong with your head?" He'd noticed my head wound, because there was blood on my face. That wound happened before we boarded the cattle train. The Nazis had marched us from the ghetto in a long line, four people across, to a field beside the train tracks. Their plan was to let us rot in the field, if need be, until the trains returned from Treblinka to pick up the next group of us. Just as we got to the field, an older Jewish man fainted, overcome by heat, and two Ukrainian guards pointed their rifles at me, shouting to me and another kid to pick the old man up quickly and walk him over to where most of the people sat on the ground. "*Schnell, Schnell!*" they shouted, meaning faster, faster.

I tried to lift the man, but he was a dead weight, impossible to budge. Even though this kid and I tried hard, we could not move him. As reprisal, one of the Ukrainians angrily smashed the butt of his rifle against the top of my head. I was momentarily stunned. As I fell, my head opened up and bled profusely. Luckily the Ukrainian dog left me for dead.

69

I allowed some time to pass until that Ukrainian guard got busy elsewhere. Then I struggled to my feet, shaky and a bloody mess. Once again I had to think fast. As usual, I wore extra shirts. In fact, I normally wore four shirts. The extra shirts were useful in all sorts of emergency situations—of which there were many. I ripped off one shirt and pressed it to my head to stem the blood and mask my head wound from the guards. If they saw that I was injured they would most likely finish me off then and there—another lovely Nazi custom. They couldn't be bothered tending to the sick or lame, so they killed those who couldn't stand on their own two feet. Human life meant no more to them than a snap of the fingers.

Once I hid my injury, I quickly rejoined the others in the field. We were all anxious and intensely hungry and exhausted, sitting in that open field for three days waiting for the Treblinka death train. In the meantime, I coped with my head wound as best as I could, and hoped nobody would notice.

As soon as the train came in, the Nazis loaded us into the cattle cars, but it took some time. All together, they were taking about 10,000 souls from the Bialystok Ghetto to the Polish death camps, so it was a big operation.

What I didn't tell you was what happened *before* I managed to escape from the train. Once inside the cattle car I recognized a doctor who had treated me in the ghetto, Dr. Tuva Sitron. He was standing right next to me. Right away he noticed the gash on my head, which was at risk of becoming infected. Amazingly, he had been allowed to keep his medical bag, and did a masterful job of bandaging my head so that the gauze did not cover my eyes. He was an artist with gauze! It was one of the pieces of strange luck I had—that the doctor was in the same car with me and had the supplies to fix my wound.

Today, I still have a big scar on my forehead from that blow to my head, courtesy of that heartless Ukrainian guard. Of course, like so many of the tragic and nightmarish memories from that period, my deepest scars are hidden.

After my frenzied run, when I was certain I had shaken any pursuers, I slowed down. I was still panting from exertion, but my breathing slowed and I settled into a quick walk, then a slower walk—and finally the walk of someone who wasn't being chased.

Under cloak of night I made my way back to the hayfields. Soon I came to several neat rows of haystacks, and decided I would hide inside one of them until morning. Once I was fully concealed by fresh-cut hay, I collapsed from exhaustion and fell into a heavy sleep, welcoming the temporary sense of refuge the haystack offered. It was even good to feel the prickly hay against my skin. If this is how freedom felt I was all for it!

Many hours later, I was still in a deep sleep state when I was startled awake by a sharp instrument poking into my shoulder. I cried out, surprising the man with the pitchfork more than he startled me. Once I was jolted awake, the horrors of the Treblinka train came flooding back. I was keenly aware that the farmer who jabbed me with a pitchfork was getting ready to load the hay onto his wagon. I squinted at the light as the morning sun began to rise. Realizing there was someone now partially hidden inside his haystack, the man gruffly ordered me to show myself.

"Hey, Boy! What are you doing in there?" he demanded.

I had to quickly decide how to make this tricky situation work for me. "I ran away from the train," I told him, in perfect Polish, as I hastily got up and brushed off pieces of hay. "Do you need any help on your farm? I am capable and looking for work." I hoped that this offer would deflect any questions he might have.

He gave me a knowing nod and seemed to understand right away. Thankfully, he assumed that the Nazis had put me on the train to work on German farms, and that I had run away. From my point of view, it was a fortunate misunderstanding, with thanks due once again to that critically important Virgin Mary medal, which I was deliberately now showing. If he wanted to think that I was a Polish Christian, who was I to dissuade him? Little did he know I was telling the truth—but

71

ironically I'd escaped from a different kind of train. I asked him if he had anything to eat. He gave me a bottle of milk and a little piece of pumpernickel bread. Nothing had tasted that good in a long time.

As it happened, the farmer that caused me such a rude awakening didn't need help, but his neighbor did, and he brought me to a neighboring farm. It was one I'd eventually live with, hiding in plain sight, for the next eleven months. First though, the farmer with the pitchfork took me to his own farmhouse, where his wife fed me. When I had eaten my food and washed up he drove me in his wagon to the neighboring farm and introduced me to his friend Mr. Zaremba, an older man with a very kindly nature.

He looked me over and said that as long as I was able to help him with the chores I was welcome to stay. I was sturdy and he soon saw that I could be a big help. He figured I knew a lot about farming, and in fact I did know a lot, just from growing up in a rural town like Knyszyn.

He agreed to take me in without asking too many questions, which was a blessing. Shortly we developed a daily routine. I helped Mr. Zaremba load his wagon with wheat, corn and various crops, among many other chores. In exchange I was not paid in currency. Money was scarce for everyone. But once I started working for the Zaremba family, I had plentiful food, a roof over my head and, most important, sanctuary. Once they got to know me Mr. and Mrs. Zaremba treated me like a son.

Mr. Zaremba was skinny and his wife was very beautiful—she looked like a doll. They lived simply but comfortably, even in this time of war. They were among the lucky ones who could grow their own food and raise their own poultry and beef. But they needed help badly and so, fortunately, needed me. It was a case of being in the right place at the right time but of course for all the wrong reasons. At the time none of their children were living at home, so there was no one else to help with the many jobs necessary to keep the farm running. Before I landed on their doorstep Farmer Zaremba was overwhelmed. Every able-bodied man was off at the front. During the war only the lame and feeble were left behind.

Getting to know the Zarembas, I got to know their story. One of the couple's sons, who had been in the Polish Army, had been held as a prisoner of war before I arrived on the farm. He'd now been a captive in Germany for almost four years. Eventually he would escape from Germany and return home—while I was living with his parents! When he got home, we formed a special bond. We had both escaped from the Germans and were both trying to remain undercover. Of course, he did not know my personal story or that I was Jewish. Luckily the Zarembas never asked me much about myself. I don't think that was by accident. And the less they knew of my story the better, for their protection as well as mine.

If I had grown up in a big city like Bialystok, I would never have survived. But because my family kept three horses and three cows, I already knew how to handle livestock. Although I had not lived on a farm, we had horses and cows housed in a barn in our yard. I'd watch how people handled the animals and quickly figure things out. Unlike us, the Zarembas had a real working farm. It was about fifty acres, which was a very large farm for the area. They also owned quite a few animals, including seven or eight cows and five or six horses. They had two large dogs, several lambs, and two calves. It was a regular menagerie. By local standards, the Zarembas were wealthy people, and they still are today. The farm encompassed a wide area, and the family still operates the land today as a working farm.

There was work on the farm seven days a week, and the days were long and hard. I didn't mind. I was happy to have a safe harbor, and thrived on hard work. It helped to keep the pain away. A typical day meant waking up at 4 AM. I would hop out of bed and put on my very worn clothes. Luckily Mr. Zaremba had kindly replaced my boots. At the start of the day I didn't have breakfast—not even coffee or tea. Mrs. Zaremba was always up at that time too. First she'd milk the cows, sitting on her little chair. I had a little chair too, and I'd sit with a pail of water, which I'd splash on the cows' udders and teats to clean them and make them soft for milking. Then I would begin to milk those gentle "milk machines." In no time I would have a full pail of warm milk. Actually I enjoyed milking the cows. I liked the calm rhythmic motion of pulling the teats to produce the milk. It made me think of home, because in Knyszyn my sisters used to milk our cows.

Even in those days all the farmers had machines to sterilize the milk and of course Mr. Zaremba had one to keep his cows' milk wholesome and drinkable. Mrs. Zaremba used the raw milk to make cheese, sour milk, and various dairy products, which were fresh and tasty. These luxuries found their way to the family table. After a few weeks in the Zaremba household I began to put back some of the weight I'd lost during my time in the ghetto.

After the milking was done Mrs. Zaremba collected fresh eggs from the flock of chickens in the barnyard. At 5 AM it was my job to take all the cows and horses out of the barn and drive them to the field so they could graze. Around 8 AM, I brought the animals back. By then a meal had been prepared in the kitchen. There was plenty of breakfast for all of us, which sometimes included some local friends of the Zarembas. The cows stayed in the barn from 8 AM to noon because it was too hot in the sun. After noon I'd take the cows out to the fields again so they could feed off the grasses. While they grazed I would often plow the field as well.

I came to enjoy the rhythm of the day. I had many different kinds of chores and I was kept very busy all afternoon, which suited me just fine. Sitting around being lazy was not for me. After the cows finished grazing I would feed the pigs and tend to the vegetable garden. There was a large plot near the house in which all of the family food was grown. They had plenty of vegetables, most of which Mr. Zaremba would take to town to sell in the market. Food was scarce everywhere so he was a welcome sight as he drove his cart, heavy with produce, into the town square each week. At that time Mr. Zaremba had only horses and a plow to work the fields, which was very laborious. After the war they bought a tractor, which saved them a lot of time and manpower.

Between 4 PM and 5 PM I brought the cows in again and started the second milking. I knew that it was of paramount importance that I disguise my true identity in any way that I could. To prove to the Zarembas and their neighbors that I was not Jewish, I was willing to do anything that was asked of me. Trouble teaches you everything.

I was very busy all day, but my efforts didn't stop there. I had developed a secret night life. Once everyone was sleeping I'd go back to the forest and bring food to the people hiding in the ditches. I couldn't forget those people who were so near yet so far, concealed in the depths of the forest. I'd steal food from the Zarembas and smuggle it into the forest under cover of darkness. I estimate that about a thousand people lived in the forest—both Jews and Christians. The Jewish partisans there were fighting for survival.

One night, about four weeks after I arrived at the farm, when I was in the forest, someone called out to me. I was surprised to be addressed by a guy who recognized me. He had known my father and was also a butcher. He told me quietly about a woman with a toddler living in a nearby ditch. He said he brought them food every night. Still, the woman was in dire need of milk for the baby. When he told me the story of Itka, the mother, and Asa, her eleven-month-old baby, I realized to my astonishment that it was the same mother who had jumped from the train car behind mine. She and her baby daughter had been hiding in this forest ever since.

Years later, thinking about the old German guard who told her to "run if she had healthy bones," I understood that many older Germans who fought in the war actually hated the Nazis and loathed Hitler. The Nazis didn't send this guy to the front: instead they made him a policeman. Thanks to him, as well as her success in hiding in the forest, Itka and baby Asa survived. As I mentioned earlier, Itka is gone now, and her daughter has made a good life for herself in Israel. One of the small miracles we can be thankful for.

Eventually I got to know some of the forest-dwelling people. I was close to some of the Russian partisan forces, but they also didn't know

I was Jewish. It seems unbelievable now, but this was how many people survived the war—a very large hole would be dug under a big tree, creating a hidden bunker where men, women, and children lived. In the winter they washed with snow, and during the hot summer they'd wipe themselves clean with leaves and bathe in a nearby stream.

It was such a contrast to the way we lived on the farm, where food was not a problem. Mrs. Zaremba was a fine cook. Her food was good and very tasty. It was not like the Jewish cooking I was used to, but it was solid Polish-style food, and I was grateful for every bite. There was all the milk you could want, and there was always fresh cool water from the well. Mrs. Zaremba baked her own bread, which was delicious and filling. We ate meat twice a week, and once a week we had chicken. We also had a variety of vegetables for lunches and dinners. We drank tea, sometimes with sugar or chicory in it. Artificial coffee was available, not real coffee. It came in tablet form, and it was awfully bitter stuff!

After a full day of chores and sneaking into the forest at night to help the Jewish and Russian partisans, I'd return to the farm to sleep. In the winter I slept in the kitchen on straw. We had blankets and a fire to keep us warm. During the summer I slept on hay in the barn. We didn't need blankets because it was warm. I slept in the same barn as the horses. During the day I rode horses bareback since they were working horses. Luckily I was very familiar with handling horses. The cows, pigs, lambs, and a coop full of chickens were kept in another barn next door.

When he returned from being a prisoner of war, the farmer's son would sleep in the barn too. He had been forced to work for a German farmer, and had escaped. He was terrified that the Germans might catch him. If they did they'd shoot him for running away or, at best, send him back to Germany. The Germans would conduct surprise searches of houses in an entire village during the night to keep people off guard. That's how they'd snare runaways, who would quickly be returned to Germany.

By the time I went to bed, I was tired but never able to be deeply asleep. I would stir at the smallest sound. A door opening or closing, or just a movement nearby, would bring me to my feet. I was hyper alert, like a soldier with PTSD. Even now, years later, I only sleep about three and a half hours a night—and nobody needs to wake me to go to work.

While I slept in the barn, I'd have nightmares or flashbacks. I could not help these episodes, but I had to keep quiet. I never cried out while I was dreaming, or I would have given myself away.

Like the majority of Poles, the Zarembas were Catholics. The farmer and his family attended mass every Sunday so I went to mass too, at the little church of St. Stanislaus in the village. It was my only option. The family never forced me to attend, but they would have become suspicious if I'd stayed at home on a Sunday morning, and I couldn't risk that. I learned to act in a Christian manner. I prayed with them and the rest of the villagers, who consisted of about fifty or sixty other farmers and their families. If any of the villagers had a notion that the Zarembas were concealing a Jew they would have been in grave danger—as would I—and I couldn't take that chance for any of us.

Every Sunday at Catholic mass, when it was time for communion, which is a sacred rite, the priest would approach me with the communion wafer, and I would let him slip it onto my tongue like a regular Christian kid. When the wafer is blessed—meaning consecrated by the priest—it is transformed into the body and blood of Christ. That is the Roman Catholic belief. By taking part in communion, I allowed the people to assume that I was a Christian. I never said I was a Christian, but it was implied by my actions. In other words, I tried to blend in and not make waves.

There were only about 120 people total in the village, and all of them called me Vonka. It was the name Walter Sr. gave me. I originally told him my name was Walter Travinski—a name I made up on the spot. He then told me that *his* name was Walter. "We can't have two Walters. You are now Vonka," he said. And so it was.

As idyllic as my sojourn on the farm as the farmhand Vonka might seem, and certainly it was preferable to most other alternatives, I was never completely free of fear. During my months there I would occasionally hear chilling stories about Poles turning anyone in to the Reich that they suspected was Jewish. Some Christians were only too happy to catch a Jewish person and deliver him or her to the Germans, who repaid them with five or ten liters of kerosene and ten pounds of sugar. So on Sunday when I went to church I had to pretend to be one of them to make sure that no one would suspect the truth. But deep inside I knew I would always be a Jew.

By the end of June 1944, bombs were going off and the Russians were about five miles from the village, and actually routing out Nazis. The Germans ran and did not stop running because they were scared of the Russians. If the Russians thought you were German they would shoot you on the spot because that is what the Germans had done to them in Russia. "See a German, kill a German," was their slogan. One day I heard that the Russians had made it to a nearby farm. I didn't say a thing to anybody, but knew it was time for me to escape once again. I took the cows out that morning as if it were a normal day, but then I took off, leaving the cows standing in the field. I felt so bad that I couldn't say good-bye to the Zarembas, and thank them, but that was the way it had to be. I ran about three miles, then saw a Russian truck on the road and waved it down. The truck, full of Russian soldiers, came to a stop. In my good Polish I asked the driver where he was headed. He said they were going to Bialystok, approximately sixty miles away. I said I was from there, and asked for a lift. He agreed and told me to climb up in the front with him, so I did.

I returned to Bialystok on July 1, 1944. When I got there I was shocked to see that the city had been reduced to rubble. Almost nothing was left standing. The once wonderful city where I had lived with my family, and also where I had suffered the terrible indignities of the ghetto, had been virtually obliterated. Now it was time to find a new life in some other part of the world. But where was I to go?

8

A Bittersweet Liberation
July 1, 1944

After being jostled in the big army truck, along with a bunch of exhausted Russian soldiers, who looked and smelled as bad as can be, we finally got to Bialystok. I thanked the driver, and hopped out of the truck, so pleased to return. I don't know what I expected—the mind plays tricks, and after great trauma it is easy to create a fantasy of how things should be, despite all contrary evidence. When I got out of the truck, what I saw around me sent me into in a state of new shock. As I mentioned earlier, the city was now 90% rubble.

As I looked around at what used to be the ghetto it was hard to comprehend the destruction. Almost nothing was left standing. As I picked my way through the debris, I looked for familiar landmarks and familiar faces. I was desperately hoping that some of the beleaguered Jews I remembered had escaped from the Nazi death machine. I had not been to the city since the Uprising and my head was spinning. Once again I had nowhere to stay, nowhere to live, no one to turn to. And once again my Virgin Mary medal would save the day.

When I finally got my equilibrium, I began looking for the nearest Catholic Church that hadn't been smashed to the ground. My hopes were not high, because I knew that the Nazis had decimated numbers of priests and taken many of them to the various camps, along with the Jews, homosexuals, Gypsies, and other groups that didn't conform to the Nazi code of ethnic purity. I wandered the streets of the nearly destroyed city, thinking what to do, and soon found myself walking by St. Nicklaus, a church where some of my Gentile friends had been altar boys before we were all

79

divided by the ghettoization of the city. I stood for a moment outside the door of the priest's house, wondering what my next move would be, when suddenly a crone of a woman opened the door a crack and peered out.

"Tak?" she said, impatiently, and poked her head out the door, nervously looking about.

"I have just come back to town and am looking for my family," I said. I had no intention of asking her for help, but she spied the medal on my neck and opened the door a bit wider as a signal to come in. Once inside, she closed the door gently and put a finger to her dried lips as a warning to be quiet. Then she crooked her finger, letting me know that I should follow her. We walked down a short hall to a drafty kitchen.

"Mr. Josef is resting, but if you sit on that stool," she pointed, "I will bring you some bread and broth. It isn't much but we cannot do better right now."

She left the room and returned with a plate, a bowl and a cup. These pieces had been fine china at one time, but now they were cracked and broken remnants of the war, just like the rest of us. Soon she produced a small but welcome meal and eventually produced a smile. I ate while I told her part of my story, but only the acceptable part. After about half an hour, I heard some footsteps in the hall. Suddenly a tall 40-ish man, dressed in work clothes, his hair tousled by sleep, was gazing down on me.

"Who do we have here, Mme. Pataska?" he spoke in Polish, but with an accent that told me he clearly was not born in Poland. Puzzled, I looked up from my bowl of thin broth.

"I have not asked his name, Mr. Josef. But he is a hungry Bialystok boy who's come back to find his family."

"So," the newly awake man looked down on me, questioningly.

"I am called Vonka. I just came into town from a nearby farm where I was a lad of all work. I was doubtful that I would find anyone—but I had to try, even here at the church."

Through the grapevine of macabre rumors, I'd heard that the bloodthirsty Reich had murdered many priests right in their Monasteries and other dwellings. This had happened in Warsaw, Bialystok and other cities and towns. I didn't want to mention these atrocities, strongly suspecting that the man who stood before me was a thinly disguised Jesuit priest. But I rose and looked into his eyes, to let him know that I understood he was in a delicate position.

"Well, Vonka," he spoke my name with an inflection that was unmistakable—I could tell he knew my game. "I have only lately come here myself. Our people needed reinforcements. And my own identity is necessarily a bit clouded, shall we say. But you can call me Josef. We have a big place here and it is empty. If you need a room you are welcome to stay, but, sorry to say, we are on very short rations."

"I know the city well, Sir. A lot has been destroyed, but perhaps I can find some food to share. Would that help?"

"Certainly." He sounded hopeful. "We have local people who come to our kitchen door every day looking for meals. Mme. Pataska here, who is a fine cook, sadly has to turn them away."

"Do you have any zloty?" I asked, a bit boldly.

"I have come from a country beyond the fighting. I have not come without funds. But there has been nothing to buy. And what little food there is, is rationed by the government."

"If you can give me some currency, I will not come back empty-handed."

"I have to believe you, young man. If you were not an upright fellow, you wouldn't be wearing the Blessed Mother so proudly."

Then "Father" Josef left the room. Feeling a bit sheepish, I finished my meager meal. He soon returned with a handful of zloty and gorsy in a little leather pouch. He put it in my open hand. After I pocketed it, he shook my hand.

"Trust me, Sir. I will not take advantage of your hospitality for long, but will do what I can while I am here."

****

After a few hours sleep on a hard mattress in a small, sparsely furnished room—but one that seemed like a palace after my bed of straw—and further refreshened by a much-needed sponge bath, I walked out into the chaos that was Bialystok. I was dressed in some simple clothes given to me by the priest because I had left the farm with nothing but the very worn clothes on my back.

Amid the destruction it took me a little while to get my bearings. The first thing I did was to head back to the fallen bricks and mortar that had once been the ghetto. There were a few buildings standing, rickety from the great thundering bombs that had been dropped nearby, but standing nonetheless.

As I was nearing Polna Street, I saw an old woman dressed in the long shapeless clothes of a Bubbe, wearing a babushka, and carrying a wicker basket. She was crossing the street just steps ahead of me. I knew her name but didn't want to call out to draw attention to myself, so I hastened my steps until I caught up with her—which wasn't hard because I was fast and she was slow. Coming abreast of her, I gently tapped her on the shoulder. Startled, she looked up, appraising me for a moment.

"Malach!" she gasped, beginning to cry out. "Is it you?"

"Quiet," I implored her, in a whisper.

"But, but," she sputtered. "It is *you*?"

"Yes, *Froy* Cohen, it is me."

"I thought you were dead. I thought you were *all* dead! I should be dead too,"

Once she got over her initial shock, I took her shopping basket from her. It was heavier than I thought. "Can we go somewhere private where we can talk?"

"Tak, tak," she said quietly. "Follow me, but not too close." After the dehumanization of the Nazi tyranny, we had all become more than a little cautious.

After we walked a block or two, with me following behind like a dutiful errand boy, we came to a distressed building just beyond what used to be the ghetto.

She stopped and we stood outside for a minute. "Do you live here?" I asked, hoping to hide my surprise.

"Where else?" she said with an unmistakable inflection. "Do you see a palace anywhere? Come, come," she whispered. Lifting her skirts, she took small uncertain steps over the rocky ground. She led me around the side of the building, and opened a small door. She stooped down and made her way down a narrow flight of uneven steps. I came after, and in a second we were in the basement of what at one time had been a fine family home.

Froy Cohen took the shopping basket from me and began sorting its meager contents.

"You live here," I repeated, sensing that her hearing wasn't the best.

"Look around, Malach. I have been burrowing here ever since the Uprising."

"You were a friend of my aunt, Hafka."

"True, but I haven't seen Hafka or no one else you would know since the ghetto was destroyed. You think it was bad then, when you were running and doing things for us? It is much worse now."

She apologized for not having any water. She hadn't been able to go to the well, which was tainted anyway, but she did have two broken chairs, which she clearly considered a luxury. We both sat down, very carefully.

"This area was blown to bits," I said stating the obvious. "How did you survive?"

"They left me for dead. Those Nazi bastards left me for dead. In the *mishegas* that followed the Uprising the thugs were running like crazy to hunt down young healthy kids like you. I played like a mummy and it worked. One of the brutes stood over me and shouted: *tot, tot* to the other Nazi bastards. *Die alte Dame ist tot.* Plenty of people were *tot*, but not me. Soon they moved on, and I've been here ever since, scratching out an existence."

"Are you here alone? How do you manage?" I had a million questions, but only time for a few. "One or two others share this dungeon, and we get food any way we can," she said. "I wish I could tell you that I knew about Hafka," she shook her head dolefully, "but I'm sure she was among those they took to Treblinka." Though I was not surprised, this was still hard to hear. "It breaks my heart to tell you, Malach," she continued, "but all of those people are gone. The Eppermans, the Klotzes, the Leibmanns. So many were taken away. I have nightmares about it, all the time," Bubbe Cohen, close to tears, bowed her head, then looked away. "If you think you're going to find somebody alive, sadly you're wasting your time."

"Perhaps I could try back in Knyszyn…"

"Of course, you can try, but I fear you will find the same story. I hear that all those villages are *bupkes* as well."

I rose, careful not to tip the unstable chair, and gave her a pat on the shoulder. I hoped seeing me would give her some comfort, yet knew she was beyond that. She had seen too much and lost too much to find peace. But she was flinty and gave me a sharp look. "Malach, you were always the busy one, on the go. I'm sure you have much to do."

"True enough, *Bubele*, I am on a mission of sorts, but if I can I will come back today with some rations for you."

"*Ach*, that would be a *mitzvah*. If anybody could do it, you can."

"I will do my best."

"You, young man, are a miracle worker. All your cleverness made life in the ghetto somewhat bearable for us." She wiped a tear away, and I turned and made my way up the narrow steps, determined to do something to help this frail old lady, living in such misery.

****

As soon I was out in the beautiful Polish sunshine again, heaven over my head and hell beneath my feet, I searched out some old contacts in hopes of finding food and other supplies to help those left suffering in Bialystok. After all the destruction it was hard to know who was who and what was what, but I still had my unerring instinct for survival and a nose for the right connections.

None of the many Jewish businesses were left—the kosher butchers, the kosher bakers, all wiped away as if they never existed. But I had traded with the Gentile merchants when I was in the ghetto, and now I gambled that some of them were still around and doing business. I headed toward Lipowa Street to see what I could find. I was glad to leave the confines of what had been the ghetto. Too many horrible memories there. Lipowa Street, which had been a lovely thoroughfare before the war, was in shambles, but in better shape than the area that used to be the ghetto. That open-air prison for Jews was no more. At least, treating us Jews as if we were no better than animals in a menagerie was over. I could take some comfort in that.

Despite these concerns I did have a mission, as Bubbe said, and could not delay. I was hoping to find a Gentile Pole named Cazimir. He used to do business out of a little shed behind Lipowa Street. He kept a very low profile, because a lot of his business was not on the up and up. It was how people survived in that terrible time. Here and there I would stop people in the street and ask about Cazimir. People shrugged and seemed not to know or understand. For once, I was getting both discouraged and hungry. I had almost reached the end of what used to be the business district and began to speculate about other options when I heard light footsteps coming up behind me. *Good, not a gendarme,* I thought. I didn't have the correct papers—or any papers at all. I felt a tug on my shirt and a kid's voice: "Mister, mister!"

I turned. A boy of about eight stood before me. A typically handsome Polish kid with fine features, blond hair and alert blue eyes. I bent down.

"Are you looking for *an old friend,*" he said in a low, excited voice.

"In fact I am," I said. "Can you help me?"

"I think I can...if you come with me."

Having been one myself, I knew the kid was sent as a courier. How I was spotted I will never know. Without another word I followed him through a warren of winding, narrow back streets. In a few minutes we came to a little hovel of a shop that had been carved out of the chaos.

The boy put out his hand for a tip, and I gave him a couple of gorsy. "Papa will be out in a minute," said the boy, and ran off with his new-found wealth. In a moment or two Cazimir appeared. A bit older, a bit more grizzled, but the same open Polish face.

He looked me up and down. I had certainly grown since he last saw me and developed muscles from working on the farm. "Malach?" he asked.

I smiled, pleased to see one familiar face in this now alien city.

"It is you. I never expected to see you again."

"I am here in the flesh."

"That is good news. Unbelievable, in fact. Come in. Come in and tell me how I can help you. "

Cazimir was one of several black marketeers I had worked with during my time in the ghetto. He was the best, the sharpest, and to me felt the most reliable. It only took me a few minutes to explain the situation I had found at the priest's house. Amazingly, Cazimir came with me to the parish house where I had been met with such unexpected kindness. I introduced him to the housekeeper, Mme. Pataska, and in a few minutes it was arranged that he would come with meat, eggs, vegetables, and bread once a week and be paid by Mme. Pataska. Since everything was rationed, this was not strictly legal, but I knew I could trust this man. As long as Josef had money, he would come, and Mme. Pataska could help feed those in need.

While we were together I also bought a piece of mutton and some potatoes from him and took them around to *Froy* Cohen. She could not believe it when she saw the food, which she would cook on an open fire. I also gave her directions to the parish house, which was not far. I instructed her to say, "I am Vonka's friend." She promised to go there for food when she needed it. I cautioned her to be discreet. I had devised a fragile system, but I had seen shakier arrangements work and I had to trust that this would work too. From now on, it was all about trust.

Despite all the uncertainty, I felt satisfied that in my short time in Bialystok I was able to do some good for a few people, but I also knew I needed to move on. I felt I must go to Knyszyn, despite the comments by *Froy* Yetta Cohen. Before I left town for what might be a long time I was drawn to some of my old spots. Bialystok was not a big city compared to Warsaw, but it was vast compared to my hometown. Still, the heart of Bialystok, the part that I knew well, was fairly small. I decided to take advantage of the summer light and take a last look at the city of my boyhood.

First I went back to the parish house to pick up a few things and put some food in my stomach. As I said goodbye to Mme. Pataska and Josef, I could tell they were both grateful and relieved. As I shook Josef's right hand he raised his left hand and made a "sign of the cross" gesture above my head. It was a Christian blessing. I took it and, with the usual mix of hope and fear, set out again.

Soon I found myself near Kosciusko Square, at the center of town. Mercifully, the old clock tower had survived and stood at the head of the Square. It was the same clock tower where I used to meet Haskell Greenstein and his brothers before we'd head out to the forest to cut up and play with abandon, only to come home when we got hungry, knowing that dinner would be waiting. How simple it seemed then! I admit I got a lump in my throat thinking of those times, which were not so long ago but might have been in another lifetime. Now the wonderful garden in the center of the square had been destroyed, and the plantings, once so cheerful, were gray and brown.

I looked around. Where there once had been buildings, there were now empty lots waiting for new life. The saddest memory of all hit me hard when I walked to nearby Suraska Street, where the Great Synagogue once stood. The stately place of worship, beloved by the many Jews who died there, with its three Byzantine cupolas, had been on this ground since 1913. Now, where that horrible immolation had taken place, there was only dust and ash. The only sign of the old wooden structure were the heavy steel ribs of the three cupolas—one large and two smaller. They could not and would not burn, so they remained skeletal reminders to anyone who passed. I walked by quickly. If I allowed myself to think about the day of the inferno I would not be good for anything. But in the back of my mind I resolved to one day right that terrible wrong somehow.

The daylight was ebbing, so with my pack over my shoulders I set out toward a main road, where, if I was lucky, I could hitch a ride to Knyszyn. There was still some lavender light in the sky on my way out of town. As I passed the Braniki Palace I had to stop and stare. Was there no end to the horrors? The wonderful baroque building, which had been the pride of Bialystok, was now in ruins. Once there had been big windows that let in wonderful light. Now they were gaping openings, like ghostly eyes, giving the burnt-out building an aspect of desolation and despair.

My heart was heavy for my city, for my people. But I still had work to do. I wiped away a rare tear and set out to make my way to my hometown. I had no idea exactly what to expect when I got there, but I did know that Bialystok was only a foretaste of what was to come.

9

Return to Knyszyn and Hunting Landmines
July 3, 1944

Something was driving me back to Knyszyn. Surely the reports weren't encouraging. I didn't know what I would find, but I thought I owed it to myself and my lost family to go there and find out.

From the Braniki Palace I walked the short distance to the heavily traveled road leading to my home town. The bridge over the Bialy River had been blown to bits, so I had to be very nimble to make my way over a narrow steel girder that served as a temporary bridge. This was the trickiest part of getting out of the city, and took time. By the time I got to the main thoroughfare it was almost dark. I was hoping to hitch a ride on a military transport rather than with a local and his horse-drawn wagon. A Russian lorry would be much more efficient than some old dray horse pulling a wagon, but I would take whatever came along.

I admit I was getting itchy to move on—a habit of impatience I'd developed through all the upheaval. Pretty soon a farmer passed by, with a very tired looking horse, pulling a battered wagon loaded with shabby goods. As the well-worn wheels of the wagon ground along the road, I called out the name of my destination. The farmer didn't even look my way. He just shook his head and waved his arm, indicating that he was not headed in my direction.

Seeing nothing else in sight, I sat on a stump beside the road. No doubt a handsome tree had grown there before the bombs and shells destroyed it. Soon an unmistakable vibration came up through the soles of my feet—a hopeful sign. Then I heard a distant rumble coming up the road. I jumped up and put out a thumb, the international sign from any traveler who needs to hitch a ride.

Dust flew up into my eyes as a large jeep screeched to a halt. I yelled out, "Knyszyn?" The driver nodded, indicating he would give me a lift. It was another one of those massive vehicles used by the Red Army ever since Stalin mobilized his powerful forces. Despite the fact that it was summer, the driver wore a heavy military jacket and a thick wool hat. As I piled into his jeep, he gave me a big grin, complete with missing front teeth, but he had a friendly manner that took me by surprise.

"Where to, young man?" His voice was deep but warm.

"My little hometown. It is 29 kilometers northeast of Bialystok."

"Okay, you are lucky, since I am heading that way. We'll be there soon."

It was hard to take in that this Russki was willing to help me in any way. I was not sure how he would feel if he knew I was not just a Pole but also Jewish. Fortunately, in a twenty-mile ride there wasn't much chance of his discovering that. In September of 1939 when the Red Army invaded Poland they were as bad as the Nazis. It was no fun to be under the Russian thumb if you were a Pole. But then, in June of '41, when Germany broke their pact and invaded Soviet territory, everything changed. The Reds, who had been technically neutral, joined the Allied Forces to defeat the Nazis, then became a fighting machine to be feared on the Eastern Front.

"My name is Ivanoff," the driver said in basic Russian, which I fortunately could not only understand but also speak. "Son, what do you think of this Great Patriotic War?"

"It is hell on earth," I said, thinking that he'd asked a silly question, but grateful for the ride.

"Yes, it's been very ugly for us too. We too have lost millions of men, and many more were taken prisoners."

"*Da*," I said indicating that I understood what he was saying. War is a hard teacher, and I'd learned some Russian while in the forest fighting with the partisans.

90

"But I see that is changing. Those bloody Germans are on the run." He changed the subject as he changed gears. "Why do you go to Knyszyn? It is not in good shape there. Nothing in Polish territory is in good shape."

"I was born there," I said flatly, as if this should be the obvious answer and serve to close the discussion.

He nodded, keeping his eyes on the road. There was very little traffic, but once in a while a large Russian lorry would speed by us, heading in the opposite direction, its huge headlight beams almost blinding us as they approached. The road was in terrible condition, so our progress was slow. Once the driver got a bit lost, but since I knew the route well I was able to redirect him. After a bumpy ride, we were soon on the outskirts of town.

"Stop here, please," I shouted, straining to be heard over the roar of the jeep's engine. Thanking him with *spasibos* I jumped out of the jeep, truly grateful for the ride, and apprehensive about what I would find in the town of my birth.

****

Quickly, I made my way to the town square, or what was left of it, and looked around at the little village that had once been my home. It was dark, but I could see clearly enough that it was in pretty bad shape, though not as bad a shape as Bialystok. I knew that most of the Jews had been taken away, so I wasn't sure what I would find. Except for my quick forays into my home town as the Malach, to find food and trade supplies, I had not been to the town square since that snowy morning of November 1942 when we'd been ordered from our homes and taken to the Polish Army Camp. Once we Polish Jews had been the backbone of the town, and in dozens of other predominately Jewish towns in Poland, and in large cities such as Warsaw and Bialystok. Now that backbone had been ruthlessly ripped out and destroyed. How would it all be rebuilt? I could only shrug, because I didn't know. What I did know in that moment was that I was hungry and needed to find a place to sleep. I grabbed my backpack, and to my delight, discovered that Mme. Pataska had stuffed two thick sandwiches into my bag without saying a word—a happy surprise for a change.

Our old house wasn't far from the town center. The house itself was almost in rubble but—to my amazement—the small barn where we kept our livestock was still standing. Gingerly, I opened the big creaky barn door and went inside. In there I found shelter, ate my sandwiches, and fell dead asleep.

When I was a kid I was always very busy with chores. There were so many tasks with such a large family, and I had my share of jobs. But in my spare time I had a hobby: I raised pigeons. I loved my pigeons, and my father built a special cote for them behind our house. Before the Germans came I had at least a hundred pigeons. I fed them every day and raced them for fun. There were other pigeon fanciers in town; and my friend Mordechai Hurwitz and I especially loved our birds. We used to get together and play with our pigeons, racing them when it wasn't the Sabbath. I knew each and every bird that I had raised from a hatchling: they all had names. Occasionally a pigeon would go missing and I used to suspect that our neighbor Reb Mishler would steal one for his dinner. Mishler was a strange one. The thought of my pigeons being eaten upset me—but not half as much as what happened to them when those sadistic Germans came to town.

One day in June of 1941, when Mordy and I were racing our pigeons, we heard a huge bang! Bang! It came from nowhere. We were startled out of our skins and scared. We could not imagine what was happening. Then one of my pigeons dropped to the ground. Then one of Mordy's. We were both too worried about our birds and too nervous to look around. When we finally did, there were two German soldiers, standing several meters away. They were leaning on their standard issue Gewehr rifles and grinning like monkeys. They could see the look of dismay and anger on our faces. But we knew if we spoke up we'd be next. Those Krauts were always trying to show us who was boss. Pretty soon they were wielding their rifles again.

"Go on, Jew boys," they shouted, in German, "Release another bird. We're having fun."

Though it was said in a playful tone, we knew it was no joke. Mordy and I both swallowed hard. Reluctantly, we each released another bird. The hapless birds took flight. In seconds more shots rang out and the birds fell to the ground. Mordy and I just stood there, paralyzed with fear that this was going to go on until we had no more birds left.

Once the second pair of our precious birds lay dead at our feet, the Krauts called out. "Go on *kleine kinder*, take those birds home to your *mutters*. They will cook them for your dinner." Then they picked up their menacing-looking rifles, gave us a small Hitler salute just to rub it in, and laughed as they walked away. I shuddered inside. We would rather have had our birds return to the forest then be fodder for German guns.

Suddenly I was stirred from my thoughts by a distinct cooing sound coming from somewhere. Of course it was pigeons, but where were they? I looked up and saw a pigeon in the tree behind the barn. Then I looked toward the sky. The broken chimney of my father's house was still partly intact, though the house was almost destroyed. Atop the chimney were half a dozen of my pigeons, little troupers who'd survived. I could hardly believe my eyes or ears.

"Coo, coo," I cried out excitedly to all the birds.

In a flash, and with a mad flutter, the pigeons flew down from the chimney and landed on my shoulders—just like old times. I recognized Tevi, Avi and the others. On seeing these old friends, I could barely contain my joy.

We were all survivors, and that warmed my heart. But I was still perplexed about my next move. I knew that Knyszyn was but a way-station. After I spent some time with my pigeons they returned to the chimney. The birds had been on their own for a long time and were no longer pets.

A few hours later, I awoke with a fresh start as dawn seeped through the cracks of the aged barn. The early light hit me in the eye.

The first image my blurry eyes could focus on was a giant cobweb in the corner constructed by a large black spider. Immediately I thought of my mother Esther. When I was a small boy she used to come into the barn with an old broom and knock the cobwebs down to chase away the nasty spiders. When I got a bit older that became one of my chores. Now there was no one to chase the spiders away, and no horses or cows either. The only familiar relic of the old life was one of my father's wagons, badly beaten up, but standing in the far corner of the shadowy and otherwise empty barn.

I had been gone from the town for almost two years and much had changed in Knyszyn, as it had everywhere else. I was overwhelmed with curiosity as I stepped out of the barn and showed myself in town for the first time since that snowy November morning when we were all taken away to the army camp.

Since there was no more food in my pack and I was still ravenously hungry, my first task was to find something to eat. In the July heat I walked through the center of town to the main street where all the little businesses had been. There had been a kosher bakery and several regular bakeries. Of course, Pawlowicz's kosher bakery had vanished, but Mr. Nowicki's bakery, that catered to non-Jews, seemed to be open for business. With a cap pulled over my eyes, I entered the bakery, armed with a bit of money that Josef had given me. I quickly purchased a loaf of warm bread and was paying for it when, unexpectedly, the proprietor offered me some tea.

"You look thirsty young man," he said, "I see you've bought a nice pumpernickel for your breakfast." I was surprised when he spoke to me in such a friendly tone, but I didn't want to give myself away. So I just nodded. "You don't sell tea," I mumbled.

"No, but I have some in the back. If you will be patient I will get you a cup. No charge! No charge!"

My impulse was to walk out of the shop, but I thought that would look odd in light of his rare generosity. So I stood there, holding the loaf wrapped in brown paper.

Soon he returned with two cups of tea. *Oh, boy,* I thought, *now I am stuck.*

"I thought I'd join you. It is early and I won't have other customers for a while."

"Why is that?" I asked. "This should be your busy time."

He stepped out from behind the counter and stood next to me, sipping his dark tea. "Well, sadly, the town is almost empty. So many of our friends and neighbors have left because of this dreadful war."

Left? I thought. *More like been dragged away and murdered!* But I held my tongue.

"Plus, there are almost no supplies. Flour, butter, milk—all of these things are in short supply. And what little there is, is requisitioned for the army. I am hoping that will change soon," he said, "now that the Red Army is chasing out those damn Nazis."

By that point, I had finished my tea. I handed him my cup, nodded thanks, and began to leave the shop.

"Will you be in town for a while?" he asked. "These days we get few outsiders."

I shrugged. "It's hard to tell," I said. "You know how it is these days."

I left the shop, feeling I'd passed a little test of sorts. Jews, though we made up the majority of the town at one time, were never really welcomed in non-Jewish businesses. I had known Mr. Nowicki's son before the firestorm began, and it was reassuring to realize the father had not recognized me.

As I walked a little ways down the commercial street, I saw a bench on the grass. It was dusty and broken, like just about everything else, but I sat down to have my bread and think what my next move should be. Here and there pedestrians were going about their business, but no one noticed me. Everything was very quiet, as Mr. Nowicki had said. This was certainly not the thriving little community of my memory.

When I finished the bread, which had that wonderful Polish flavor

I missed so much, I felt satisfied, but knew that somehow I would have to make provisions for food and shelter in the days and weeks to come. My whole philosophy, one that had become a way of life, one that had kept me alive, was to stay on the move and trust that somewhere, somehow I would manage. I kept expecting miracles and, frankly, they kept coming. So far I had been spared the fate of many. Deep down I knew that it was for a reason. Perhaps that reason would reveal itself one day. Meantime, I was in survival mode.

At the end of my little meal I folded the brown paper and put it in my pocket. One never knew. Right? Feeling a bit fortified, I thought I would see if I could find the old Jewish sports club, which was very popular when I was a little kid. I walked a bit farther along the old main street and, all in all, things didn't look quite as dismal as I'd heard. Nonetheless it was very painful to see the overwhelming devastation.

As I passed Kanski's gas station, which was closed because there was no gas, I sensed that someone had fallen in to step beside me. That presence made me deeply uncomfortable because we all lived with a cloud of suspicion hanging over everything. It is one of the most lasting ravages of war. While damage and destruction can sometimes be fixed, you can never shake the paranoia that comes with being hunted.

"Moishe," a man's voice whispered. "Can it be?"

The man walking beside me touched my shoulder. "I am not Moishe," I said with a muffled growl. Then I turned. I had to look at this guy, whoever he was, straight in the eye.

"Isn't your dad Mr. Solasz, the butcher?"

"Are you Max Bronski?" I asked in amazement. Could he be the same kid I knew from the sports club and from my two school years at Chada?

"Yes, it's me. My dad ran the kosher restaurant," the tall young man replied.

"I remember." At one time Knyszyn had five restaurants, all of which did a brisk business, with Jews patronizing the kosher restaurant and Gentiles patronizing the others.

"Have you just gotten back to town? And why in the world did you come?"

"Big questions, Max. But not to be answered here! I was just heading to the old sports club to see if anyone was around."

"The sports club is a hovel now and it is deserted. But I have a place nearby. If you come back there we can talk in private. The walls have ears, but we're safe at my house."

We walked a couple of blocks in the morning heat, and came to a small house, damaged but still standing. "This is it, my little palace," Max said with the same broad boyish smile I remembered. "Come, come!"

We walked around back. Tacked to the rear of the house was a little room, not much more than a shed. At one time, I'm sure, chickens had lived there. Max opened the door and we stooped to enter. He sat on the cot and I took the small chair. He pulled out a cigarette and offered one to me; cigarettes were a scarce commodity.

"No thanks," I shook my head. This wasn't a social call as far as I was concerned. "So, Max, you ask why I am here. But how and why are *you* here after these years? I didn't think that there'd be a Jew left in town. I must say I am surprised."

"As you should be, Moishe, as you should be!" He waved his cigarette and blew a puff of thick smoke.

I sensed that he had quite a story to tell me, and I wasn't wrong. Max always did have a bit of a theatrical style, and it came back to me now as he recounted his story:

"You know, little Solasz, you were quite a smart one, as I recall," he began. "I never understood why you didn't run. Why more didn't run."

"Explain, please."

"On that November night a few hours before the orders were enacted, my father came home, very worried, and said we should get out of the house, fast. As you may know, my mother died when I was small. My sisters were already on their own. So it was just Papa and me. I could tell he was very agitated. We packed up all the food we could carry and crept out of the house in the deep night with only the clothes on our back. It was freezing. I was quite scared, I can tell you. We walked into the Knyszyn woods, careful not to make a sound. The Gestapo were patrolling the town with those vicious dogs, helped by the Polish Army, who were keeping a sharp eye on us Jews. Somehow Papa and I managed to elude them. I think it was because our house was a bit out of town." Max paused for another puff on his cigarette. I was gripped with curiosity, hanging on his every word.

"When we finally got to the woods we went deep inside. It was dark and scary. There were a few other townspeople in the woods as well—just a handful. Everyone was silent and shivering in the icy air. You could hear nocturnal animals stalking around in the dark, which made the hair on my neck stand up. Somehow, in all the confusion, my father and I got separated and the night passed slowly. When dawn came I realized I still couldn't find Papa and I began to panic. He was all the family I had. Then we began to hear the commotion in the distance as people went to the Square."

"Yes, I know."

"Of course, you do—so sorry. Anyway, I was looking like crazy for my father, and I was frightened and started to cry. Our neighbor, Froy Friedman, who was also in the woods, put her arm around me to comfort me—and to quiet me. We huddled together, and the next thing you know we could hear the loud reports of German guns. From what we could tell they were shooting anyone who was not cooperating. Bang, bang. It was so loud I had to cover my ears. I was extremely frightened. I knew without Papa I'd be alone in the world."

"I understand," I mumbled and shifted uncomfortably in my seat. His story was bringing me right back to that dreadful day. Even so I had to hear it.

He continued. "The grownups in the woods were, of course, being cautious and didn't want to make a move until we knew that the wagons had moved on and the Germans were gone. So we sent out a

98

scout: Mr. Wozniak, a Gentile man who was married to a Jewess and had stayed by her side. When things seemed to die down, Mr. Wozniak went back into town, very warily. After walking the mile or two into town, he returned to the woods to report that things were clear.

There was still no sign of Papa. Anything could have happened to him, and I was very upset. Froy Friedman, who was a widow and lived alone, took me to her little cottage. She had chickens and a vegetable patch, so we had food, which put us ahead of a lot of people. She was very kind to me, but I was fretting every day for my Papa, and I kept holding my breath, waiting for word of him.

One day, as I was in the yard helping Froy feed the chickens, I heard footsteps behind me. I was nervous that the Gestapo was back, and didn't dare turn around. Then I heard my name whispered. '*Psst! Psst! Maxila.*' That could only be one person. I turned and to my great joy it *was* my father. I had thought he was dead and he had thought the same of me. We hugged and kissed, hugged and cried. It was quite a reunion, I can tell you.

I was very moved by the story, thinking of my own father, knowing I would never see him again, but I stifled my emotions and kept my composure.

"That is an amazing story," I said. "So few good stories have come out of this time." "Ah, yes," said Max, followed by a heavy sigh and another puff of smoke. "It was a happy outcome for once. But Papa did not last long after that. He had caught a chill in the woods and died six months later from influenza. His lungs were weakened, you see."

"That is terrible," I said. "But you've stayed in town all this time?"

"I stayed with Froy Friedman and helped her with the chores. She became a kind of grandma to me. Now she too is gone. She was quite elderly and died of old age not long ago. This was her house. It is mine now, not that it's worth anything. I've stayed in my little chicken coop, because no one ever checks back here."

"Are there any other Jews from that time in town now?"

"A few, only nine or ten. We all still keep undercover. That's why

I was so surprised to see you on the high street, Moishe."

"Okay, but you have to know that I am no longer Moishe. I have not been Moishe for a couple of years. I changed my name in the Bialystok Ghetto. The Germans were looking for Moishe Solasz, so I became Schlomo. That was the name of my younger brother, who died many years before."

"So you are incognito as Schlomo?"

"Exactly. Moishe died—Schlomo lives."

"Didn't I see your older brother Schmuel here some while ago? The one who was a singer?"

"Yes, Schmuel had hidden in a Christian's barn the night of the roundup and got separated from the rest of us. Before that he was at university but had to leave because he was a Jew. Originally, before the war broke out they wanted to send him to America to train his voice."

"The war was the death of a lot of dreams," reflected Max as he stubbed out his second cigarette. "Where is Schmuel now?"

"Don't ask," I shrugged.

"A bad story?" he replied, but anticipating the answer, fell silent for a moment.

"What else?" I said. "He's gone like the rest of them. But how could I know? I ask myself that all the time."

"How could you know what?"

"It's a long story," I said. "When I was in the ghetto I survived by being a courier and smuggling in food and other goods. It was high risk, I can tell you, but fortunately no one there knew my real name. I was only called 'Malach' since I was a messenger. Sometimes I would come here to town to get food and other supplies and take them back to the city. One day when I was in the village I met with a farmer who was a friend of my father's. To my great surprise I learned that Schmuel was living with him and in hiding. I didn't know my brother was still in Knyszyn and he had no idea of what had happened to the rest of us." I paused, to calm myself. "It meant a lot to me to find my brother. We made a big happy scene just like you and your father. Then he complained he was having trouble sleeping because there was noise all night, due to the Germans and the Polish Army with all of their guns. I convinced him that he would do better if he came to the ghetto, that at least it was quiet there. So he did. In short order he found a girlfriend and moved in with her family."

"I can guess how this ends," said Max, empathetically. "Let's try not to be gloomy."

He was trying to spare me from telling the rest of the story, and for that I was grateful. "Yes, there is plenty to be gloomy about. But sadness will not win the day. So, Max," I changed the subject, "are you going to stay here once this war ends?"

He seemed a bit shocked at the suggestion.

"Oh, no." He flashed a smile and ran his fingers through his thick dark hair. "I am going to America. To Hollywood in California, where they have sunshine all the time and where they make American films. They say the *machers* there, the big shots, are all Jews, so I am going to make my own way."

"Are you an actor?"

"No, a barber, but I am going to be a film star. You don't need to be an actor to be a film star." He showed me his perfect profile. "I am changing my name and I will have a bit of money when I can sell this house. Froy also left me some gold jewelry, which I am going to sell."

I was surprised by Max's ambition to become an actor. For me the war left no time or space for thinking about American films. I wished him well and told him I would soon be leaving town. We parted ways as friends, but I never saw him again after I left Knyszyn. Well not until years later, when I saw him on the silver screen in a film with the American actress Kim Novak. Some dreams do come true, as I would discover in my own life much later on. For now, I was taking things one step at a time.

****

After I left Max in his hidden chicken coop. I returned to my old house where I'd spent the night in the barn. They say you can't go home again, but I returned once again to the grounds of the boarded up property that had been demolished like so many others, which stirred a lot of memories of the way things used to be. I suddenly remembered another incident I had buried in my subconscious, a story that now came back in full force. It was one of those horrendous moments when one's childish innocence is lost forever. It happened on a day in 1941 when I was walking with my beloved little mutt Sunya. We were minding our own business—me, a thirteen-year-old kid, and a helpless little dog.

When the Germans first came to town, they didn't know who was a Jew, but Gentile neighbors were only happy to point us out. These Gentiles were paid for ratting out their neighbors so of course they put the finger on my family. That day this big German soldier calls out to me: "Hey, kid. Jew kid!" I turned in his direction and he just pulled out his pistol and shot my dog. Why? Maybe just because he could. Showing off to the other Nazi soldiers, perhaps. After he did it he laughed, and they laughed too. Such things happened all the time—Nazis flexing their muscle to show us they were in charge now.

I was distraught. I had raised Sunya from a puppy and she was my constant companion. I knew I couldn't say or do a thing or they would have shot me too. So I just picked up the poor thing, carried her home and buried her lifeless body in the field behind the barn. In the Jewish custom I marked her burial place with some stones and laid them out in a particular pattern. I would always know where to find my little Sunya. She was a victim of the war as much as the rest of us.

On this day, I was hesitant to look behind the barn, fearing that, since there had been such destruction in Knyszyn, my memorial stones to mark Sunya's burial place would have been disturbed. To my amazement, the stones were there—still in the pattern I'd created. I struggled to hold on to my composure. It was no use. Behind the barn and out of sight of the world, I wept for my little companion—and for a lot more besides.

****

One day, a few weeks after I was back in town, I was leaving the smoke shop when I heard someone signal me with a loud "Psst!" The sound was coming from the small park nearby and was clearly directed at me. I was still keeping a low profile so I couldn't imagine who might be trying to get my attention. I looked up and saw a burly man with his back turned toward me. He was dressed in the unmistakable uniform of the Red Army, complete with scruffy jackboots, a fur-lined ushanka hat, with the ear flaps down to protect him from the cold, and perhaps to protect his identity. Again I heard a loud "psst!" followed by "Hey, kid!"

I took a few steps toward him. My feet crunched the dry leaves beneath my feet. He heard the noise and turned to face me.

"Ivanoff?" I asked, a bit shocked. It was more of a question than a comment. It had been quite dark when he'd given me a lift, and so my powers of recognition were imperfect.

"Yes," he smiled, once again revealing a missing front tooth. "I am the Knyszyn taxi…once again at your service. Can we talk somewhere, more private?" he asked.

Without replying I led him to a little spot hidden behind the smoke shop. I was a bit nervous, unsure what he wanted, because clearly he wanted something. I just hoped he wasn't on some sort of illegal mission.

"I *am* surprised you're here," I said quietly. "What is going on?"

"It's pretty simple," he said with a big grin. He quickly explained that the Russians had chased the Nazis out of the area, but that the Nazis had left all sorts of dangers in their wake.

"You're a smart kid. You know the area around here well, and you speak Polish."

"Yes," I replied, *and Yiddish,* I thought, still not sure what he was driving at.

"You want to make a few rubles?"

103

"Sure. What do you need?"

"It can be a bit dangerous," he warned. Then he launched into an explanation: "My division is trying to clear up all the landmines that those Nazi swine buried in the fields all around town and all over the area. But our efforts are moving slowly."

I knew about the landmines, of course, and had been sternly warned to stay away from certain areas by other locals.

"I'm sorry," I said with a slight shrug. "I can't see how I can help."

"Well," he said—it came out *"Vell"*—"to come to the point. We have a BIG task. Me and my soldiers are here to clear all those damn landmines from the fields. But we don't know the area."

"Okay...so?"

"So, could you please join us and show us where the landmines are."

"I have some idea, but it's dangerous work."

"We won't make you actually dig up the mines. No! Just point them out so we might clear those fields. Ten rubles a day, plus some Red Army rations. Are you game?"

I didn't have to think about his offer long. After all, I was bored and only too happy to undercut those Nazi devils, even if they had been driven out. Besides, I knew that the money would ease my way out of town.

Before long I was wearing a regulation Red Army uniform, and out every day helping Stalin's brutes, and some German POWs, to demilitarize the area around the town. There were many acres of rich farmland surrounding Knyszyn. The German forces had seeded vast areas of these farms with lethal booby-traps. Landmines, a major tool of Nazi warfare, came in various shapes and sizes. The Germans were very inventive and devious when it came to building these lethal explosive devices. Such hidden killers could easily maim or destroy any poor soul unfortunate enough to trip one. Some mines were so powerful that they were designed to blow up tanks and other military vehicles. Landmines served several purposes, none of them good. It was far too dangerous to plant in the mined areas. So farmers were very limited as to the area where they could grow crops, and as a result farms were far less profitable and produced less food. The risk also kept locals neatly contained near the center of town and fearful of venturing out into the fields and nearby forests.

Once I connected with Ivanoff, I quickly settled into a routine. I would get out of my little bed well before dawn, slip into my uniform—a fake soldier is how I thought of myself—and bike the couple of miles to where the real soldiers were doing the backbreaking and risky work of removing unexploded devices from the ground.

Sometimes landmines would be buried in a pattern or grid to make them easier to remove, and others were buried randomly to make them more difficult to find. Luckily, in my area of Poland most of the landmines were set in the ground according to a pattern. Part of my job was to ask various farmers if they knew how or where the mines were buried. Most of the farmers gave me good information about the lay of the land and the approximate location of the landmines.

Once I gathered enough information I would return to Ivanoff and the Russian officer over him, and fill them in on how and where they would most likely find these deadly weapons, the scourge of World War II ground troops. Then they would make a diagram of where we estimated that the mines were hidden.

I would stand far, far back as teams of soldiers crawled forward on their stomachs in order to not set off the mines. They were followed by others, who would head into the fields with metal detectors and large metal drums. Once the metal detector gave off a clear signal that a landmine lurked below, the careful digging would begin. It was very tedious, not to say hair-raising work. Landmines came in many shapes and sizes but were all essentially the same. They all contained TNT, and had detonators or trip wires. If one of the detonators or trip wires was accidentally set off, it would be all over. Once the soldiers were able to dig out a mine, they would put it in special containers. Later specially trained engineers would undertake the tricky work of defusing the mines.

Not all landmines were metal. Some were constructed of wood, while others were made of glass to evade discovery by the metal detectors. But all contained TNT, and often contained metal or glass shards, which made the effects of an explosion even more deadly.

Teams worked with utmost care—there was no other way. So it took a very long time to clear even a small area of mines. Meanwhile there was a lot of time spent waiting around, which was very frustrating for me.

Day by day I continued to work with the Russians and collect my ten rubles. It was not a lot of money, but it was adding up. Meanwhile I was plotting my next step.

****

Three months passed. In the final month dedicated to working with the Russians I decided it was time to leave. It was deep into autumn and the weather had distinctly turned: chilly by day and freezing at night. By this time, the Russians were making a lot of progress with the landmine removal project. I decided I'd had enough of working with Ivanoff and his detail. One morning, when I arose, I went out to the removal site and put in my time to collect my rubles. At the end of the day, I peddled back to the barn where I'd left a change of clothes, slipped out of my Red Army uniform, and, without saying a word to anyone put on my mufti gear and peddled down to the main road to hitch a ride. Once again I was on my way. But to where, and to what? I still had no idea.

10

Life in the DP Camp
May 1945

It was almost hard to believe after so many long, tortured years, hiding, running, deceiving, always keeping just one step ahead of disaster, that finally this bloody living hell of a war had ended. It was just past my seventeenth birthday, and I was alone in the world. I had been alone before, but I had never *felt* so alone. Then, I had desperation and fear as my constant companions. Now I only had uncertainty. When I awoke some days, I had to pinch myself to realize that the fighting and duplicity were actually over.

I knew I had been miraculously spared because I had the courage to take action at the right moment. I had also been damned lucky. On a deep level I was determined to make the most of my life in the years ahead. I figured that I was spared for a reason—whatever that turned out to be. Meantime, I sensed that Bialystok, and perhaps even Poland, were over for me forever.

A few days after the armistice, I was back in Bialystok in Mr. Sedeski's café listening to the scratchy VOA news when my friend, Freddy, came in. "So what are you going to do now, Sam?" he asked. The "big" question and one that I had been thinking about since this conflict had ended—thank God in favor of the Allies. When we'd first heard of Hitler's death, the news had us all jumping for joy. In fact, the joy was worldwide. Before his rise, in 1933, it had been unthinkable that such a monster could exist in modern times. But Hitler, Mussolini and others who shared their evil design proved us very wrong, costing over 55 million lives. That number is staggering, even now, and instilled fear in all of us, but especially in us Jews—that genocide on this scale could happen, while our neighbors watched and remained silent.

Right, I thought. I was a teenager alone in the world, with no father, uncle or brother to guide me, or my mother's love—all erased from my life. At the same time I knew I was gutsy and resourceful. So where to go next? I believed an answer would soon present itself.

The next day, after having worked a few hours in the neighborhood butcher shop, I was having a little dish of pierogi and a beer in his café, when Mr. Sedeski came over. Without a word, he sat at the table with me and plopped a newspaper under my nose.

"Have you seen this, Sam?" he pointed at a prominent article. "Have you heard about these camps?"

I bristled at the word camp. "No, thanks! I've had enough of camps, ghettos and what have you!"

"Haven't we all!" Sedeski gave me a wry smile. He was a Christian but he'd had Jewish friends who'd been my neighbors in the ghetto and who met their fate in Treblinka. "Sam, it ain't that kind of camp. You gotta' read this."

"Okay, okay," I shot back. "I'm pretty tired now. Why don't you just tell me what all the fuss is about?"

He grabbed a cup of chicory that passed as coffee, then read the headline aloud to me and anyone else within earshot: "The Allied Authorities, in combination with the United Nations, are establishing Displaced Persons Camps to house refugees from Eastern Europe."

The article, which Mr. Sedeski read us in his raspy, excitable voice, went on to explain that the cessation of hostilities had left more than a quarter of a million Jews displaced.

Of course, I thought. Those Nazi louses destroyed our homes, villages, whole towns and cities in their madness. Now, so many people had literally no place to go back to. Where were they to go? There was no home anymore for them—or for me. So I paid close attention as Mr. Sedeski read on, and the answers began to roll out.

The article explained that temporary camps for displaced persons were being set up by the Allied victors in Germany, Austria, Italy, America, and Great Britain. They were intended to house not only Jews, but also Armenians, Greeks, Ukrainians and other nationalities who found themselves homeless and powerless following V-E Day. These camps quickly became known as DP camps, and were meant to provide temporary shelter and protection for refugees from the Holocaust, and from the greater war, until more permanent provisions could be made.

There were many thousands of Jews such as myself with nowhere to go. We were from ghettos and towns, and many more who'd been released from death camps, POW camps and labor camps. Arrangements had to be made quickly. There was the additional issue, a complex one, of survivors desperate to find loved ones they'd been torn apart from. There was always that flickering hope that they'd find family members who'd somehow survived. Some did. I knew that this was not an issue for me. The original Solasz family was gone, except for me.

"What do you think, young Sam?" Mr. Sedeski broke into my thoughts. I'd forgotten about my pierogi in his enthusiasm and my curiosity about the news.

"How do they say this works?" I asked. I'd heard about these proposed camps, but information was vague and disjointed in the early post-war days. Let me tell you, there was a lot of confusion. Thousands of souls were discombobulated in the immediate aftermath of World War II. I was one of them, but not for long.

Following the defeat of the German Reich, the four victorious nations—America, Great Britain, France and the Soviet Union—divided up German territory into Administrative authorities, to keep order and help resettle the millions of dislocated citizens. These camps were established in conjunction with the United Nations Relief and Rehabilitation Administration, or UNRRA. Of course, everyone's first choice was to send people back to their country of origin, but for many complicated reasons that was an impossible option. So DP camps became the answer, for a few years at least. This seemed like a possibility for me, but how was this was going to work, I wondered. It was surely a huge undertaking to house and care for the many thousands who would come empty-handed and in distress.

Little by little more information began to dribble out, in the papers, on radio and through the refugee grapevine. The authorities were eager to spread the word, so there were lots of notices in newspapers, posters were put up in town centers and of course the news was constantly on Voice of America.

Life was coming back to Europe in small ways. I saw how this new system was going to work. Officers from the Polish Army were acting as point people in various towns and cities to assist in the funneling of human beings from one place to the other. One day I saw a notice about an Information Office in Bialystok, near the bombed-out Town Hall. These offices were established to answer questions, give out papers, travel passes, and sometimes a bit of money. When I got to that office I had to wait for hours in a crowded room with anxious mothers and screaming babies. By time I got to speak to an intake officer it was the end of the day and they told me to come back the next day. Once I was finally able to speak with the right person, I was assigned to a DP camp in the American zone called Föhrenwald, 18 miles outside Munich in southern Germany.

The Allied countries that despised The Reich and had fought them bitterly now controlled all of Germany. Munich, of all places, was where I now had to go to register as a DP, get my papers and find a new temporary home! The irony didn't escape me. Things seemed disorganized and bureaucratic, which indeed they were. Later I learned that, in anticipation of the huge upheaval in Europe, the Allies had a peacetime refugee plan in place long before the end of the war.

It was over 800 miles from Bialystok to Munich. In Europe, especially at that time, 800 miles was a long, long way for war-weary refugees, which I realized was what I'd become—a refugee. I never truly thought of myself that way. I was not a refugee at heart, but a survivor.

Soon I found a few others like myself who were traveling from Bialystok to southern Germany. We had similar itineraries and DP camp destinations, so we formed a little group to travel together. I was the youngest, so I became a sort of mascot for this motley band. I also spoke more languages than some of the others, which came in handy during our journey.

When the day of departure finally arrived, I packed up my few belongings, said good-bye to Mr. Sedeski and my friends at the café, and, with the tickets in my hand, met up with the others at the Bialystok central railway station. As you can imagine, there was a lot of nervousness and hubbub in the air. Most of us had never been to Germany and our recent experiences with the Germans were unsettling, to say the least. Some poor souls were just plain terrified to set foot in the country. But we thought of the Americans as "the good guys," and were praying that we were in safe hands.

As we milled about in the railway station no one had the least idea what life in a DP camp would be like. Even before Hitler we Poles had been looked on as country cousins, or worse, by the better educated, more worldly Germans. Perhaps now things would be different. It was a new post-war world, or so we hoped.

While we waited to depart, some in our small contingent grew restive, and no wonder. During the war, train journeys for civilians had become very difficult, since most of the freight trains were commandeered for transporting troops to the various fronts to fight. Now things were beginning to return to a new normal, but there were a lot of hitches in the process. Finally, a freight train arrived which would transport us to Warsaw, the first station on our southwest trajectory to Munich. Clouds of steam and smoke filled the air, and the crowd all around us grew excited.

Nothing in my many ups and downs during the war had prepared me for this turn of events. The last time I was on a train, it was courtesy of the Gestapo. This was an altogether different experience. I was wary—all I wanted to do was gaze out the window at the passing countryside. I didn't know if I'd ever see Poland again.

The train lumbered on, and it was very late by time we arrived in Praja, where we had to disembark and get onto trucks to cross the bridge into war-torn Warsaw. From there we had to pile off the trucks and pile into another freight train that would leave us in Lodz, another bombed out city in Poland. Lodz had been a major textile center, but during the Occupation a ghetto was established and conditions for the Jews of the city were intolerable. It was the same story in every city in Poland. A few new refugees joined us at Lodz.

When the Lodz-bound train finally arrived, it was the middle of the night, and inside it was unbearably hot and crowded, which made it almost impossible to sleep. The train was quite shabby as well, but we were all too tired to care. It was only about 80 miles to Lodz, the third largest city in Poland, but still, another tedious journey.

The whole shape of my country had changed with the war. The Soviets had claimed a big swath of western Poland, while Poland had annexed a large part of Germany to the East and the North on the Baltic Sea. Someone once said that war and geography were interlocked and that was certainly true of Poland in 1945. As a country, my Poland was changed forever by powerful men at the Potsdam conference in the summer of 1945.

Our journey became more uncomfortable as we hurtled through the night. In the very early morning we had to board yet another train since we'd reached the border of Czechoslovakia. Each country had its own rail system and crossing a border was a very cumbersome process. The trains were boarded by guards who checked everyone's passport and identity. You were required to tell them where you were going and why. By this time I thought we would never get to our destination. But as we began to approach the outskirts of Prague I felt heartened because I knew that Germany was not too far away. We had more of this border crossing nonsense as we left Czechoslovakia. Next we were put on army trucks once more. When we got to a wide river that I took to be the Danube, I knew that we were finally in southern Germany.

In Munich the convoy of trucks stopped, and we were met by uniformed American soldiers holding signs in several languages with the names of the DP camps, since there were quite a few camps in this part of Germany: Düsseldorf, Landsberg, Feldafing, Föhrenwald, Frankfurt, St. Ottilien, and others. Such strange names to us Polish. Luckily the U.S. Army, who was organizing this transfer, had supplied translators, speaking Yiddish, Polish and other languages. Behind the soldiers holding the signs there was a long line of more military trucks, buses and jeeps—any kind of conveyance they could dredge up. It was really hard to know what this all meant. Little by little we weary travelers did get sorted out, and we were transformed into official Displaced Persons.

I grabbed my little satchel and got on the bus marked for Föhrenwald, which was about 18 miles from where we were in Munich. Right away, even through my tired eyes, I noticed how lush and green the countryside was. Munich is in Bavaria, a beautiful castle-dotted part of Germany near the foothills of the Alps. The landscape was very different from my home country, which was mostly flat. It didn't take too long before we arrived at our particular camp—which would be my home for the next three years, along with some 6,000 other persons.

I arrived there in early August of 1945. When I first looked around, I was surprised by the size and scope of the facility. The original plant was built only a few years before as living quarters for munitions workers for a big German company, but it was then used by the Germans as a camp for forced labor. It was a strange turn of fate that it now housed those of us who had survived the Nazi persecution.

In Föhrenwald I was quickly assigned to a small house that I shared with five other men. Three of us were Polish Jews, plus we had a lively guy from Budapest and a dour Slav. Most of the streets in the camp were named after U.S. states. Our house was on *Newyorkstrasse*, which I took as a good sign. At first some of the camps were mixed, Jews and non-Jews, but later Föhrenwald became an all-Jewish camp, on orders from General Eisenhower himself, and the other guys were moved someplace else. We shared with some new Jews who came from yet another camp. In this system people were always being shuffled around.

For the vast majority of people in the camps it was a way station until they could emigrate and leave the old world behind. Most wanted to go to Palestine, which was still under British control. Many, like me, hoped to go to New York or somewhere else in the U.S., and still others wanted to go to Australia or Canada. Often the outcome depended on where they had relatives or connections, or on what country would take them. It was a waiting game in the DP camps.

While we settled into a routine and waited for the next chapter, daily life in Föhrenwald was not unpleasant, and certainly far better than what we had left behind. We arrived at the camp in its early days, but as more and more DPs came in, the camp quickly filled up. It was the size of a large town and was self-contained, with goods, medicine and other needs supplied by the U.S. army and a range of international charities.

While enjoying life in a DP camp is unimaginable to most people today, it was the best thing that had happened to most of us in a long time. A sense of hope and optimism began to take hold. Soon lots of marriages began taking place, and babies were born. Schools were established for young children. World ORT, a Jewish charity based in London, set up training schools for those who'd lost out on education. Women and girls were taught things like sewing and needlework, while boys and men were taught carpentry and other skills to prepare them for a life beyond this artificially created world.

The camp had a large communal dining room, and meals were on schedule, just like being in the army, which in a strange way we were. The camp was run under the auspices of the UNRRA, and the director of the camp was Henry Cohen. Henry was a young veteran of the U.S. army. He went to great lengths to ensure that residents were treated well and that things ran smoothly, which most of the time they did.

After we were in the camp for a few weeks, I got a chance to use my butchering skills—but started under the radar—it wasn't encouraged. I was able to find a big empty basement that no one else was using, and that's where I set up my butcher shop. I would get hold of 20 pounds of coffee or chocolate and trade it for a lamb. There was a small PX in the camp and I was able to get credit by trading some goods to make my meat purchases. In my leisure time I also got into boxing and soccer, and bought a motorcycle, which I loved. Surprisingly, there were lots of activities in the camp. Thanks to American ingenuity different sorts of sports were organized. There were even musical events and a camp orchestra as well as live theater. There was a camp newspaper and a monthly magazine. It was hard to believe how quickly denizens of Föhrenwald emulated life in the pre-war world. Such normalcy gave us a sense of comfort.

When I learned that there was a Golden Gloves boxing program I was quick to sign up. Other than running from the Gestapo, I hadn't had a chance to participate in any sports, and I enjoyed the competition. Winning is a part of my nature, and I won every chance I got. Golden Gloves boxing began in Chicago, but the U.S. army offered it to us here. I relished it and did well.

Practically as soon as I arrived at the camp, I saw that there was a regular group of guys training for the Israeli army, even though Israel was not yet a state. It was still Palestine, and would be for three more years. My dream was to go to New York, since I had relatives there, but I saw going to Palestine to fight for a new country as a first step toward New York. At that time it was easier to go to Palestine than the U.S. But it wasn't even that easy to go to Palestine if you were a DP.

Under what was then the British Mandate, only 1,500 Jews a month were permitted to immigrate to Palestine. With so many thousands of Jews trying to go there the wait could be very long. There was a faction in the camp that was dissatisfied that it would take them endless months to get to Palestine. At one point they caused a big kerfuffle and problems for Mr. Cohen by demonstrating on *Rooseveltstrasse* in the center of the camp. U.S. Army Military Police, who were non-armed Jewish police, kept order in the camp and quickly shut down the demonstrators. They were not to be deterred and emigrated illegally, only to be sent back to the camp when the British authorities discovered them, since they carefully checked all the boats arriving in Palestine.

At Föhrenwald there was both a Yeshiva and a Torah School within the camp, along with the presence of a rabbi, who made the camp a center of Hasidism in the American sector. Zionism, a form of Jewish nationalism with the objective of a Jewish homeland in Israel, took hold big time. This was a natural reaction to the horrors of the Holocaust. To the millions of Jews everywhere it seemed more important than ever to have a Jewish nation.

All of this distraction kept me busy and the days passed quickly, but I was getting antsy. Three or four times a week I went for Israeli Army training. Sit-ups, push-ups, learning to handle a gun—a skill I already had—were preparing you to fight for a Jewish homeland. I believed in the cause, so I went to the sessions. I knew putting my name on the list to immigrate to Palestine would speed up my leaving the camp.

Meanwhile, between my boxing and army training I was getting fitter and fitter. And, of course, cutting meat builds muscle, so I was becoming quite confident that I would do well in the army. Still I waited and waited for my turn to come up, to get into the monthly quota. By early 1948 there was still no ticket to Israel in my hand, so I finally decided to join forces with the *Aliyah Bet*, a group of brave and desperate Jews who sought refuge in the Jewish homeland. *Aliyah Bet* were the illegal immigrants who tried to sneak into Israel, needing to get past the British naval patrols that protected the waters off Palestine. Sometimes these journeys were successful and sometimes they ended in disaster, but they were always risky. Many refugees drowned at sea in faulty boats, or were sent back to the DP camps, or interned in Cyprus. It was a confusing mess. Even so, I felt that moving forward was better than staying still, and decided to take a chance.

The *Aliyah Bet* missions had gone on since the early 1920's, but they really slowed down during the war, for many obvious reasons. Once there were thousands of Jews stagnating in DP camps the missions began to ramp up. Those of us who lived in the American Sector were technically not permitted to connect with the *Aliyah Bet*. But sympathetic UNRRA officials often turned a blind eye to the *Aliyah Bet* emigration because they knew, first-hand, how badly we wanted to leave the DP camps behind and get settled somewhere. There was a definite process to making your way illegally into a country that didn't exist yet and was still under British control.

A group of us who were in army training in Föhrenwald decided to make the trip together. We soon learned that if we made our way to Leipheim or Bad Reichenhall, two other camps in the American sector, we could begin our illegal trek to the Holy Land without too much hassle from the UNRRA. Of course there was no telling what would happen if the British caught us.

Once in the Leipheim DP camp we were either picked up in trucks that were disguised, or traveled by rail to conceal our illegal migration to Italian ports such as Bari on the Adriatic Sea. There we would embark on the perilous journey to Palestine.

It took many hours on the road, but when we finally got to Bari I looked out at the Adriatic sea. An unmistakable lump in my throat told me that I was leaving my family behind forever, since their remains were in European soil, and yet again travelling into the unknown.

"Monsters exist, but they are too few in number to be truly dangerous. More dangerous are the common men, the functionaries ready to believe and to act without asking questions."

—Primo Levi (1919-1981),
Jewish-Italian chemist, author and Holocaust survivor.

Sam's father with first wife and daughters Miriam and Marsha. Both sisters died at Babi Yar

Sam's paternal grandparents

Sister Miriam

Miriam, Schmuel, Marsha

Sister Dina

Uncle Dave and parents

Jews forced into the ghetto

Cattle car to Treblinka

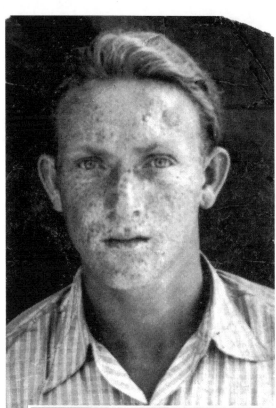

*Sam at DP
Camp from
1945 to 1948*

About to board the General Harry Taylor, Jan. 1951

Sam and Rose on their wedding day, June 1957

Sam starting Master Purveyors, August 1957

Dome of the Great Synagogue after the massacre, 1942

Sam with rediscovered partial frame of Dome

Rebuilt Zaremba farmhouse

Scott, Diane, Rose, Sam, Mark

Sam and F. Chaim (aka Ephraim) Katzir, President of Israel from 1973 to 1978

Sam and boyhood friend Haskell Greenstein (middle) with mayor of town in Israel named for Bialystok, Poland

Sam in NYC in one of the seven ambulances his family donated and sent to Magen David Adom, Israel's emergency medical service

124

*Mordekhai Tennenbaum Medallion ,Commemorating the heroes
of the Bialystok Uprising, that was presented to Sam in 1976
by President of Israel, F.Chaim Katzir*

UNITED STATES OF AMERICA

Form approved.
Budget Bureau No. 43-R076.2.

DECLARATION OF INTENTION
(Invalid for all purposes seven years after the date hereof)

No. 68874

United States of America,
District of New Jersey. } ss.

In the .... District .... Court

of .... The U. S. .... at .... Newark, N. J. ....

(1) My full, true, and correct name is .... SAM SOLASZ ....

(2) My present place of residence is 364 Seymour Ave. Newark Essex New Jersey

(3) My occupation is Butcher (4) I am 23 years old. (5) I was born on May 5, 1928

in Knuszhin, Bialistok, Poland (6) My personal description is as follows: Sex male

color white, complexion light, color of eyes blue, color of hair blond, height 5 feet 9 inches, weight 160 pounds,

visible distinctive marks none race White, present nationality Polish

(7) I am not married; the name of my wife or husband is .... we were married on ....

at .... ; he or she was born at ....

on .... and entered the United States at ....

on .... for permanent residence in the United States, and now resides at ....

(8) I have no children; and the name, sex, date and place of birth, and present place of residence of each of said children who is living, are as follows:

(9) My last place of foreign residence was Wolfratshausen, Munich, Germany (10) I emigrated to the United States from

Bremerhaven, Germany (11) My lawful entry for permanent residence in the United States was

at New York, N. Y. under the name of Szloma Szolarsz

on January 22, 1951 on the SS General Harry Taylor

(12) Since my lawful entry for permanent residence I have not been absent from the United States for a period or periods of 6 months or longer, as follows:

DEPARTED FROM THE UNITED STATES			RETURNED TO THE UNITED STATES		
PORT	DATE (Month, day, year)	VESSEL OR OTHER MEANS OF CONVEYANCE	PORT	DATE (Month, day, year)	VESSEL OR OTHER MEANS OF CONVEYANCE

(13) I have not heretofore made declaration of intention: No. .... on .... at .... in the .... (Name of court)

(14) It is my intention in good faith to become a citizen of the United States and to reside permanently therein. (15) I will, before being admitted to citizenship, renounce absolutely and forever all allegiance and fidelity to any foreign prince, potentate, state, or sovereignty of whom or which at the time of admission to citizenship I may be a subject or citizen. (16) I am not an anarchist; nor a believer in the unlawful damage, injury, or destruction of property, or sabotage; nor a disbeliever in or opposed to organized government; nor a member of or affiliated with any organization or body of persons teaching disbelief in or opposition to organized government. (17) I certify that the photograph affixed to the duplicate and triplicate hereof is a likeness of me and was signed by me.
I do swear (affirm) that the statements I have made and the intentions I have expressed in this declaration of intention subscribed by me are true to the best of my knowledge and belief: SO HELP ME GOD.

(Original and true signature of declarant without abbreviation, also other name if used)

Subscribed and sworn to (affirmed) before me in the form of oath shown above in the office of the

Clerk of said Court, at Newark, New Jersey

this 20th day of August, anno Domini 1951. I hereby certify that

Certification No. A7,944,152 from the Commissioner of Immigration and Naturalization, showing the lawful entry for permanent residence of the declarant above named on the date stated in this declaration of intention, has been received by me, and that the photograph affixed to the duplicate and triplicate hereof is a likeness of the declarant.

[SEAL]

WILLIAM H. TALLIN,

Clerk of the U. S. DISTRICT Court.

By .... Deputy Clerk.

Form N-315
U. S. DEPARTMENT OF JUSTICE
IMMIGRATION AND NATURALIZATION SERVICE
(Edition of 11-1-41)

16—10119-9 U. S. GOVERNMENT PRINTING OFFICE

Sam's Declaration of Intention to become a U.S. Citizen. August 20, 1951

126

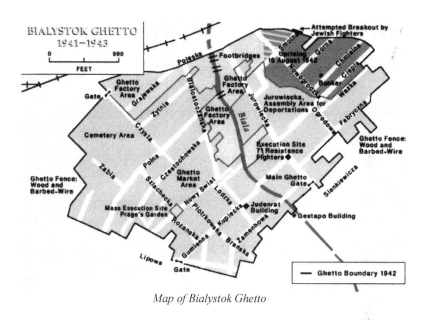

Map of Bialystok Ghetto

Map of Treblinka Extermination Camp

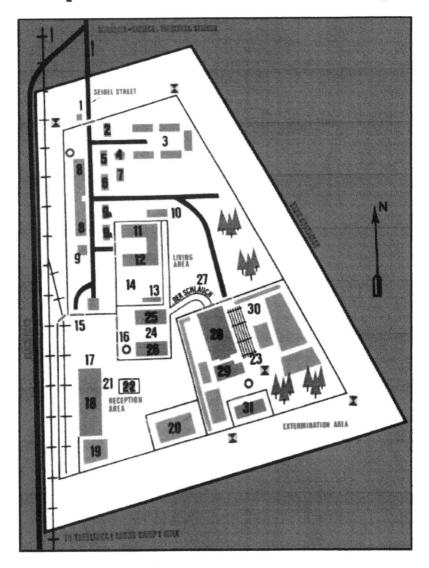

Key to Treblinka Map

▬▬ Roads
+ + + Railroads

Map of Treblinka extermination camp

128

Sam with sons Scott and Mark at Master Purveyors

Sam and Rose

Sam's grandchildren protect him from the rain on visit to Treblinka

11

Helping Palestine to Become Israel

It may seem strange that I had never seen the sea before I got to the Greek islands. But Poland was mostly landlocked, and I hadn't had the luxury to travel. I knew the Biala River and had seen the magnificent Danube during my time in Germany, but a vast sea where you could look to the horizon without seeing an inch of land—that was completely new to me, and a bit overwhelming. Especially since I guessed that all of us refugees had to board old cargo ships, and other less trustworthy ships, which, to make things worse, were usually dangerously overcrowded.

The Mossad Aliyah Bet, a branch of the *Haganah*, facilitates Jewish immigration to British Palestine, in violation of British restrictions, through an underground network called *Brihah*, which means "flight" in Hebrew. Together the Mossad and the *Brihah* coordinated all of this complicated travel from the DP camps to Palestine. This *mishegoss* was necessary to get around the strict British immigration quotas and naval blockades that were looking out for illegal immigrants like me. It was not a perfect system. Nine times out of ten these missions failed and would-be Palestinians were sent back to either the DP camps or to Cyprus, where the British had established a big detention camp.

Standing on the dock of a small Greek Island, I could hardly believe how fresh and salty the air smelled. It was a new sensation. I stood there alone for a few minutes when, through the noises of the crowd around me, I heard someone call my name. I looked over my shoulder but didn't see anyone who appeared to be looking for me. The dock was packed with travelers like myself. Most were carrying suitcases. Many had children and squalling babies in tow. The Mossad was emptying out the DP camps as fast as they could, with my fellow refugees coming from all over Europe. Jews had been migrating to Palestine for many years, but now, in the aftermath of the war, it was more important than ever to carve out a Jewish homeland. The dream was that a Jewish homeland would offer perpetual protection from monsters like Hitler. Hitler, of course, was dead, but he'd laid the groundwork for others, and anti-Semitism was on the rise again in Poland and elsewhere. It is hard to believe, but in one Polish town over 40 Jews who'd survived the death camps went back home, only to be murdered by local Polish fascists who conducted their own pogroms. There were plenty of reasons to go to Palestine. But there was also a big problem, since the Palestinian Arabs had also viewed it as their homeland since biblical times.

Musing on all of these big questions, even though I was tired from my journey, I was suddenly jostled by someone at my side. "Hey, Solasz," I heard. I looked around and to my great surprise, Haskell Greenstein was standing right next to me. I had not seen him for several years and had no idea if he was living or dead. Excited to see my boyhood friend again, I gave Haskell a big hug. Trust me, I had not hugged anyone in a very long time. I could hardly believe my eyes. Haskell had grown a bit taller than me, and was very thin. The expression in his eyes told part of his story. I knew we would have time to compare notes about our grief and loss, but before we could say more, a man with a bullhorn cried out to get the attention of the anxious crowd. We were told to form lines, which quickly became very long. We were directed to check in with official-looking people who were sitting at long tables in a big drafty shed next to the dock. Greenstein was in the first part of the alphabet and Solasz was in the second half of the alphabet so we got split up for a time—again.

After we checked in, which took quite a while, we were assigned to a particular ship, and given an estimated departure date. Demand for passage was high, so there could be a few days wait. Eventually I was told that a Greek cargo ship would transport us to Palestine. Once we were assigned a vessel and day of departure it was always a "wait and see" situation. Soon it was evening and the heat had cooled down considerably. The Mossad organizers had things under tight control and directed all the men and boys to bunk in a large shed next to the dock. The women, girls and young children were accommodated in a similar shed nearby. A plain meal of a heavy soup and bread was provided. It was tasty, and to those of us who were used to DP camp food this Greek fare was a welcome change.

To get through the night we were each given a threadworn blanket. This was roughing it for sure, but after what most of us had endured these sheds were suitable digs. Once all this business was over, I looked at the slip of paper I had been handed. On it were my transit number, the name of the vessel I'd been assigned, and time of departure. We were supposed to sleep in this big shed but it was a restless night for me. Anticipation of the adventure—or misadventure—ahead kept many of us from sleeping. I grabbed a couple of hours at best. With first light there was commotion all around me, since many of the men were leaving first thing that morning.

Once the numbers of people had thinned I easily found Haskell, who was still sleepy and didn't seem ready to get up. I shook him on the shoulder and he groused at me: "What you doing, Solasz? Cut it out." Then he realized where he was and that we were together again by a miracle. Soon a man came along and yelled that if we wanted breakfast we should hurry. Since we'd slept in our clothes, it didn't take any time to show up at the makeshift canteen where they were handing out coffee, tea, Greek bread and pastries. We were carefully watched so that we didn't take more than our share. Food was still scarce and there were so many to feed.

With our meager rations, Haskell and I found a couple of crates on the dockside and sat down. Pretty soon an old rabbi came over and sat beside us. We were not pleased that he interrupted our reunion. Of course, the first thing the rabbi did was ask us if we were doing our daily Talmud and Torah studies. We pretended we didn't understand him. I didn't like being rude to the old man. I knew my father wouldn't approve. But I also knew that he saw us as prospective young followers. I smiled at him and Haskell shrugged, so he stood up, shook his head and tottered away. Certain rabbis were recruiting followers but I was going to Palestine because I believed in the cause, not because I wanted to be locked into Jewish practices day and night.

It was a fine morning with the sun shining and Haskell and I could hardly believe that we were free after all. I quickly learned from Haskell that he'd lost his parents in Auschwitz, but that his two brothers had gone to Russia, and all three Greenstein brothers survived. I admit I was a bit jealous because I could not make the same claim. Haskell, I later learned, had been on the same train from which I jumped, but instead of being taken to Treblinka he wound up in Majdanek, was then taken to Lublin, and eventually to Auschwitz. He managed to survive all of that. A lucky man indeed!

Right now our minds were on other things. Even though we were enjoying a moment of peace on the noisy, busy wharf, Haskell and I both knew that we were heading into more uncertainty. Not only was the sea journey risky, it was also by no means certain that those of us on this Jewish pilgrimage would arrive safely. Trust me, there were many hazards ahead. For now, all we had to do was wait. And hopefully not for long.

It was late February 1948. I was almost twenty and itching to get on with my life. When my father was twenty he was already married with a young family. But this was a very different time and a different world, for sure. I admit that deep down I had mixed feelings about going to Palestine. For one, I was eager to get to New York, but knew I had to be patient on that score. Also, the Jews and Arabs in this Promised Land had been fighting each other for many years. It was another perilous state of affairs. There was a prevailing fear that a major war could break out at any time. *So what else is new*, I thought. This tribal conflict is precisely why the British were mandated by the League of

Nations in 1922—in the aftermath of World War I—to keep peace in the region, and the battles are still going on.

Haskell and I were both on the passenger list for The Caserta, a broken-down cargo ship that was scheduled to leave from Bari, a town in Italy, and travel through the sea-lanes of the Adriatic, and then through the Ionian Sea until we got to the Mediterranean and eventually to the coast of Palestine—if we were lucky.

When I compared experiences with Haskell, it turned out that he too had been training to join the Israeli Defense Force, which was in the British sector of Germany. The *Haganah* was training recruits in all the DP camps to prepare to fight for the new country. It was amazing that we came together as part of the *Aliyah Bet*. Naturally we were both a bit apprehensive about what lay ahead, but, as with every other strange situation I'd encountered, I sensed that somehow I would prevail. Right now, though, all I could think of was making it to Palestine in one piece.

The following day we were relieved and excited to learn that we were to depart that afternoon. I didn't fancy another night in that drafty shed. Our ultimate destination was near Haifa, a large port in the North of Palestine. When we finally were able to board The Caserta, we discovered that there would be over 600 people on that old tub. It didn't look very seaworthy to begin with. But the Mossad didn't fool around. They wanted to get people resettled as fast as possible. This was supposed to be a stealth mission. How do you sneak so many people into a country without being noticed? I was curious to find out.

The trip was supposed to take about two days, and was set to arrive in British waters after dark, to avoid detection. The politics we were heading into was beyond complicated, and we would learn even more as we moved toward our destination. By late November 1947, with Harry Truman, the U.S. President, the UN General Assembly Partition Plan had divided Palestine into designated areas, creating a Jewish State and an Arab State. They carved up the territory like a jigsaw puzzle, in a random way, while leaving the Port of Haifa in the Jewish State, and the capitol

135

of Jerusalem in the Arab State, but under U.N. administration making it a supposedly neutral area. It was quite confusing.

While this huge, overcrowded ship plowed through the dark waters of the Adriatic I tried to snatch some sleep. We had hammocks below deck that were incredibly uncomfortable and there were some among us who were crying and sobbing, so deep was their fear. They had never been on a big boat before. There were a lot of people who became seasick, even though the crossing was not rough. But the famous story of *Exodus 1947* was in everybody's mind. Less than a year before, *Exodus 1947*, another ship ferrying illegals, had been successfully turned back by the British Navy in an ugly sea battle, which left several people dead and many wounded. It was unpleasant food for thought.

In the early morning, I went up on deck to get some air, and could hardly believe my eyes. The light was brilliant as we passed the Greek islands. The beauty all around us was beyond description. After so much grayness and destruction in Europe, the white cliffs of the islands, dotted with blue domed churches, made it hard to believe that this was also part of Europe. It seemed a world apart.

Pretty soon Haskell was up and grumbling that he couldn't get any sleep. He'd brought a pair of cheap binoculars. We took turns looking at the new world around us, struck by the terrain as we passed by the craggy shores of Greece and then the coastline of Turkey, heading toward Cyprus.

After we had a piece of stale bread and some dreadful coffee we were approached by a man who identified himself only as Ari. We knew someone would meet us, but we didn't know who. Ari was from the *Haganah*, and he was on the ship to organize and assist a group of us who had trained to join the militia, which included me and Haskell. Ari told us to meet him later for a briefing prior to landing in Palestine. When we were assembled, there were about 20 young guys and one woman, whose name was Hadassah. We got into a sort of huddle and Ari, who was a Lieutenant in the *Haganah*, explained the dangers of landing in Palestine for illegals like us.

It was a bit daunting, to be sure. The blockades were very effective at deterring immigration, and some of us were openly skeptical that we were going to make it. However, the Lieutenant explained that there was yet another plan in the likely event of a blockade. *Huh*, I thought, *Tell me more, Lieutenant.* In a low voice, Lieutenant Ari explained that later that night, when land was in sight, members of the *Haganah* would run out to meet us in fishing boats, too small to be intercepted by the British. Those of us who were coming to fight for the homeland would be picked up and quickly ferried to a port where buses would be waiting to drive us to secret bunkers. We would be forced to hide once again since we were illegals. *Would I ever again be legal*, I wondered.

"Lieutenant," I asked, "how are we to get to these boats? It's a long way down." The ship we were on was enormous. He told us that they would throw a rope ladder down off the back of the ship, then we would climb down the ladder and jump on the small boats waiting below. The water seemed very far beneath us and it was dark and churning from the ship's big engines.

I hesitated to speak up, but finally I said, "Lieutenant Ari, I can't swim!" I tried to hide my concern, but then several others chimed in, admitting that they couldn't swim. It was a daunting prospect.

"Don't worry guys," the lieutenant said a bit too cheerfully. "We'll have experienced swimmers waiting in the boats in case you get into trouble. We'll look after you. You're fighting for Palestine now!"

When the hour came and we were about ten miles down the coast from Haifa the Lieutenant gathered us together. We had to be very quiet. It was hard to keep so many young guys quiet. Everyone was eager and excited. We all had our ideas of Palestine. For the more devout among us, it was a dream destination—the dream of a Holy Land was within their grasp. My stomach was upset. Dropping down into that black water was a new kind of horror to me.

The Lieutenant had everything under control. He lined up us recruits, making sure that the best swimmers went first. Haskell and I were at the end of the line. When the Lieutenant gave the signal, the guys ahead of us, one by one, began climbing down the thick rope ladder as it slapped across the back of the ship. It took a lot of strength to do this. The experienced swimmers were the first to shimmy down the ladder. I peered over the railing and watched them head down to the boats below, which looked like toys bobbing in the darkness.

Some of our group were murmuring prayers in Hebrew as they began the descent. When it was finally our turn, the Lieutenant said to Haskell and me, "Whatever you do, don't look down. Take it slow. One rung at a time. And hold on tight." *As if he needed to say that!* I thought.

He then tapped me on the shoulder, signaling it was my turn. I hoisted my leg over the edge of the railing, and put my foot on the first rung. By then a mist was rolling in, and the wooden rungs on the old rope ladder had become slippery. Luckily I had a lot of strength in my arms, but I was very unsure of my footing. With each step I thought of a member of my family. Step one, Mam. Step two, Tate, and so on. I was almost at the last rung and feeling a bit more confident when my foot slipped. I lost my grip and felt myself plunging into the water. Quickly, my head popped up and I heard someone calling *Aliyah, Aliyah!* They didn't know our names so everyone was just *Aliyah*—one making immigration to Israel as an illegal.

I was a bit disoriented, but then I saw a big light penetrating the mist. "*Aliyah*, over here!" The voice was insistent, and I knew that it was not far away. "Stay there, I am coming."

I couldn't see who was calling, but I could sense that the voice was coming nearer. I was freezing in the icy water. My instinct kicked in and I began paddling wildly to keep from sinking while I spat out foul oily seawater that kept getting in my mouth. I couldn't swim, but I knew that swallowing that water was the beginning of the end.

"Here, grab hold!" Suddenly something landed beside me. It was a white safety ring. I reached out and grabbed it. It was slithery under my fingers but I held on. Slowly the ring was being pulled toward a little fishing boat as I managed to keep a good grip on it. I could hear the guttural growl of the boat's motor revving up.

Without warning I felt someone reach out and clutch my free hand. Two strong guys grabbed me by the shoulders and hoisted me into the boat. When I got my bearings I saw that Haskell was already in the boat.

Above, the Lieutenant whistled loudly, his signal that all of the new recruits were safely off the ship, including Hadassah, who was, of course, strong and an expert swimmer.

Once we had all safely disembarked from the cargo ship, the little flotilla of fishing boats cut through the night, speeding toward the shores of Palestine.

****

The next morning I was sitting in a low-ceilinged, dusty bunker where we'd been secretly taken. Meantime I heard that the big ship we just left was turned back by the British, as so many were. Where those poor people landed I'll never really know. I was not clear about the set-up in Palestine, and was curious to find out. As soon as I was taken to the *Haganah* camp, the militia gave me a fresh set of clothes, a uniform and a gun. It didn't take me long to realize that Palestine was quite a bit hotter than central Europe, where I'd spent the last three years. The beads of sweat on my brow told the story. After all, Palestine was more than half desert. I had no idea where I was, really. We'd been smuggled into the country in the middle of the night. I did know that it was boiling hot—in many ways.

I was sitting around in the small structure with a few other *Aliyah Bet* recruits, rolling dice to pass the time, when a gruff-looking man in army fatigues blustered into the room. He had a sidekick, a scrawny little guy with a clipboard.

"*Shalom*," he greeted us. "Welcome to Palestine!" His booming voice was far too big for the room. "I am Sergeant Blitzstein, and this is Private Geldof." A few of us looked up, but didn't rise.

"Stand up, you baboons! You're not in some slacker DP camp now. You're in the Irgun!

As tired as we were, we stood up as smartly as we could manage. This guy meant business. "Geldof here is going to take all your names and ID cards. You will each be assigned a bunk and a fighting unit." Then he checked our regulation guns and rifles.

Haskell was not in the room. After landing we'd been split up in all the commotion that morning. I wondered if he was in another *Haganah* group and hoped we'd meet again.

The *Haganah* had been around since 1920, when it was a loosely organized militia of farmers who were protecting their farms and kibbutzim from attacks by Palestinian Arabs. By early March 1948, when I got to Palestine, it was a paramilitary organization with all the trappings of a regular army. The *Haganah* had been busy during World War II, supporting the British who defeated Rommel in North Africa, among other conflicts. As members of *Haganah* we were still part of the Jewish underground in Palestine known as *Irgun*. The leader was another Polish Jew like me by the name of Menachem Begin. By chance, Begin had been a friend of my father's back in Poland. In fact, there were thousands of Polish Jews everywhere in Palestine. For most of these refugees this was the "Land of Milk and Honey," after the pure cruelty of planned annihilation. But let me tell you, in those early days life in Palestine was hard going.

In a brief orientation, Sergeant Blitzstein informed us that we were in Jaffa, an ancient port city near Tel Aviv. At that point I only knew a few facts about the geography of Palestine, so there was a lot of learning ahead. I did have some idea of the politics and conflicts because, back in Bialystok, my father and his friends used to meet at our house and talk over the political news of the day—often about Palestine and Israel.

Now, with all that had happened, I was in another kind of underground. There were actual hidden tunnels that kept us out of sight. When the Sergeant got through with his orders, Geldof came around to each one of us with papers to sign. Believe it or not, everyone had to sign a contract to fight in the underground. After we got all the paperwork out of the way we were taken to a military medical center.

There we were thoroughly checked out before being taken by bus to the Army Camp Hasik Gimmel four miles from Ramla toward Jerusalem, an ancient city about 20 miles from Tel Aviv. I soon learned that Ramla, where we would be stationed, was almost in the dead center of Palestine. Quickly we were taken to a bare bones barracks in the camp, where we would officially begin our lives as Israeli soldiers—but we were still illegals.

Later that day I asked after Haskell, and learned that he'd been assigned to another army camp and another brigade somewhere else in this raw land. There was talk of a State of Israel on every tongue, which was an exciting prospect. I wondered what my father and his pals would have thought if they knew I was in Palestine and would soon be fighting for a Jewish nation. I'd like to think that they would have been quite proud.

For more than 50 years, serious conflicts, skirmishes and battles between the Arabs and the Jews had been popping up. This ongoing civil war was mainly over rights to the land and territories, especially when Jewish settlers began establishing kibbutzim. But there had never been an all-out hot war, which *was* on the horizon now.

When I got to know my fellow recruits, most of whom had come from various DP camps in Europe, I saw that there were many similar stories that had brought us to Palestine. When we were in Europe, we were all engaged in battling our own personal horrors. In a strange way, that was an isolating experience. When I began mixing with Jews from everywhere else in Europe I realized the great commonality of our journeys.

I was taking army life in stride and had made two good buddies, Izzy and Spike, who would be my compatriots during the coming war. *How bad could it be after everything else I'd been through? But was I ready for a real army*, I wondered. I'd had six weeks of training at a separate DP camp in the German forest, and I knew how to put together and take apart a gun from my time in the ghetto underground. But training at Ramla was no joke. It was very rigorous because they were trying

141

to quickly build a professional army out of green recruits. Furthermore, every recruit had to live by the clock. I was not so crazy about that. Every single minute of the day was regimented and there was no free time. Still, all the activity kept my mind off the past and made me feel that I was working for something big that would help my people.

As each day of training flew by, I fell into my bunk at night, with my body racked with aches and pains from the rigorous routine. I was suffering from a new kind of exhaustion. The intense sun that beat down on us all day also didn't help.

During my first weeks in Palestine, things were a bit irregular since we were still illegal Jews who'd run the British blockade to set foot on the coveted soil. Now we all waited to see what was coming. While we were still in a civil war, the Golani brigade was busy mostly quashing skirmishes between Arabs and Jewish settlers. Our main area of operation was in northeastern Palestine, including parts of Galilee and the Jordan River Valley.

After all our waiting, the day of days finally came on May 14, 1948 when David Ben-Gurion, chairman of the Jewish Agency for Palestine, and a leading Zionist, proclaimed that Israel was an independent Jewish state. That night, at midnight, the British withdrew. This was the news that Jews in Palestine and throughout the world had waited for a very long time. The tom-toms had been beating for a long time that this declaration was coming. In fact, a resolution by the United Nations General Assembly on November 29, 1947 laid the groundwork for the State of Israel to ensure that Jews had a land that was all their own, and U.S. President Harry S. Truman recognized the new nation that same day. Ben-Gurion read a definitive proclamation at the Museum of Tel Aviv in front of a large celebratory crowd of newly-liberated citizens. Cries of *Mazel Tov* were in the air, and there were a lot of strangers hugging strangers. We learned that from that day forward some major chunks of Palestinian territory would now be known as the State of Israel—referred to by most Jews as *Eretz Yisrael*. It was a day of jubilation, complete with cheering crowds, fireworks and plenty of excitement. Now Haifa at last became a legal gateway for Jewish immigrants. No more being smuggled in, or being turned away by the British. No more underground tunnels. I must admit that I felt a certain thrill that I was there at the birth of a new Jewish democracy.

Sorry to say, the excitement was short-lived. The very next day, May 15th, after the British formally withdrew, the Arabs declared war on the infant state—barely one day old. On the morning of May 15th Arab forces began streaming over the borders of the new country. Suddenly fighting forces from Egypt, Jordan, Lebanon and Syria, together with expeditionary forces from Iraq, poured into Palestine. Soon other Arab states followed. Soldiers, complete with weapons and tanks, mortars and grenades—all the trappings of real war—seemed to come from everywhere. The invading forces took control of the Arab areas in a show of brotherhood, but they didn't stop there. They immediately attacked Israeli forces and several Jewish settlements. It got really bad really fast.

Right away, my unit was given orders to go to the city of Tiberias, several miles north of Ramla, on the western shore of the Sea of Galilee, where Syrian forces were attacking Jewish settlers. Those poor people were practically defenseless. Some of the settlers knew how to handle a gun, but were no match for the trained army of King Abdullah of Jordan. They were desperate for reinforcements. We were not so well-trained, but we were organized and had passion on our side, or at least a thirst for revenge.

For three days I engaged in hand-to-hand combat with some pretty fierce Arab fighters and fended off armed attacks—beating back the Syrians as I fought alongside other members of my brigade. We soon ran the Syrians off, suffering only a couple of casualties and some minor injuries. A bullet grazed Izzy, but he was a tough guy from Minsk and it practically ricocheted off him. As soon as that action died down we were busy defending two kibbutzim in the same region. Some in my brigade were behind high man-made embankments of sandbags, facing Syrians, who were behind their own sandbags—a cheap commodity

143

in the desert. The Syrians did a lot of damage to the kibbutzim, but the settlements remained in Israeli hands. All of this conflict became known as "The Battles of the Kinarot Valley."

After the statehood of Israel was declared there were some immediate and very important developments. All illegals like myself immediately became legal. After skirting the powers-that-be in Europe and Palestine for so many years it was a great feeling. Instead of having to conduct activities in stealth, we were honored to fight for Israel, and this included, Izzy, Spike and Haskell, who was in the Negev brigade. I personally heard Menachem Begin, leader of the Irgun, announce this news in a stirring radio address. Listening, I could only think of my father with a heavy heart. I deeply wished I could have shaken Begin's hand at that moment, on behalf of my father and the thousands of Polish souls who died dreaming of a Jewish homeland.

On May 26, 1948, a couple of weeks later, the Israeli Defense Forces or "IDF" came into being. That action brought a number of squabbling Israeli militia groups together and they became a single, unified and much more powerful army, which today is still one of the best armies in the region. By October 28th of that same year Israel was able to adopt its own flag. That brought a new sense of reality to the country. The familiar white and blue standard with the central Star of David is now known throughout the world.

The detention camps in Cyprus and the DP camps in Europe soon began to empty out, since Jews could now freely come to Israel. At one time there had been about 28,000 Jews in the Cypriot detention camps, living in very difficult conditions. By December 1948 the Cypriot camps were finally empty.

The founders of the new country envisioned a haven for Jewry from all over the world. Each new settler helped to gain parity with the large Arab population. Each baby that was born in Israel was a cause for celebration, and helped deepen our roots on Jewish soil.

As for me, I was active every day in the IDF, so happy to be a part of that newly launched force. When we had a bit of free time, I would hang out with Izzy, Spike and some others, playing cards, smoking and talking about women. But there was plenty to keep us busy—right up until March 1949, when the IDF secured the southernmost Israeli town of Eliat. Eliat, where the River Jordan flows into the Gulf of Aqaba and then into the Red Sea, was crucial to the economy and development of Israel. Both the Golani and Negev brigades participated in this pivotal final operation of the war. I finally ran into Haskell there, which was cause for our own celebration.

After the fighting ended in an Israeli victory, the clamor of war died down and many of the soldiers became reservists in the IDF, which had been a conscription force. Many of my fellow infantrymen were only too happy to remain in Israel. By then some had girlfriends and even wives, so they'd found a basis for their lives. As an inducement to remain in the country we were each offered free land and all kinds of perks. The new Israel Government was hungry for settlers. My General, Uzi Nakeys, gave me a nice little house and even gave me a store in Ramla, so I could operate my own butcher shop. For six months I operated a business out of that store. I was making decent money, but I found life in Ramla pretty dull. I hadn't abandoned my dream of New York City, USA. I wanted to do big things, and knew that I could. However, at that time, you couldn't immigrate to the U.S. from Israel, but it was possible to come to America from Europe. Not easy, but possible. That was what I wanted: a life where everything was possible in a land where everything was possible.

So, after eighteen and a half eventful months, watching with my own eyes and heart as Israel became a democratic state, I locked up the store, gave back the house in Ramla, and returned to my DP camp, Föhrenwald. It was October 1949.

"We are alive. We are human, with good and bad in us. That's all we know for sure. We can't create a new species or a new world. That's been done. Now we have to live within those boundaries. What are our choices? We can despair and curse, and change nothing. We can choose evil like our enemies have done and create a world based on hate. Or we can try to make things better."

—Carol Matas (born November 14, 1949), internationally-acclaimed author of 45 books for children and young adults. Quote is from Daniel's Story, a Holocaust memoir.

12

A Long Journey to a New Life

After the heat and dust of Israel, where the grit in the air was sometimes so thick it would get in your eyes and make them sting, it felt good to get back to the damp, greenish-grey fall colors of Bavaria. Once I was finished with the Israeli Defense Forces I had wired ahead to ask if there was a place for me in Föhrenwald. When I got word from the United Nations Relief and Rehabilitation Administration (UNRRA) office that I could return, I hustled back, by land and sea, traversing old ground and some new ground until I arrived in the Munich station a few days after leaving Ramla.

The camp operated a van to take people to and from the train station. When I got back to Föhrenwald I realized I'd actually missed it. That is a funny thing to say about a DP camp that provided temporary shelter for refugees, but it was the closest thing I'd had to a home since my family was rounded up in 1942. Then I was a boy and now I was a man, and men have different perspectives than boys—or at least they should.

I'd had an amazing and unforgettable time in Israel, and felt really good about my participation in the war. But I had come back to Germany with a purpose. I was not going to waste another minute until I reached my ultimate destination—the USA! When I got to the camp I went directly to the UNRRA office. I walked in, and there was Dina. She had assisted Henry Cohen when he was in charge of Föhrenwald, and I was glad to see that she was still there. Any connection is a good connection when you are alone in the world.

"Sam!" She looked up with a surprised smile. "So glad you made it. How are you? You look much stronger and healthier than when you left us."

"Trust me, it wasn't the Israeli army food that did it. It was the army itself. They worked you really hard and trained you harder. Plus I was baking in the sun all the time."

"Well, whatever it took, you look good. I'm sure you want to get settled," she said warmly as she handed me a set of keys and directed me to the cottage that would be my home while I was there. It might seem odd that a German national was working in a camp for Jewish DPs, but because of the UN we had nationals from all over working in Föhrenwald. Dina was a pleasant German woman who lived in the town of Wolfratshausen, not far from the camp. She was a war widow with a couple of kids and really needed the job. Ironically, having the DP camps in Germany was a boost to the local economy. As you can imagine, the Germans were really on the ropes after their blistering defeat by the Allies. Wolfratshausen was a typical Bavarian village with a certain charm. Because it was nestled into the foothills of the Alps it was removed from the line of fire, so the village had only been lightly damaged by the war.

I was glad to see Dina, but I was even happier to find my bed. I'd been travelling for several days and was exhausted. Since I knew the camp well, I had no trouble finding my new berth. This time I had it to myself, since my fellow refugees had been leaving Europe as fast as they could. By now many had gone to Canada, South America, Australia, the U.S., and Israel—anywhere they could resettle. Such arrangements were not easy, and I knew I had a challenge ahead.

As soon as I caught up on my sleep I hitched a ride all the way to Wolfratshausen, just to see some familiar sights. I knew it was market day, and local farmers would be coming into town with their wares. After the war, Germany was in chaos, to say the least. There were severe food shortages and no work, as most of the big factories and plants had been destroyed. This situation caused inevitable strikes and riots. Now, thanks to the Marshall plan of 1948, things were finally getting a little better. To resurrect Europe from the ashes, the U.S. infused 12 billion dollars into the European economy—which is always a lot, but was an especially whopping amount of money at the time.

When I got into town, the day's market was just winding down and the farmers were packing up. Luckily, I spotted a familiar face in the thinning crowd. I didn't waste a moment. "*Guten Tag*, Kurt," I said, tapping the gnarled man on his shoulder. He looked much older than his actual age, since he'd spent his life outdoors on his little patch of land.

He turned and looked me for a long moment. I could see he was puzzled.

"It's the butcher from the DP camp." I said, finally. "Don't you remember me?"

"*Ach*," he smiled. "Sure I do. It is young Sam." He reached out to shake my hand. Since he'd been working all day, his hand was grimy but I shook it to be cordial. "You look so different," he gazed up at me. "More grown up. How can I help, *Herr* Sam?"

"I am back at Föhrenwald for a while. How is your business doing?

"Well, you know, young Sam," said the old farmer, "animals keep breeding and calving, but we have to feed them to keep them alive and healthy. We lost quite a few good animals during the war." He shook his head sadly. "Finally, now, we can get food and supplies. So bit by bit things are getting better."

"*Das is gut*," I said and gave him another friendly clap on the shoulder.

Old Kurt didn't dare say it, but I could guess what he was thinking. The Nazi trolls had nearly destroyed his beloved country, but now that Konrad Adenauer, a longtime foe of Hitler, was Chancellor at last, Germans could try to forget about their shameful past.

They could try, I thought as I took my leave, *but they can never really live down the ignominy of Hitler, and how so many of them, even if they didn't actively participate, did look the other way.*

If you think it was odd being a Jew in post-War Germany, you would be right. It was a very uneasy truce. I had no bitterness against people like Dina and Kurt, a woman who lost her husband and a man who was far too old to fight. They were also victims of Hitler's mania. I could be friendly but never warm to my former enemies.

****

By the next day I was off to the HIAS office, which was on Mel-strasse in the camp. HIAS, as I explained earlier, stands for the He-brew Immigration Aid Society and is a venerable organization initially founded in New York to help Jews who were persecuted by the Russian pogroms back in the last century. The HIAS office was a collection of offices they shared with several other charities, most of them Jewish charities, also based at Föhrenwald, to assist refugees in a thousand dif-ferent ways. People and organizations came from all over the globe to aid those of us who were displaced by war. It was rather heartwarming, really.

When I entered the HIAS office there was lots of bustle and com-motion because of the large demand for their services. This included finding lost loved ones separated by the tumult of the Shoah, helping refugees locate family members that had emigrated to far parts of the world, and all sorts of other support. Often this was a near impossible task, since so many vital documents such as birth certificates and mar-riage records went up in smoke during the catastrophe.

I waited for a very long time in the HIAS office until I was final-ly able to get the attention of a little bald man sitting behind a desk, whose name turned out to be Stanley. He was an American with thick overtones of Yiddish in his voice, so I guessed he had once been an im-migrant himself. I explained to Stanley that I had relatives in America, probably in Brooklyn, New York or somewhere in New Jersey, or so I thought. My information was a bit vague because my father's relatives had gone to the states in the late 1920s, around the time I was born.

I knew my father's father was a rabbi somewhere in New Jersey, but there were hundreds of rabbis in New Jersey, and my uncle and aunt were likely living there too. Ever since the Nazi invasion in 1939 we'd lost touch, and now ten years had gone by. In fact I didn't know whether my family members in the U.S. were living or dead. They undoubtedly had no idea if any of my immediate family had survived—though I'm sure they suspected the worst.

To get to America there were a lot of hurdles. The biggest was that I had to have a sponsor—a relative or close connection—who would vouch for me. President Truman and his Congress had passed the DP Immigration Act of 1948 to welcome Jewish refugees to the shores of America. Still, there were a lot of obstacles, and finding a sponsor was the biggest one. To make sure that a DP would not come to America in poor health, dire need, or broke you had to have someone to speak up for you. My best bet was to find my father's family. I badly needed to locate my grandfather or uncle. I also dreaded telling these virtual strangers, who lived so far away, that I was the only survivor out of my huge family. I knew it would break their hearts. While it was clearly vital that I locate them, at this moment that seemed like a long shot.

I explained all this to Stanley, who was kind but firm. He listened to stories like mine all day every day, and tried to appear interested. When I finally finished my familiar tale, he looked up, put his pen down and explained that HIAS would do everything they could, but it could take many, many months to find my relatives, arrange for passage to New York, and make all the other necessary arrangements. The biggest stumbling block, he emphasized, was locating a sponsor—if they could even find any of my relatives. Many people waited years to get to America, and sometimes they wound up in Australia, Canada or someplace else that was not their first choice. I was determined to make my way to New York, and would not settle for less. I had fought too long and too hard to give up now.

I pressed him again and Stanley again promised that HIAS would make every effort, but said he could make no guarantees. He had a "Don't call us, we'll call you" kind of manner. I resolved that I would make this work somehow. I'd paid my dues and I was not prepared to

151

wait much longer. To complicate matters I had no papers and no passport. As you can imagine, all our family records had been destroyed long ago. My only forms of identity were my papers from the DP camp and for the Israeli Army, but they wouldn't cut any mustard when it came to my immigrating to a new country. I had to get a DP Card. There was also a medical exam, because TB had become a big problem in some of the camps. People with tuberculosis were not welcome in a new country until they returned to health.

****

Things were humming along. Surprisingly I'd been able to connect with some of my other DP friends who had also gone to Israel and likewise returned to the camp. But the next week I still hadn't made any progress with HIAS. The next morning I went straight into town again. The air was crisp. It was a sunny afternoon and I was in no hurry to catch the bus back to camp, so I walked along the little main street minding my own business. Suddenly I felt a firm tap on my shoulder. I was startled. After all my time being hunted by the Nazis, I was still a bit jumpy.

"Hey, Buddy," I heard a friendly voice and turned around. "Is there anything to do around here for fun?" I was face to face with an American GI who was trying to communicate in pidgin German. He was of medium height, with dark hair and slightly Semitic features. He was with two other GIs who were both taller and blond. The three were likely stationed at a French military barracks, which wasn't too far from town.

I noticed that the name sewn on his uniform was Nussbaum, and took a chance. "*Ich sprech kein englisch*," I said, explaining that I didn't speak English, and followed with, "*Farshtet?* Do you understand Polish or Yiddish?"

"Sure," he said, speaking in Yiddish with a big grin. "My parents were originally from Krakow, but I was born in the Bronx."

This was a new word to me. "Bronx, what is that?"

"Just the best part of New York City. Good old Bronx. My home-town."

"You're from New York City?" I was trying to not get too excited.

"Yep. Have you ever been there?"

"Not yet," I said firmly. "But that is where I am going!"

"Great. How are you going to get there?" I'd piqued his curiosity. By then his buddies, bored with our chatter in Yiddish, had wandered off.

"I don't know. I just returned from Israel. I was in the IDF. But I can't get to the U.S. from Israel. Not now. So I came back to Germany."

"Oh," he said as the penny dropped. "Are you from the DP camp?"

"Yes, I'm living there right now. "But I need to get to New York. And soon."

"I hear you, pal." He stuck out his hand in that friendly American way, and said, "Ray."

"Sam," I replied and shook his hand. I explained about HIAS, and all the difficulties in finding my relatives. As an American Jew, with immigrant roots, he totally understood.

"Look Sam, I know you're in a tight spot. I think I might be able to help you. But I've got to catch up with my buddies. Can you meet me here tomorrow about the same time?"

Emphatically, I said I could and would. "Yes, of course."

"Then it's a date. Keep your chin up, Sam."

Up until then I'd met very few Americans, but he had that breezy quality that I'd seen in American movies. Sometimes in the camp they showed American films with subtitles. That was always a big event.

I had no idea what my new friend Ray had in mind, but you can be sure that I would be in town the next day, no matter what.

****

Since we'd happened to meet in front of the small tobacconist shop, I was waiting there the next day at 4:00 PM sharp. In fact I was half an hour early. I admit I was a bit nervous, because I had no idea what Ray had in mind. But meeting a Jew from the Bronx seemed like some kind miracle to me.

I hoped I didn't look too conspicuous as I stood alone on the street in this little village. Everybody knew everybody in town and I was a stranger, so I didn't want to attract any attention. After a while I started walking up and down the street while keeping an eye out for the GI. I had been there for half an hour, and still he was a no-show. For a few minutes the whole encounter seemed like it might have been a fantasy. Could I have dreamt meeting Ray? Was he standing me up? I was beginning to doubt my own senses, but I was determined to stick it out. Another 15 minutes went by and by now it was getting cold. Then I heard my name.

"Hey, Sam!" I turned, only to see Ray hurrying in my direction. "Hey, buddy, so sorry I'm late."

I was so relieved that I didn't care that my teeth were beginning to chatter. "I'm glad you're still here," he said, a bit out of breath. "I was worried that I'd miss you. Let's go into the *gasthaus* and get some beer and *schnitzel*. My treat." That sounded pretty good to me. And it was nice to hear Yiddish again, especially spoken with a New York accent.

Once we got settled at a dark corner table and had some beer to restore us, Ray said, "I'm really sorry I was late, Sam," and then went on to explain. "I am in the medical corps at the base, and at the last minute one of the dependent wives went into labor. It was her third kid and it was coming fast. I had to drive her in the ambulance all the way to the hospital outside Munich. She screamed all the way. Whew! We just made it too!"

"Sure, sure. That's okay. I knew you wouldn't let me down." I filled Ray in on some of the details of my situation. It turned out that he had Polish relatives who were also trying to get to New York, so he knew the ropes. "So you are working with HIAS?" he asked.

"Yeah," I said. "But they are not very encouraging. And I'm not sure where my family is. I have a notion that they are in Brooklyn and maybe also somewhere in New Jersey."

"HIAS has helped a lot of people, but there are far too many people needing their help, and there is a lot of red tape. Miles of it."

"You said you thought you could help."

"Right. Here is what I have in mind."

Ray was a high-energy guy and I liked that in him, being a high-energy guy myself. He enthusiastically explained that it would be a big shortcut if I could send a letter directly to HIAS in New York. I could also give a copy to Stanley at the camp. I needed to explain my situation clearly and then HIAS in the city would see that it was printed in the New York newspapers.

"Great," I said, "Only one problem: I can't read or write in English."

That's no problem at all. I can!" With that Ray pulled out a sheet of paper and an envelope. "Here's the deal, Sam." Ray jotted down something on the envelope: "425 Lafayette Street, New York City, NY." Above that he wrote HIAS in big letters. "This, my friend, is the address of HIAS headquarters in New York. This is the real deal."

I listened with rapt attention as Ray Nussbaum, my new guardian angel, explained that he had a plan. Together we were going to compose a letter telling the story of how I was looking for my relatives. I would put in as much detail as I had about them, which wasn't that much, and he would write it out for me in English. He would mail the letter to New York from the Army Post Office on the base. I would take a copy of the letter to poor beleaguered Stanley in the camp office. Typically, HIAS would print letters from DPs who were looking for relatives in *The Jewish Daily Forward*, which was, and still is, a Jewish newspaper published in New York. Hopefully *The Jewish Daily Forward* would print my letter, and do it in both their English and Yiddish editions.

I was practically jumping for joy inside as Ray rolled out his idea. *Perhaps his plan would do the trick*, I thought, hopefully. As if reading my thoughts, Ray said, "Trust me. This can't miss. Your father's relatives are bound to see the letter. Every Jew in New York reads this paper!" I was secretly thrilled but tried to play it cool, like this sort of thing happened every day for me—which it certainly didn't.

Then, as if presenting me with dessert, Ray told me the best part of his plan: "I am being demobilized in a few weeks, meaning I'll have soon finished my stint with Uncle Sam, and be sent back home. After I kiss my Ma and shake my father's hand, the next thing I'm going to do is go down to Lafayette Street, march into the HIAS office, and speak with the boss there about you."

"What will that do?" I asked, naive to the way things were done in the U.S.

"You'd be surprised, Sam." Ray gave me a warm smile. "You'd be surprised."

****

The next morning I marched over to the HIAS office and presented Stanley with a copy of the letter. It felt like a special gift. He looked at it a bit skeptically, then looked me up and down over his spectacles. "Well, what do you expect this will do, Mr. Solasz?"

"I expect it will get me home soon."

"Home? Aren't you a bit mixed up? You've never even been to New York."

"*Das ist wahr*," I said, affirming the truth of what I said. "But I know it is home."

"Very well, Mr. Solasz. Keep me informed. If you make contact with a sponsor, please let me know so HIAS can make the proper arrangements for you."

"Okay, Mr. Stanley," I said, and left his office.

During the next few weeks I kept in touch with Ray. The last time we met at the *gasthaus* he told me that he had a girl back in the Bronx and that he couldn't wait to see her again. They were getting married soon. That sounded pretty nice to me. I wished I had a nice girl waiting for me. Not a frumpy *fraulein*, but a smart stylish American girl. That was part of the dream.

As I shook hands with Ray and wished him well, he repeated his

156

promise to go to HIAS on Lafayette Street, wherever that was, and make my case to the big *macher* at the headquarters, convinced that this "was the ticket" as he put it. I gave him my address in the camp and promised to see him in New York when I got there. Then he sped off in a battered old Ducati motorbike he'd borrowed from the motor pool at the base.

Now there was nothing to do but wait. And wait and wait and wait.

****

My many ups and downs during the wars in both Europe and the Middle East had taught me to be patient, which is not really my nature. Back then I was always in the thick of the action. Now time was moving like molasses. Fortunately I was very busy with my little butcher business, went to a few social events at the camp, kibitzed with some of my neighbors. Meanwhile I watched this one and that one leaving from the camp as they headed off to a new life somewhere. The bright spot of my day was going to the camp mailroom to see if any letters had arrived. Every day my box was empty.

One day, as I was leaving the mailroom, I bumped into another friend from the camp, Paulina, a sweet motherly type. I must have looked a bit downhearted because she asked, "What is the matter, Sam?"

"I'm fine," I replied, but I guess I didn't convince her, because she repeated her question, this time sounding even more motherly.

"*Ach*," I shook my head. "I am hoping to hear from relatives in the states."

"You're still looking for a sponsor?"

"Sure. And day after day I hear nothing."

"Don't get discouraged, Sam. I know that it's taken some people months to connect with a sponsor, but it usually works out in the end."

"Thanks, Paulina." I managed a smile. "I really appreciate the encouragement."

I continued with my routine. Working at the business. Going into town every week to see Kurt. It was a bit on the boring side, especially after the harum scarum of the last ten years. Every morning I went to my mailbox, and when it was empty once again I felt a little downhearted. One afternoon I told myself—why bother? Still, I found myself in the vicinity of the mailroom and couldn't resist. I put my hand in the box and guess what, there *was* a little envelope sitting there. I opened it, and to my surprise, it was from Ray. As I unfolded the flimsy airmail paper something fell out and landed on the floor. I bent to pick it up.

Wow! I thought. It was a little snapshot. It was a picture of Ray in his uniform, grinning like a fool, and standing next to a pretty, petite brunette who was wearing a nice suit, a big flowery hat and carrying a bouquet. I turned the snapshot over and on the back was written: Ray and Antonia, married January 15, 1950. *Antonia*, I thought, *that's an Italian name*. When I looked harder at the picture, they were standing in front of a church. He married a *shiksa* I thought with some amazement. In my world it was practically unthinkable for a Jew to marry a *shiksa*. Antonia was lovely and Ray looked like the cat that swallowed the little yellow bird. I knew that my parents would have certainly frowned on such a match. *I guess America really will be different*, I thought. Oh, well, I didn't have any girl at the moment. Frankly, I didn't see the point, since I was planning on leaving Europe as soon as possible.

Ray's note was brief, telling me how happy he was and what a great girl he'd married. I was happy for him too, but knew that his old-country parents could not be overjoyed to welcome Antonia into the Nussbaum *mishpocheh*. Just before he signed off, Ray confirmed that he'd been to HIAS on the famous Lafayette Street and they'd promised to print my letter in *The Jewish Daily Forward* and perhaps other New York papers. He told me to have patience— that it would happen. All of this was written in Yiddish.

My heart leapt at reading that. But, knowing that I was still playing the waiting game, I went back to my informal butcher shop.

For many days I did not darken the door of the HIAS office again. I just kept putting one foot in front of another. One day a friend named Gertrude stopped by. "Any news yet, Sam?"

I shook my head. "I am just going over there to check now. It's taking forever."

"After what you've been through, a little waiting is the easy part."

"I suppose," I said, as I started to walk over to the mailroom.

"*Viel Gluck!*" she called after me.

I didn't feel particularly lucky, despite Gertie's encouragement, but as I reached into the mailbox I put my hand on a letter. I pulled it out and opened it nervously. It had a U.S. stamp so that was good. My hand shook a little as I began to read the letter. It read something like this:

Mr. Solasz:

My cousin, Saul Rosenbaum, read in the Jewish paper that HIAS is looking for a sponsor for someone who claims to be my nephew. Right away he contacted me to let me know that someone is looking for the Solasz family.

Are you who you claim to be? All of my family died in the Shoah. How can you possibly be my nephew? I will need proof. I cannot sponsor anyone who is a faker or a phony. Some Jews have brought relatives over from Europe who turned out not to be relatives at all. I won't do bubkes for a stranger pretending to be family.

Dovid Solasz
E. 34th Street
Brooklyn, NY

The letter was written in a mixture of Polish and Yiddish, but it was cold in any language. Still, it was the long awaited response, and better than no response at all. Clearly this man wasn't going to make it easy. Now I must think what to do.

The next day I went over to the HIAS office in the camp. Stanley wasn't there. When I asked after him, I was told he'd been transferred to another DP camp, which turned out to be a lucky break for me. A very nice woman by the name of Sonia Marcus asked me to sit down and tell her my story. She already had a file with my name on it, which she pulled out of her desk drawer. I was a bit reluctant to show her the letter from my uncle. His response was embarrassing, but I needed to ask her advice.

She took a minute to read the letter, then put it down a bit sharply. "This happens sometimes, Mr. Solasz," Sonia Marcus was warm and friendly. "Don't be discouraged. Jews who got to the U.S. well before the war cannot really imagine how bad it was for the Jews who were caught in Poland and other countries when the Nazis rose to power. They think that they know, but they really don't. Don't be too hard on your uncle. I have seen these sorts of letters sent to other DPs. Unfortunately this man's skepticism is not so unusual. But there's a way around it."

I felt better just hearing her say that. Then we got down to cases. She asked me to call her Sonia, then told me she was going to help me write a letter to my uncle. In the letter she was going to put down every bit of information I had about my family. Names, dates, the hometown, any and everything I could think of to assure my uncle that I was who I said I was. I should also send a picture, she said. Maybe they'll see a family resemblance. She had a little camera and took a snapshot of me. When we had everything together she would send it in an airmail pouch to HIAS on Lafayette Street. That was the fastest way to get it there, she explained.

"At least," she said, "we now have your uncle's address in Brooklyn. That's a key piece of information. Someone in the HIAS office will send your new letter directly to your uncle at his home."

"Miss Sonia, you think this will work?" I rocked back on my heels, which meant I was edgy. My pride dictated that I should be taken at my word. After surviving by the skin of my teeth so many times, now my

160

own family wanted me to pass some sort of test. It was humiliating.

Sonia reassured me that this second letter would do the trick. She had seen it work for other DPs. At least I wasn't alone.

****

Miss Sonia Marcus was so confident that she immediately began making arrangements for my passage to the U.S., because she said it could take a good while to get my name on a list for a transport ship, and she wanted to make sure that I didn't have to wait much longer.

I needed a DP Card, and had to go into an office in Munich to get that. She gave me an identity card and a letter from her that I was a client of HIAS. Bit by bit I was making progress. Then a few months later another letter came from my uncle. This time it was a bit friendlier and contained two America dollars, as a gesture of his softening I supposed.

All together I got three letters from my uncle, and eventually he agreed to sponsor me, which didn't cost him a penny.

****

It wasn't the warmest welcome from my family, but I needed a sponsor and had to swallow my pride.

I decided to go into Munich to look for some presents to bring to my uncle, who finally agreed to sponsor me, and also for my father's sister who had immigrated to the U.S. My aunt and her family lived in Newark, New Jersey and my uncle and his family lived in Brooklyn. Yes, as it turned out I also had relatives in Brooklyn—but didn't everybody?

Although eighty percent of Munich had been destroyed during the war, by late 1950 the city had come back a bit, and there was a small but very nice shopping street in the center of town near the *Rathaus*. It was December and the city was all dressed up for Christmas, as only German cities can be. I must say it brightened my mood to see the greenery and lights and *tannenbaum* trees everywhere. The whole idea for the Christmas tree originated in this country. It was confounding to me that a country that could have such warm and lovely customs could also have such a bloodthirsty history. It is a puzzle to me to this day. However, despite all that, I found the lights and decorations quite cheerful. As I walked around the *Marienplatz* I was looking in little shop windows, which were crammed with woodcarvings, music boxes, porcelain figurines and all sorts of the goods that Germany was famous for before the war, but found nothing I could bring to my Jewish family in the states.

As I walked along, I saw people on a street corner singing some lovely music—hymns and carols I supposed. Though I wasn't familiar with any of the music, it was still beautiful. Then I stopped in my tracks. I found myself in front of a famous beer hall where Hitler had begun his lethal campaign to win over the German masses with his harangues.

Just looking at the beer hall, I had chills up and down my spine. I was so angry I could have spit on the ground, but Munich was a very tidy place, despite the destruction that was still apparent everywhere. So I calmed myself, and continued walking. Suddenly I saw that a lot of other pedestrians had stopped and were looking toward the sky. *What is this*, I thought, a bit concerned, but couldn't resist looking up as well. To my amazement the Glockenspiel clock in the Rathaus tower—which had been miraculously spared during the bombing raids—began its wonderful routine, with almost life-size figures performing traditional automated dances. The little show lasted about 15 minutes. When it ended I looked at my watch. It was time to catch my bus back to Föhrenwald.

****

First thing the next morning I headed straight over to the mail room. My heart skipped a beat when I saw that Miss Sonia Marcus had left an envelope in my box. My hands shook as I opened it.

December 11, 1950

Dear Sam,

I am writing to let you know that I've secured a berth for you on the USNS General Harry Taylor, departing from Bremerhaven on January 12th 1951. Please come to the HIAS office at your first opportunity to make further arrangements.

Best regards,

Sonia Marcus, HIAS Executive Director, Föhrenwald DP Camp.

"A storyteller can attempt to tell the human tale, can make a galaxy out of the chaos, can point to the fact that some people survived even as most people died. And can remind us that the swallows still sing around the smokestacks."

—Jane Yolen (born February 11, 1939), author or editor
of more than 280 books, of which best known is
The Devil's Arithmetic, a Holocaust novella.

13

A Rocky Ride to a Very Big Voyage

As soon as the cock crowed the next morning, I hopped out of bed, and before even getting a cup of coffee began making lists of things I needed to do in the short time I had before I left Germany. There were people I wanted to say good-bye to, errands I needed to run, and everything else. I'd had a terrible night, as you can imagine. Excitement had been my companion and sleep didn't come easily. Throughout the night I kept turning on my bed light and looking at Miss Marcus' note to make sure it was true, that I was really going to America! I had less than a month to get everything in order. After so many years of waiting and planning, a month seemed like no time at all.

I knew that the HIAS office didn't open until nine o'clock in the morning and it seemed like I had hours to fill until I could seal the deal. Until I met with Miss Marcus, and talked with her in the flesh, I was afraid this whole opportunity would go away, that it had all been a dream. In one way I was afraid to get too excited and tempt fate. But in truth I couldn't contain my pounding heart. My real life was about to begin!

After I finished my little "to do" list, I looked at the wind-up clock beside my bed. It told me I still had two hours before HIAS opened. So I shaved, dressed and waited. When I thought of the big move ahead, my stomach did flip-flops.

I would never say it to anyone, since he *was* sponsoring me, but I had to admit to myself that my uncle's attitude was grudging at best. I also kept reminding myself that these New Jersey and Brooklyn kin would never replace my own family—as much as I wanted that to be the case. No one can ever replace your parents. No uncles, aunts or cousins could ever step into the shoes of Mam, Tate, my brother Schmuel and the rest. Before I allowed myself to get too deep into memory, I made a cup of coffee and a thick slice of toast with jam. The next thing I knew it was almost time for HIAS to open.

I rushed out the door and raced around to the HIAS office. It was a foggy winter morning in Bavaria and the dampness felt good on my face, calming me somewhat. By the time I got to the office I could see my breath in front of my face. And there was Miss Sonia Marcus, standing at the front door with a key in her hand.

"Oh, good, you're here, Sam!" she said, smiling broadly with her eyes lit up. Her smile made me feel optimistic. "Yesterday I was in Munich," I blurted out excitedly, "I didn't get your note until I returned to camp, and by then the office was closed."

"That's all right, Sam," she said, sensing my concern. "No harm done. Everything is in order."

She turned the key in the lock and motioned for me to come in. We didn't waste a second. The soul of efficiency, she had all the paper-work ready. There was even a packet of papers for my uncle explaining his responsibilities as my sponsor. "This is just a formality," she said, handing me the papers.

Together we went over all the details. There were tickets for my passage, and the logistics of how I would get to the ship, the General Taylor, docked in Bremerhaven, a major German port on the blustery North Sea. Then she kindly warned me that crossing the North Atlantic in January, even in a vessel as big as the General Taylor, could be a bit rough—which turned out to be a major understatement. Miss Sonia explained that a few other DPs from the area were also going on the General Taylor, so HIAS would escort a group of us to the ship, well in advance of its scheduled departure.

"This is one appointment you can't afford to miss, Sam. These ships are…"

"Oh, I am very good at being on time, Miss Sonia. The IDF taught me that." In my excitement I cut her off.

"I'm sure you are," she smiled, indulgent of my nervousness. "I'm just telling you that these navy vessels are extremely punctual. It's the law of the sea."

"I'm sure it will be much different from those old tubs that the Haganah used to get us to Palestine. Except for those, I've never been on a real boat."

"I think you *will* find this a bit different. You will be crossing the North Atlantic. It should be an adventure. And don't call it a boat. The General Harry Taylor is a *ship*."

"Right, Right," I said, wondering what the difference could be.

"The ship departs on January 12th and makes her first port on January 20th in Halifax, Nova Scotia. Quite a few of our DPs are resettling in Canada, so they will disembark there. The next port is New York on January 22nd. I will wire your uncle in Brooklyn to let him know exactly when you will be arriving."

"You will?"

"Your sponsor must be there to meet you. Otherwise the immigration authorities will detain you and you risk being sent back. So it is not just nice: it is critical that he meets you. Do you have any idea what he looks like?"

"Unless he is the twin of my father, I have no idea what he looks like."

"That's one reason we sent him your snapshot. It will help him identify *you*. There will be hundreds of people on the ship."

I'm sure I looked confounded at that news. "That's why," she paused, "I have made you this sign," saying that with a flourish. It was on bright yellow paper and had my name printed in big black letters, bold enough to be seen at a distance. "When you disembark in New York, hold this up so your uncle can find you."

"Okay, Miss Sonia. That is so nice. Thank you," I said appreciatively.

Efficiently, she gathered together all the paperwork, including the DP papers and the sign, and slipped them into a large brown envelope that was stamped HIAS and marked "Confidential" in red ink. "To make sure they are secure, I am going to put them in our safe here." She instructed me to come by the office the day before I was to leave to collect the envelope. "*Sicher*," I replied in German. "How could I forget?"

"We will have a little parting gift for you then," she promised.

"How can I thank you?" Let me tell you, I was very touched by all this woman was doing for me.

"You can go to a new country and have a good life, Sam," she said. "You sure do deserve it, after what you've been through and what you lost in your young life." She stopped, and looked sad. "When you smile you remind me a little of my son," she said quietly. "I lost him in the war, at the Battle of the Bulge."

I couldn't conceal a shudder because I knew what a terrible event that was.

"When Charlie didn't come home to Baltimore, I felt my life there was over, so I decided to join HIAS and help survivors like you who still have a future."

I was very moved by her story, but what could I say? I had a large lump in my throat and could hardly speak. I mumbled good-bye to Miss Sonia and left the HIAS office with one foot in heaven and one in hell. I always knew that I wanted to do my best for my family. Now I also wanted to succeed for Miss Sonia Marcus of Baltimore—wherever and whatever that success would turn out to be.

****

For the next several days I was in a whirlwind, making final preparations for my trip, one that I suspected would end my connection to Europe for many years to come. There were lots of last minute things to do. I had to close up my little business and say good-bye to my friends in the camp. There was even a small farewell party for a few of us lucky enough to be leaving. The gathering was festive and also sad, for we knew that we would most likely never see each other again. Even though, by its very nature, Föhrenwald was a transient place, people did form attachments. It was a bit contradictory because everyone wanted to be someplace else, away from their bad memories of the Reich, yet here we all were in Germany having mixed feelings about leaving. The irony didn't escape me.

My own feelings, however, were not really mixed. I was counting every hour until it was time to go back to HIAS and pick up my packet that had been so well prepared for me by Miss Marcus.

A few days passed, and then as if by magic it was the eleventh of January 1951. I had my instructions and followed them to the letter. At the appointed time I went back once more to the HIAS office. Miss Sonia was not at her desk when I walked in the door. For a moment, I began to panic. What if she had left suddenly—just like Stanley? But a moment later I heard her distinctly American voice: "Oh, there you are Sam! Please sit down. I will be right there."

She was in an adjacent office talking with a colleague, but in seconds she returned to her desk. She pulled out the big manila envelope and handed it to me. She explained that I should be at the main gate of Föhrenwald the next morning at 10:00 AM. "We are taking several other DPs who will be your shipmates. There is a bus that it going to leave at about 10:30. "Do you have any questions, Sam?" she asked, as she finished.

"No, I don't think so Miss Sonia," I replied, a bit uncertainly, as I reached into my little satchel and pulled out a thick package triple wrapped in brown paper and tied with twine. A bit hesitantly I handed it to her.

"Why, Sam!" she said with genuine surprise. "What is this?"

"I saved you two nice steaks and some of my special sausages."

"Oh, that is very sweet. Thank you so much."

She put the package aside and reached into her purse. She pulled out a small envelope and handed it to me. I didn't ask a question, but I looked at her and she couldn't miss my confusion.

169

"It is just a little gift from HIAS, a bit of money for you to have in case of emergencies." Miss Sonia said sweetly.

For once, I didn't know what to say. I just took the envelope and put it in my pocket. Later I discovered that it contained five dollars—a generous gift.

Miss Sonia then shook my hand. After thanking her again, I nearly raced out the door in my eagerness to get on with my mission.

****

The next morning at 9:00 AM I was standing by the main gate of the camp with a leather satchel that held my few belongings. I knew I was an hour early. I was alone, and I didn't care. The air was very fresh in Bavaria and on this January morning, it was frigid as well. As I looked at the distant mountains for the last time, flakes of snow began to fall. I had a sinking feeling when I felt the first sting of snow on my face. It took me right back to November of 1942 when we were all transported to the Polish army camp. But I did not have enough time to delve into the misery of that particular memory because at that very second the big bus pulled up that was to take us to the ship.

I must remember to call it a ship, I thought, but I still did not know the difference. As soon as the bus came into view, other passengers began to stream toward it. When there were about twenty people standing in line the driver finally opened the door. There was an unfamiliar woman from HIAS on board with a clipboard and list. One by one she checked off our names in alphabetical order as we climbed aboard the old green Mercedes bus. My name was among the last—followed by Tauszig, Weisberg and Zuckerman. I didn't know any of the others. But that was okay with me. I had bigger things on my mind.

As the driver started up the diesel engine again, with a big chug-chug, I took one of the last free seats where there was room for me and my one suitcase. It was in the rear of the bus. Finally the bus began to roll away from the camp. I looked out the back window for my final view of Föhrenwald in the falling snow. There was Miss Sonia in a big loden cloth coat waving good-bye to me, and to everyone else also leaving the camp forever.

****

It was about 500 miles from Munich to Bremerhaven—about an eight-hour drive under the best of conditions. Bremerhaven is a port on the North Sea, a short distance from the commercial city of Hamburg. I knew it was going to take a while to get to our destination, especially since the roads were getting slipperier every minute. Our route to a new life would take us from one end of Germany to the other.

Despite all the horrors, I had come to appreciate southern Germany with its lakes and mountains, the Zugspitze being the highest point in the Bavarian Alps. There was the beautiful Chiemsee—a vast mirror of a lake—and the darkly romantic Black Forest. This part of Germany was very lush, but it was the only part of Germany I knew. *The Germans once had so much, and look what they did with it in two world wars: such craziness!* I thought, as we rolled along and I gazed out the smudged window. Then I tipped my cap over my eyes and dozed, knowing we were in for a long ride.

After a couple of hours on the road I was jolted out of my deep sleep by a sudden loud thumping sound coming from the front of the bus and a collective panic from my fellow travelers. "*Mein Gott!*" I heard a woman yell. I tipped my cap back and opened one eye. My fellow passengers were in an uproar. In front, the bus driver called out to everybody to calm down. The commotion quieted. As the passengers waited nervously, the driver got out of the bus to assess the situation. When he came back he announced that it wasn't a serious accident. The icy road had caused the bus to slide, and one of the front wheels was now on the shoulder of the road. In short, the bus was stuck.

Hearing this, people began to give in to mild hysteria. Everyone was thinking the same thing. One woman spoke for everyone when she stood up and shouted: "Driver, you've gotten us into a real mess! Now we are going to miss our ship!" At that everyone started to yell and scream at the same time.

The driver stood in the front of us and faced down the frightened crowd. "Calm down everybody! Please. I know these roads and we will get help soon. We will make your ship with time to spare."

The woman from HIAS with the clipboard stood and faced the other passengers. Her voice was calm and controlled. "He is right. There is no need to panic. We are not in any danger. And these roads are very well maintained. We will get help soon." Sure enough, in a few minutes a big brown truck came along and gave the bus a big push that set it back on the right path. Soon we were once again on our way.

Once we were safely *en route* the woman from HIAS rose once again. She spoke quietly but firmly: "Prejudice in any form is despicable. I heard one of you mumbling *Nazi* under your breath when you thought the driver caused this accident. You should know that our wonderful driver today is a survivor of Auschwitz. His name is Aaron Gregor Frankel. He fought bravely in the Warsaw Ghetto Uprising, and was one of the few who managed to survive." She didn't have to add: *He has suffered like you, so please be respectful.* It was implied in her every syllable.

Some of my fellow passengers were greatly chastened, murmured apologies, and then fell quiet, settling back in their seats as the bus moved on, a bit slower but still making cautious progress. As I observed this little scene, relieved that the trip had resumed, I reflected that even we Jews, who suffered the worst kind of racial prejudice and torture, were not immune to false assumptions and bigotry. *I suppose such bias is part of the human condition,* I said to myself, and then began to doze again.

When I woke up, I was hungry and knew it was time to eat the meat and cheese sandwiches I'd packed for the journey. As I ate, I looked out the window and saw a sign that indicated that we were close to Nuremberg, a city on the northern edge of Bavaria. As we all know now, the famous trials that took place there, beginning in 1945, had meted out a smidgen of justice to dozens of Nazis war criminals. I took no small amount of satisfaction in knowing that vipers like Hermann Göring, the highest-ranking Nazi criminal to be tried and convicted, committed suicide the night before his execution. Or that Rudolf Hess, who was Hitler's Deputy Führer for several years, had spent time in Spandau prison, before he too committed suicide, in 1987. Those bastards deserved everything they got and much, much more. At least some justice had been dispensed at the court in Nuremberg, setting a new standard for international law.

By the time we drove past Nuremberg, the snow had gotten quite a bit heavier. The bus seemed to be making good time despite the conditions. Then the bus began wheezing a bit, as we began some steep climbs. I guessed we were going through the Harz Mountains—a highland area in Central Germany. On the downward incline the bus slipped and slid a little, and I was white-knuckling it until the vehicle gained traction and began to resume its normal speed. I looked at my watch. We'd been on the road for five hours, but still had a way to go. All I could think of was getting to the General Taylor and being on my way.

Soon it got very dark very quickly. I could feel that the bus was driving on the downside of a hill. When we got to a lower elevation the snow and sleet stopped pelleting the windows and the sky cleared. After a while I could see some stars and a sliver of wintry moon, even through the almost opaque bus windows. Once the weather cleared the bus flexed its real power and began to speed along on the now flat terrain. I could sense that the people around me were all getting agitated. You could almost see a cloud of tension in the air. Everyone who was a DP faced an uncertain future, including me, but at that point in my long journey to what I considered my destiny in America. I felt more excited than fearful.

After we encountered what seemed to be some big bumps along an unpaved road the big green bus finally came to a halt. The driver paused a few minutes, not yet opening the doors, as the bus gave what

I liked to think was a final wheeze of relief. That was no easy ride!

Once again the lady from HIAS stood and gave us our strict instructions. All of the passengers, she explained, were to spend the next few hours in a large waiting room that had been prepared for our arrival. Coffee and sandwiches would be provided. The ship would be taking passengers on promptly at 6 AM the next morning, which was just a few hours away. Until then there would be more waiting. Finally we had our orders, and the driver, who we now knew was the heroic Mr. Frankel, opened the doors.

One by one our HIAS chaperone checked our names off her list, then handed us off to another escort who was to lead us to the waiting area. The woman explained that from this point on we were in the hands of the Military Sea Transport Service or MSTS.

As soon as I stepped off the bus the icy air, blowing in from the North Sea, pierced through me. It took only seconds for me to realize that my warmest clothes were not warm enough to sustain me through the journey ahead. Still, it felt good to get some air in my lungs again, even if it cut like a knife, and to stretch my legs after spending hours on that cramped bus.

When I had a moment to look around, even by the dim light of the moon, I could see that I was standing in the middle of a muddy field, with marshland all round. The ground felt distinctly squishy under my feet. The land, a brown desiccated greenish grey, was flat as far as I could see. *How very different from Bavaria*, I thought. Northern Germany seemed to be an unbroken vastness, with lots of rivers and streams.

Before I had time to think about it too much, a member of the U.S. Navy appeared, and said he was there to escort us to the waiting area. I collected my belongings, and along with my fellow passengers was shepherded toward a large low building with a big sign in English— that of course I could not understand. I was glad to get inside. Even if the waiting room was chilly, there was hot coffee, soup and sandwiches waiting. It had been a long trip with little to eat, so people descended like vultures on the simple food supplied by Uncle Sam. Then we all huddled together for warmth.

At the first light, everyone began to stir. The cold dawn of northern Europe was very different from the warm light of the south. Still, it foretold an exciting day ahead. Just then a shrill whistle split the air. My heart skipped a beat. It was finally time to board the USNS General Harry Taylor. Or, at least, I *hoped* that's what it meant.

Another Navy guy, who was apparently a translator, stood on a bench to make announcements in several languages, because there were hundreds of DPs getting ready to board. They had come from camps all over Germany and Austria. We were told to get out our paperwork, which meant more clipboards and lists. Because there were so many passengers, the translator told us, it could take hours to get everyone on board, so the more everyone cooperated the faster it would go.

The USNS General Harry Taylor, named for a U.S. Chief of Army Engineers, had long served as a troop transport ship. In 1944 she took thousands of U.S. military personnel to fight in the Pacific theater—to such hellholes as New Guinea and Guadalcanal, where the combat was arduous and the chances were slim of returning home in one piece, if at all. In 1945, at the end of the war, the General Taylor was put to a happier use, bringing veterans from Marseilles, France home to the U.S. By 1950, the General Taylor was being used regularly to transport troops, dependents and large numbers of refugees from Europe to the U.S., Canada and many other places.

It is hard to imagine the relief all those men and women returning from the European theater must have felt when they boarded this ship. Perhaps they felt excitement and trepidation close to what I was feeling now, as I paced in the waiting area, anxious for my group to be called.

After what seemed like standing in line forever, I finally heard someone call out, in several languages, "Everyone with names beginning with R-S-or T please come to the main gate." I was clutching my DP card and boarding pass as if my life depended on them. Once I finally got to the front of the line, I showed my papers to a member of

175

the crew. He looked at them, then said: "Sir, please go to quay number three. The Taylor is docked at Pier Five." As he said this he handed me a card with directions in several languages. When he opened the door, I stepped outside, and got my first glimpse of this large working enterprise. I was almost overwhelmed. The port itself was enormous, with a wide variety of vessels everywhere. There seemed to be dozens of them. More military personnel were stationed outside, holding signs that pointed the way to the General Taylor.

It was a much longer distance from the waiting area than I had supposed, and it had not gotten any warmer. There was a lot of people pushing to get to the boat—okay the *ship*—so I was sort of carried along with the crowd. When I finally got my first look at the vessel that was to take me across a whole ocean, its size and complexity were a bit overwhelming. The General Taylor, painted gray, was over 500 feet long I guessed, and very high, too, with three or four decks that I could count. There were several smokestacks and lots of gizmos and gadgets, which I couldn't identify. *This is sure not like the old buckets that took us to Palestine*, I thought. As I approached the gangplank I finally knew the difference between a boat and a ship: the General Taylor was a *ship* for sure!

As I waited for my turn to go single file up the gangplank—a kind of moveable bridge that is used to board or leave a ship—I thought about the scary night when I arrived in Palestine and had to jump off the back of the boat. This was the exact opposite of that experience.

As I stepped aboard the General Taylor at last I was still only 22 years old. I felt that I had lived ten lives, in my various stages of survival. Now there was a new life ahead, just as unknown as the others were. Breathing a huge sigh of relief, I got down to the business of crossing the North Atlantic.

Next stop: New York.

14

Finding Solid Footing In My New Country

Once I set foot on the General Taylor, I could not have imagined how much hullabaloo there was. There were hundreds of people—in fact the number was close to 700, as I discovered later. The passengers included U.S. military personnel, going back home after being stationed in Germany or elsewhere in Europe, plus lots and lots of refugees who, like me, were coming from camps like Föhrenwald. As people like me found ways to emigrate, the populations of the DP camps shrank. In fact, by 1952 only two DP camps remained: Föhrenwald, which closed in 1957, and Wels in Austria, which closed in 1959. It is hard to believe that fifteen years after the war there was still a need for a DP camp, but the process of repatriation and resettlement could be painstakingly slow—which is why Miss Sonia was such a hero to me. I had her to thank for securing my passage on the General Taylor.

When I think back on it, even today, I can still recall the commotion as people boarded in a somewhat chaotic fashion on that freezing day. Everyone was trying to find their accommodations on this enormous ship, and let me tell you, the accommodations were very modest. It was, after all, a ship originally designed for soldiers and sailors.

Before we boarded, we had all been assigned a bunk or cubby and given cards with our assignments. Since I didn't speak English, I held my card up to a young guy wearing a khaki uniform. He directed me several floors below deck to a men's dormitory with four bunks on each wall, stacked like a big sandwich. The quarters sure didn't look comfortable, but since I was getting where I wanted to go, I could put up with it for a few days. I had endured much worse.

I was the first one to find this little cabin, so I was quick to put my stuff on the middle bunk—the international sign for "This place is taken." Pretty soon I heard two voices chattering in Polish. Soon someone called out, "Hey, Larry, look it's *Ginji!*" When I heard my old nickname, the Yiddish word for ginger, meaning redhead, I was startled and looked around. "Yeah, *Ginji*, Where've you been? I can hardly believe my eyes."

To my amazement, the newcomers were Larry and Abe Graboski. Astonishingly, they were assigned to the same cabin. The Graboskis were twin brothers from Poznan, Poland that I met in the IDF. I hadn't seen them since. They were good looking guys, and funny as hell! When they suddenly appeared, I thought that this voyage might not be so tough after all. They had aspirations to make it in America as comedians or actors. The real miracle was that they had both survived the war and were still together—though they'd had their own heartbreak. Once we'd shaken hands and compared notes on the past few years, I asked them not to call me *Ginji* again, because I didn't like that nickname. I felt a little bereft—though I wouldn't tell them that. *If only one of my siblings had survived,* I reflected. *In truth they used to call me Ginji. But oh well, what is the point of thinking about that now.*

While I was catching up with the Graboskis, I heard the massive engines of the ship come to life. The deep growl seemed to be coming from the bowels of the earth, causing a shudder that came up through the floor and even through to the soles of my shoes. The power of the General Taylor was something to experience. Knowing we were finally leaving Bremerhaven, I got excited and raced up to the main deck to watch as this massive vessel slowly made her way out of the busy port.

When I looked over the railing, down to the dark water far below, I saw that four or five tugboats were busy pulling the General Taylor away from the pier and guiding her out to the open water where she could go full steam ahead. These tugs were good-sized boats, but from my perspective, high on the main deck, they looked like toys messing around in the harbor. Yet they did the heavy work for many of the bigger ships that couldn't maneuver away from the pier without their help.

I was fascinated to watch this process for a while, along with dozens of other passengers who were also watching, crowded along the railings. There were so many people on one side of the ship I wondered if it could tip over. Then, as a fierce wind whipped up, I remembered that I had a job to do, a job that would take me below decks, where it was not exactly warm, but a bit warmer.

Before I'd left camp, Miss Sonia had given me a note to take to the Purser of the ship. He was a big deal, and it took me a while to find him. The note was an introduction from HIAS and requested that I be given a paying job on the ship. This Purser fellow, who had on a pretty fancy uniform, glanced at the note and told me to report to the galley, Navy talk for the kitchen, which was somewhere below decks. He scribbled another note for me, and told me to report for KP, whatever that was. I was slated to cut meat throughout the voyage for the officer's dining room.

For the first couple of days it was easy to get lost on the General Taylor. Though there were signs on every door, they were all in English, so I spent a lot of time wondering where I was. Eventually I found my way to the galley, then found the right place by following the noise and the aromas coming from the big, busy kitchen. After all, it was an enormous task to feed some 700 people, crew and passengers, three times a day.

When I entered the galley no one even noticed me. There were pots the size of oil drums on enormous stoves, and a whole crew of men was standing at a long table cutting, chopping, dicing and slicing. There was a big kitchen at the DP camp, but I'd never seen a setup like this.

I was standing by the door and somehow felt invisible. Then suddenly a big fellow with sweat stains on his shirt and a grubby apron noticed me and came over. He took one look at me and said: "*Sprichst du Deutsch?*" By my clothes, shoes and haircut he knew that I was a refugee. But I was very surprised that he greeted me in German. Fortunately I was then, and still am, fluent in several languages, including German.

Each day for the next thirteen days I reported to the galley, and was glad to have something to do to pass the time. Even better, I was being paid one dollar a day! A dollar went a lot further back then. And when you're penniless every little bit helps.

I had a bit of free time when I wasn't working in the kitchen. I would hang out with the Graboskis and we would brag and boast about how we were going to be big successes in New York. No doubt about it: for three guys who'd seen the worst of humanity we still had plenty of moxie and hope.

During the day I would occasionally come up from the galley and check on the ship's progress. I was fascinated when I could stand on the deck or gaze out a porthole to literally see the world go by. After we left Bremerhaven, the General Taylor made her way through the icy North Sea, passing the coasts of The Netherlands and then Belgium. All of Europe had suffered greatly during the war, but these countries more than most. Now we were in a new decade, signaling a different era where things were turning around. The sea air felt good on my face even as the wind buffeted me about. Sometimes I had to cling to the railing to keep it from blowing me overboard.

Every day there would be a map in the main area of the ship that would chart the progress of the General Taylor and let us civilian passengers know where we were. It was exciting to check the map and realize that each day we got a bit closer to North America. Once we passed through the North Sea we entered the Straits of Dover. As soon as I spotted the white cliffs, I knew we were entering the English Channel. It was a narrow and often choppy body of water that separated Dover, England from Calais, France, and was a mere 20 miles wide at its narrowest point.

Every person who lived through World War II knew the famous song about the "White Cliffs of Dover," sung by Vera Lynn. To my amazement there they were. Unmistakable in their beauty, these pure white chalky cliffs rose high above the sea as we entered the Dover Straits. They were a welcome sight, since I longed to see the world for myself. Now I felt as if I could almost reach out and touch these cliffs that had mercifully kept the Krauts at bay.

The English Channel is about 350 miles long, and, after a bit, we were headed to Le Havre, France, where the ship picked up a few more DPs. I could not believe that they could squeeze more passengers in, but they managed, along with supplies for the galley, including some sides of beef and pork that would keep me busy for the rest of the voyage.

Making port in Le Havre meant we were halfway through the channel and beginning to make for the open sea. This is where the trip got interesting. Traversing the North Atlantic in January is no joke, and on some days even this immense ship pitched and writhed as the ocean sent up angry curls of water, crested with foam. Crewmembers remained cucumber cool, but many of the DPs began to panic and became fearful. People were sick all over the place and it was not pleasant. The thrashing seas kept the medical corpsmen very busy. I had seen some pretty rough stuff in my time, so I was not fazed by a little seasickness. But in our little dormitory below, the Graboskis and I would sometimes hear the ship creak and groan, and I admit that was worrisome. At times it sounded as if the ship was breaking apart. It didn't sound good, I can tell you.

After a couple of days, the storm passed and things settled down to a more normal routine. On deck I was able to look for miles in any direction and not see a speck of land. That was incredible to me, coming from a land-locked country like Poland. It was hard to comprehend the vastness and power of the sea, but I was beginning to get an idea.

One day I looked at the ship's progress and it said that the next day we would arrive in Halifax, Nova Scotia. This made me very happy, since it meant that New York was next. On the morning we arrived in Halifax, we remained there for several hours, since a lot of DPs were disembarking. It took several hours to make sure every passenger got off safely, and the ship had to be thoroughly searched to make sure that there were no stowaways. Sometimes DPs, bound for Canada, would hide, hoping to sneak off the ship in New York instead. The crew and the immigration people conducted this search efficiently, since they knew the routine. Determined immigrants would hide in lifeboats, closets or any nook or cranny where they thought they could get away with it. But the crew was onto them, and it didn't take long to rout out the three men and one woman on this trip who had been bold enough to try to outsmart the authorities.

Abe, Larry and I watched with some interest as these stowaways were hustled ashore and wondered what would happen to them. The immigration people were very tough and would think nothing of putting them on the next boat back to Europe. But that was conjecture, and we didn't have time to think about it since there was only one more segment of the trip left before the ship made port in New York.

****

January 22, 1951. At long last we had arrived. It is hard to imagine what a momentous day that was. I didn't sleep for one second the night before, thinking about the uncertain prospects for my new life. To distract ourselves, the Graboskis and I played cards all night. I'd said good bye to the galley cooks. Of the thirteen dollars I earned cutting meat on the General Taylor, I spent three on little incidentals like chewing gum and snacks, but still had ten dollars left in my pocket. At least I was not arriving penniless in New York, which made me feel good.

At dawn I was up on deck with my few belongings, and Abe and Larry were with me. An elderly aunt, who lived in Elizabeth, New Jersey, was sponsoring the twins, and I was meeting members of my father's family for the very first time. Thanks to the war, we were all being thrown into the arms of strangers. It was an odd feeling, but I forgot all about it when I spotted the statue of the lady in the harbor. I'd been dreaming about the sight of Lady Liberty for many years. She had been welcoming strangers like me to America for a long time and held the promise of liberty and freedom. The moment I spotted her torch poking through the early morning fog my eyes grew misty. Suddenly all of the emotions that I'd been holding back began to get the better of me. I snuck a sidewise glance at the twins. They too looked like they were about to cry.

Before I got too *verklempt,* I looked over my shoulder to see the dark towers of lower Manhattan rising to unimaginable heights. They were so muscular and impressive that they took my breath away. *Europe has nothing like this,* I thought, and I forgot all about my welling emotions. "Hey, guys," shouted Larry Graboski. "We're really in New York Harbor, at last! We've made it!" A general cheer rippled through the crowd, assembling on the deck. There were a lot of *mazel tovs* in the air.

I could not take my eyes off this famous skyline. Its boldness and power signified this country's promise for my new life. Of course I knew I had a few stumbling blocks to overcome. The biggest was that I didn't speak English. I knew that the U.S. wasn't like Europe, where most people spoke a few languages so you could always find some way to communicate. *Oh, boy!* I thought, but I wasn't really worried. I knew I would figure it out, like I'd figured out so much else.

I was thrilled as the General Taylor steamed up the Hudson River, which I learned was named after some early New York explorer. *Well, New York,* I thought, *here comes Schlomo Solasz*! I felt like a new kind of explorer. In no time we were making progress up the river. It didn't take long before a fleet of tugboats appeared to guide the big General to a pier on the west side of Manhattan. It was still early in the day when the ship finally docked, and the pier was bustling.

As the ship was maneuvered into its space along the pier, I managed to get a spot on the railing so I could see what was going on dockside. It sure was a busy scene. Taxies, buses, trucks, all sorts of activity. Bremerhaven was a country town compared to this. Then there was the noise. Horns honking, people yelling in various languages, and lots of photographers that seemed to meet every ship just in case there was someone famous on board. On this old ship, loaded with DPs, I think they were out of luck.

Before I could meet with my family, there were lots of formalities.

Every immigrant had been given a number and I was no exception. Before the rigmarole began I had followed Miss Sonia's instructions and pinned my identification to the lapel of my jacket. First, immigration officers came aboard and we were all lined up in the mess hall to be checked. Then officials from the city Health Department came aboard and gave everyone the once over, which took more time. Some people were detained for medical reasons, but I passed with flying colors.

After those formalities I raced up to the main deck to see if I could spot my family, but we were pretty high up, and I could only see the tops of people's heads. Also, it was pretty dark where my family was waiting. In those days there was an elevated highway, which ran along the West Side by the piers, and it cast a shadow on everything below.

The moment the gates of the deck opened and we were permitted to disembark I raced down the gangplank, with the Graboski brothers on my heels. There were loads of people waiting to meet the ship, and it was at that point that I carried the yellow sign with my name in big black letters. It seemed that Jews from the five boroughs and all of New Jersey were waiting to greet DPs. By this time nearly half a million DPs, Jews and others, had immigrated to the U.S., so it was becoming an old story. But not to stakeholders like myself, for whom this was a life-changing moment. There were a lot of tears and hugs as people found their sponsors.

What I discovered on the pier was that the inspections were not yet over. There were more officials from customs waiting for us, and we were put in a sort of a holding pen until we could be screened one more time. They called out numbers, and when you heard your number you had to have a meeting with someone in control of your future. I was sitting on a bench with a few other refugees. When I finally heard my number I went to a table that had been set up and I showed a guy there my DP card with my picture inside. He checked off my number and tried to read my name aloud. He looked up at me, a bit puzzled: "How do you say that, son?"

Miss Sonia had coached me to say in English: "My name is Schlomo Solasz." So that was exactly what I said to this guy: "My name is Schlomo Solasz." I tried my best, but my accent was heavy. The guy wasn't having it. "Schlo....what? Not anymore. Here in New York your name is Sam." *Sam,* I thought. Okay. I'd had several names in my time, starting with Moishe, so I nodded and thought, Okay, I guess I can go with that. I was now officially Sam Solasz. A new name for a new beginning.*

After this process I was free to go. Suddenly I heard my old name called out by someone who *did* know how to pronounce it. The name *Schlomo Solasz* rang out over the noisy pier. I held up my sign and made my way through the crowd with my luggage.

Immediately, I spotted a man in a fedora and dark suit. It was hard to tell, but I did see a faint family resemblance and he had sent a blurry photograph for me. I made a beeline for him. He held out his hand and said, "Welcome Schlomo, I am your Uncle Dave." I said, "I am now Sam!" "Well, Sam," he replied, "I'd like you to meet your Aunt Jenny and Uncle Harry." He introduced me to a plump and pleasant lady in a dark coat, with a fancy fur collar. It was a cold day after all. Aunt Jenny was my father's sister and she and her husband Harry, a short man in a plaid coat with a warm friendly face, lived in Newark, New Jersey. They had brought their son Bernie with them. He was about my age. They had also brought a card from my aunt Anna, my father's oldest sister, who lived in Florida.

It was tricky trying to connect with all these new family members at once. Looking around in between handshakes and hugs I spotted the Graboskis, on the other side of the dock. I could see they had found their aunt. I gave them a wave and smiled because I knew they were going to be okay. Soon my newfound Uncle Dave gave me a nudge: "Come on, Schlo—er Sam. My wife, your aunt Lil, has prepared a big lunch in Brooklyn. We need to go." But I wasn't quite ready to leave, though I didn't know why.

*The name Sam rather than Schlomo was used up to this point for convenience, but this is the moment I officially became Sam Solasz.

Then I heard a man with a deep voice, yelling: "Any butchers on the ship?" This was music to my ears. Better yet, he was speaking in Polish. Uncle Dave nudged me, again. "Wait, wait," I insisted, "I have to see what he wants. This could be important." "Ah, okay," my uncle said in a grudging manner. I was concerned because I didn't want this new relationship to get off to a rocky start, but I also didn't want to waste an opportunity. My uncle, afraid to lose me in the crowd, was on my heels as I looked for the person who was calling out.

I heard the same man call out in Polish again and raised my hand. Soon he found me in the crowd and was quick to tell me what he wanted. I was plenty curious, I can tell you. The man, wearing an expensive-looking coat and a Homburg hat, explained that he was the General Manager of Hygrade Meats. I never heard of it, but it apparently was a very big company. It seemed that local businessmen, in need of laborers with special skills, read the shipping arrivals in the New York papers and regularly met the ships, looking for workers.

While I was trying to pay attention to this man, my uncle was tapping me impatiently on the shoulder, but I wouldn't be deterred. After all, this man was looking for a butcher. It seemed too good to be true. "My name is Bill Belgin" he began, "I am the general manager of Hygrade. We are a big company. Are you looking for work cutting meat?"

"I certainly am, Sir," I said quickly in Polish. I knew the money in my pocket wouldn't last long, and I certainly didn't want to ask my uncle for money.

"We only sell high quality products and I have about six hundred people working for me at our plant in New Jersey. We can use another good butcher. If you come with me now, I'll give you a try."

"He can't come now," Uncle Dave interrupted. "The boy has just gotten off the boat, and my wife has made a big lunch. We must go to Brooklyn right now. The whole family is coming." *Or what's left of it*, I thought.

Thankfully Mr. Belgin ignored my uncle. He handed me his business card: "If you can come by the plant later, we'll give you a fair tryout and see what you can do." I shook Mr. Belgin's hand as I took the card. Then, rushing through the mob on the pier, we caught up with Uncle Harry and the others, and Uncle Dave went to get the car. Standing on the edge of the commotion, I turned to get one last look at the General Taylor. At that moment, I noticed a huge ship in the next berth. It was shiny and picture perfect, with a black hull and a white strip painted around the top. This gleaming vessel was so flawless in every detail that it didn't look real.

"What is that?" I asked Uncle Harry, pointing at this handsome ship, with its smart red and black smoke stacks. "That is the *SS United States*. A brand new American luxury liner that will cross the Atlantic in real style," said Uncle Harry. At that moment a chauffeur-driven Packard pulled up on the pier in front of the liner. The driver opened the rear door and an elegant woman emerged draped in furs, as the chauffeur took her matching luggage out of the trunk. Magically, a porter appeared and stacked the luggage onto a trolley. Then the woman, followed by the porter, made her way toward the magnificent liner. She was carrying a small black dog.

"Isn't she beautiful? And very fast, I heard." my Aunt Jenny commented.

"Are you referring to the ship, or that swanky woman, mom?" said my cousin Bernie. "Either way she's a dish." *A dish*, I thought. *Why would you call a woman a dish*? Clearly I had a lot to learn.

Shortly, a horn honked. It was Uncle Dave driving a tan Dodge sedan. He was clearly anxious to go and we all piled into his sedan. As we pulled away, I took one final look at the pier. Sadly, the *SS United States* made the General Taylor, which seemed so substantial in Bremerhaven, look a bit shabby and forlorn, but she had brought me safely across a great ocean.

Today, as I look back, I realize it was at that very moment that I firmly left the old world behind—for many many years to come.

"The force that has overcome Europe and destroyed entire states within days could cope with us, a handful of youngsters. It was an act of desperation . . . We aspired to only one thing: to sell our lives for the highest possible price."

— *Mordechai Tenenbaum (1916-1943), resistance fighter in Vilna, Warsaw, and leader of the Bialystok Ghetto Uprising of August 16, 1943.*

15

Attaining the American Dream
Sam the Butcher

As we crammed into Uncle Dave's 1945 Dodge heading for Brooklyn, there was a lot on my mind, so I was a bit quiet. When he pulled out into midtown traffic, I could not believe the chaos and congestion. The noise of the car horns, truck horns, police sirens, and everything else didn't seem to bother anybody but me. And there were the biggest buses I'd ever seen, plus hundreds of taxis, most of them bright yellow, careening all over the place. I felt as if I was in the midst of such confusion. When I spoke up, Aunt Jenny turned and said, "Welcome to New York, young Sam."

"You'll soon get used to it," shouted Uncle Dave, as he barreled toward Brooklyn.

In those days there were vendors with horse-drawn carts by the sides of the roads selling vegetables and all sorts of goods, which only made the congestion worse. Not to mention the hoards of pedestrians crossing the streets and avenues—all at the same time. I'd never seen such dense crowds. But it was the height of the buildings, soaring all around, that really made me stop and look. I craned my neck at this city that brushed the sky.

Then we crossed the Brooklyn Bridge and soon were in another borough, where things were a bit less hectic, but only a bit. Brooklyn was pretty crazy too. I admit to a sense of anticipation as we crossed that famous bridge. Brooklyn was a legend, even to people like me. Every Jew in Europe knew someone who lived in Brooklyn, New York. There were other groups in Brooklyn: Irish, Poles, Italians, Germans, but as far as I was concerned Brooklyn was a very Jewish place.

When we finally pulled up to a modest building near Ocean Parkway, Uncle Dave said, "Well, this is it." I looked up to see a solid looking house with a little grass in front. It didn't look fancy, but it was much more solid than anything I'd experienced since the war. My uncle's apartment was a two bedroom walk up in this house, and quite modest, but neat and tidy.

I was hungry, but before we could eat, Uncle Dave proposed I get a shave and a haircut for my job interview. We got back in the car and he drove us to a little barbershop. I saw a sign that said "Shave and a Haircut 35 Cents." Nice of Uncle Dave. While my hair was cut Uncle Dave had a shave. When he was done I saw him give the barber some change. I started to walk out the door. "Hey David, didn't you tell your nephew the shave and haircut are not for free?" I stood there, not believing my ears. Dave gestured to me. "Of course. Sam, pay the man!" he commanded.

My ten dollars was buried deep in my pocket and I practically had to cut my pants to wrestle the bill out, but I did. I gave the barber 50 cents and said "Keep the change!" I thought my uncle would have a heart attack. "He's the boss. Bosses don't get no tip," he stage-whispered. As it turned out, Uncle Dave's cheapness—miserliness—was legendary in the family. Still, on my first day and my first time among my American family, it hurt.

One thing Uncle Dave wasn't wrong about. When we got back I saw that his wife, Aunt Lil, had prepared a wonderful lunch of Jewish dishes, many of which I hadn't eaten in a long time. Though the food was enjoyable, the conversation was tense. I knew that Harry, Jenny and the others were curious to hear my story, but my mind was really on getting to the plant in Jersey and trying out for that job. Besides, I didn't want to talk about those terrible days. But they were all ears, which made for a strained lunch, and a rather odd homecoming.

I didn't really know these people, and the 35 cent fiasco aside, I was bitter that Uncle Dave had made me jump through so many hoops before he agreed to sponsor me. Also, I sensed a little smugness on the part of these people that came to America and were saved from so much suffering. They weren't any smarter than my family, just a lot luckier. And, I have to admit, terrible as it may be to say, a small part of me resented them for being alive while my entire family was dead. Not that any of it was their fault. I'm just saying that I had mixed emotions all around, so things were strained.

Of course they had a good idea what had gone on in Poland from reading the papers during the war, and from the Jewish grapevine, where lots of tales of atrocities were floated for American Jews. New York was by far the most Jewish city in America, and Newark, New Jersey, where Harry and Jenny lived, was right behind.

One thing I was not ambivalent about: I was enjoying the meal, especially when they served a wonderful noodle Kugel. It was a real treat, since it's usually reserved for holidays. I enjoyed that part of the meal the best. At last, my new Uncle Harry broke the tension, "Lil, thank you for the wonderful lunch!" said Harry, "It was delicious, but I know that our nephew is anxious to get to that plant and show off his stuff."

"Sure, sure," said Aunt Lil, a little miffed that she wasn't being given her due. I suddenly saw that she was the queen bee type. "That's right," said Aunt Lil. "Saul was a wonderful butcher. I'm sure his Sam is too."

"First," I said, as I stood up from my seat, "I would like to thank you, Aunt Lil, for such a special meal. It could almost be a Seder." "Yes, thanks, Lil," her husband, Uncle Dave, added for show.

Harry grabbed his coat as a signal to everyone that this party was over. "I've got to get to Jersey through the traffic. So we better leave now. That man at the plant will be waiting." Everyone said a quick good bye. I shook Dave's hand. I didn't feel comfortable giving Aunt Lil a kiss, even if she did make a noodle Kugel that reminded me of Knyszyn, so I just gave her a little hug.

****

Uncle Harry drove his huge Buick Roadmaster as fast as the law allowed to make sure I got to the plant quickly. He was a man with a good heart! I could tell that his driving made Aunt Jenny nervous as she sat beside him in the passenger seat. Cousin Bernie was in the back with me. Before I knew it, we were on Springfield Boulevard in Newark, pulling up in front of a business that had a sign that said *Dave's Luncheonette*.

"Why are we stopping here, Pop?" Bernie asked. "Keep your shirt on, Bernie. It's on the way to the plant. I want to check with cousin Dave." "Dave's a lot of hot air, Pop, even if he does own this store and a few taxi cabs," Bernie noted.

"Bernie, what are you, some stuck-up college kid? We have to let Schlomo, er, *Sam,* meet his relative!" *Another relative! Another Dave! This could be confusing*, I thought. Next thing I knew, we were in Dave's Luncheonette. Bernie was annoyed that we were wasting time, but Harry seemed to know what he was doing.

First I got a brief introduction. Dave, who was working the grill behind the counter, turned out to be the son of Anna, my aunt who lived in Miami. Dave was a bit surprised that we stopped by. But he was a local businessman, who kept his ear to the ground and bought a lot of meat for his business. Harry made me show Cousin Dave Mr. Belgin's card. Dave seemed impressed.

"Hygrade's a good company. Good meat," said Dave. "They're based in the Midwest. Michigan, I think. But they have a big operation right here in Jersey." "Right," said Harry, "We're taking Sam over there for a tryout this afternoon. What do you know about this Belgin guy?"

"I don't hear nothing bad," said Dave, while flipping several burgers to satisfy his hungry customers. "And you know what they say about how fast bad news travels. A few people from the Hygrade shop are my regulars. He must be an okay guy or I would know. He's from Krakow but came here well before all hell broke loose."

The next thing I knew, Harry hustled me out the door and in a few minutes we'd arrived at the Hygrade Company, in an industrial part of

Newark. When I got out of the car I saw that there was a high fence all around that protected the Hygrade Company, and the gate was locked. There were a couple of workers hanging around, having a smoke. I didn't know whether they spoke Polish, so Uncle Harry helped me out.

"Hey, you guys," he yelled. "Do you know Mr. Belgin? He is expecting my nephew here." Harry made this sound like the most important appointment of all time. One of the workers scuttled inside, and in a minute Mr. Bill Belgin himself came out to meet me at the gate. "Give us a couple of hours," he said to my uncle, and then took me inside.

He gave me a white coat, some gloves and a couple of knives, plus a steel sharpening tool. Then we went into a huge room where the serious business of meat cutting took place. Butchering was second nature to me. I had done it almost all my life. I whipped through several basic tasks in no time. Then he asked me to make some sausage, using this big machine that ground the meat and processed it through some casings until the links came out. Again I completed these tasks in no time and was looking for something more to do.

Next thing I knew, Mr. Belgin came over to where I was working and led me into his office. He even asked me to sit down. In Europe, a boss of six hundred people would never ask a worker like me to sit down. *This guy has big responsibilities, and he has time for me?* I was a little amazed, and on pins and needles, waiting for whatever he was going to say.

I didn't have to wait long. "Mr. Solasz: I know you just arrived from Europe, so I really appreciate you coming in today. You do fine work and very fast, just the way we like it at Hygrade. Do you have any money?"

"No sorry, I don't." I felt a bit embarrassed to say I had nothing, but that nine dollars and fifty cents in my pocket was all there was between me and being broke. To my surprise, "Bill," as he'd asked me to call him, reached into his desk, opened the cash drawer, and slapped something into my hand. It was a twenty-dollar bill. Now I was even more amazed.

"We would like to have you join us here at Hygrade as a meat cutter. We can give you regular hours and a weekly paycheck. Would you be interested?" I was a bit stunned, so I merely nodded a response. "Okay," said Bill. "That's great! When can you start?"

"I am staying here in Jersey with my relatives. I can start tomorrow."

And that was it. Landing in New York, meeting my relatives and getting a job in one day. That day in January 1951 was a pretty momentous one.

I walked out and stood by the gate. Harry got back in his car and swung by to pick me up. He didn't ask me anything, just looked at me with a big question in his eyes. I pulled out twenty dollars, which really meant something then, and told him that I was starting my new job in the morning.

That night, around Jenny's table, the family members were all in a good mood. I think they were relieved that I got a job, and wouldn't be a drain on them. I was more than lucky that Mr. Belgin met the ship, and also that he spoke Polish. There were some big Polish neighborhoods in New York in those days, but finding a Polish-speaker as a boss—well, that was just plain amazing.

Once Jenny and Harry knew I had real work they went into action. I wanted to be at the plant at 5:00 AM the next morning. Jenny got up at 4:00 AM to make me scrambled eggs, and packed two hearty sandwiches for my lunch. Harry was up and ready to drive me to the plant, so that I got there at 5:00 AM sharp. In fact, they had to open up the place for me. By the time I'd sharpened my knives and got set up for the day, the rest of the workers had punched in and the plant was really humming. In fact, it was a beehive that hummed all day, up to quitting time at 4:00 PM.

My life continued in that routine for a long time. Cousin Bernie, who got stuck sharing his room with me, used to pick me up from work every day on his way home from school. Bernie was one of Jenny and Harry's two sons and a daughter and a student at Fairleigh Dickinson

College in New Jersey, which was a very big deal to his parents. Harry, who was in real estate, drove me to work each day. This support from all of them was remarkable.

Jenny and Harry lived in a solid middle class house that had belonged to my late grandfather. They'd raised their kids there, so the three were real American kids. With my heavy accent, my experiences in Europe and Israel, and my losses, I was a bit of a different character. Cousins Bernie and Ralph led fairly carefree lives, going to school and working, while I had become hardened. They spoke a smattering of Polish and Yiddish, but I couldn't communicate in English. So each night, when we had a few minutes, Bernie would try to coach me in American English. At the plant I spoke Polish, Yiddish or German all day long. In that environment, I wasn't going to learn English, and since I planned to make my life in America a big success, English was important.

For nine months I lived in that house and got into a familiar routine. I liked my work and was well respected at the plant. Most importantly I was salting away money. Then one day I found myself in the living room answering a lot of questions from the family about my experiences during the war. They had a general idea, of course, and knew that I was the only survivor of my family—that whole sad story. But then Aunt Jenny got a bit sniffy or defensive, I don't know which. She said: "Well, you do know, Sammy, that we didn't have it so easy here."

"What are you saying?" I replied, because I couldn't believe my ears. "No one was beating or starving you or taking you to the ovens and killing you."

"Well, no. But we did have rationing. It was hard to get butter, eggs and meat—and petrol, too."

"Jenny!" said Harry, tossing down his newspaper, and nearly jumping out of his chair. "What are you saying to the boy?" I was not a boy, but to Harry we were all boys. "Ma," Bernie chimed in, "Dad is right. Be quiet. You don't know what you're talking about. No one can ever know what Sam really went through."

My aunt got huffy and walked into the kitchen. Harry just shrugged. I was very upset and stormed out of the house. Bernie came after me trying to make things right: "I'm so sorry, Sam. Ma gets that way sometimes. I don't think she knows how to handle the ugliness that your family went through in Poland."

"She doesn't know what she's talking about!" I was spitting mad.

"It's no excuse. But I've seen it with a lot of Jews here, and Ma is no exception," Bernie was trying to calm the waters. "They are filled with guilt that, thanks to a lucky choice they abandoned the old country, leaving family behind to suffer the horrors of….you know."

"I *do* know. So you think she feels guilty?" I was really angry and challenged Bernie. We were having a hot argument. I was sputtering in Polish and Yiddish, while Bernie was struggling with Polish, mixed with English. It's a wonder we communicated at all.

"In a nutshell, yes. She loved your parents Saul and Esther, and the rest. Whether it seems fair or unfair, she feels their loss in a very big way. But she can't express it, because she knows it can't compare to your own suffering." He paused, then continued:

"I've come to realize that American Jews of Ma's generation, who still have their hearts in Poland, Russia or wherever, are eaten up by guilt and remorse," Bernie said. "But yes, that doesn't give her the right to say what she said," Bernie wound down. I knew poor Bernie was trying his best to rationalize his mother's behavior, and smooth things over, but I wasn't having it.

****

The next day I was still so angry with Jenny that I left that house forever. I told the bosses at Hygrade that I would be leaving my job. They were very sorry to see me leave and said I would always have a job there. I told them I had unfinished business, and that when I returned I would definitely be back to work for them. Then I bought a ticket that would take me back to Europe.

After what Jenny said, I was determined to never go back to her house. I was outraged that she dared to speak to me that way, and make that kind of comparison. I stayed outraged for a long time, but I stayed on good terms with Harry, Bernie and the others. My flare-up with Jenny was actually fortunate in a way, since it prompted me to take action on some necessary business. I needed to go back to Germany to tie up important loose ends. Before I left Munich, Miss Sonia had informed me that I needed to apply to the German government for reparations. In 1951, Konrad Adenauer, the first chancellor of the Federal Republic of Germany, who'd been a war prisoner, set up a major program of direct financial reparations for Holocaust survivors throughout the world. The Germans also had to pay reparations to the State of Israel. It was the German government's way of acknowledging that they had committed tremendous wrongs against Jews like me, my family and so many others. It was all very complicated, but at Miss Sonia's urging I had applied to be part of the program. I began the process before I left Munich, but now it was time to finish it. So I would be going back to Föhrenwald for a few more months.

When I told Bernie and other relatives and coworkers that I needed to go back to Germany, they were horrified: "Aren't you afraid to go back there, Sam?" I was asked again and again. That was not the case. I was going back to the sector where the Americans were in control. The Nazi regime had been eradicated in 1945.

But this made me realize, once again, that American Jews are limited in fully understanding how it was for us. They saw the situation in Europe through one lens—a very outdated lens that did not show them the entire horrific picture. Also, I'd gotten my Green Card just six weeks after I'd arrived in New York, so I was very confident in my ability to come and go to and from the States. I had a newfound sense of security that was very different from the uncertainty of being a stateless DP.

Always a planner, I had saved enough money to make the journey so that I wouldn't have to work for a while. Once I got to Munich, I was free to spend my days at the Rathaus applying for the program, going through a lot of red tape. It was important to me to do this. It was not about the money—it was about a shred of justice and a scrap of dignity. There would never be justice. The reparations program, which meant I would get regular disability checks from the West German government for the rest of my life, was a small vindication in itself, so I pursued it.

To my disappointment, Miss Sonia was not at the HIAS office any more, but there was another capable woman there who took up my cause and guided me through the complicated reparations program. I spent three months in Germany untangling my application and completing the paperwork. When I finally had it squared away my savings were almost gone, so it was time to go back to the States. When I returned to New York, Bernie picked me up at the pier and drove me to Jersey, but I didn't go back to Uncle Harry and Aunt Jenny's. Instead, I moved in with cousin Dave, renting a room from him in the apartment he lived in over his Springfield Boulevard luncheonette. A very sociable guy, Dave worked hard and long hours, in tough conditions. But he had a steady business and liked most of his customers, so he got up before dawn each day to fire up his griddle.

On my first morning back, I went to Hygrade to see what the situation was there. My boss, "Bill," welcomed me back enthusiastically. I was as eager as ever to put in a day cutting meat and doing it well. At the end of my first day back, Bill tapped me on the shoulder and signaled me to come into his office. *What does he want,* I wondered, because that was not the general way of things. Most butchers didn't hang out in the general manager's office unless there was a problem. I didn't have to wait long. Bill slipped an envelope into my hand. It was thick and felt as if it was filled with cash, but I was not about to look inside just then.

"What is this?" I asked. "I've been off the payroll for three months. You don't owe me nothing."

"Well, Sam," said Bill, as if we were old pals, "we're just glad to have you back at Hygrade."

"Okay, but what is this?" I held up the envelope. "This is your back pay," said Bill, cheerfully. "There was a pay raise while you were away, and we didn't want you to miss out."

I was astonished, but naturally I didn't argue. I thanked him, took the envelope and left his office. As I stood outside the gate that afternoon, I counted the cash. They'd given me my regular pay, plus the raise. Six-hundred-dollars. In December 1951 that was a lot of money in one lump sum. Six hundred dollars would go far.

While I waited for Bernie, the envelope in my pocket made me feel that I had a secure future at Hygrade. When you lived through as much uncertainty as I had, it can be very hard to trust, or really feel you belong anywhere. Now I was prepared to think a bit more seriously about building my future.

****

It was approaching 1952 when I completed my business in Germany and returned to Hygrade. For the next six months I lived in my little rented room with cousin Dave, his wife and their two little kids. The apartment was small; most of all I longed for my own place. I had also continued to depend on Bernie for transportation to work. Occasionally Dave would suggest that we go to dances at the local Reform Jewish Center so I could meet girls. Since Dave was happily married he had no problem going up to girls in a relaxed, friendly way and chat them up. I was not so confident, especially since I was still learning English. However, I was getting better. But right then I was focused on building a nest egg, and worked as many hours as I could get. I was always happy to work overtime, and, since I was their top producer, I got first choice to grab extra shifts, especially at busy times like the holidays. I quickly learned that Americans loved their meat for occasions: Memorial Day, Labor Day, Fourth of July. The American institution of the cookout always raised the demand for quality meat, so I didn't have much free time.

Before I knew it the years flew by. By January 1956 I was a full-fledged American citizen and very proud of that. I also now had my own apartment and a new 1953 Pontiac convertible.

****

One day, out of the blue, a man named Lou Solomon, another Hygrade manager, asked me if I would be willing to transfer to the Hygrade operation in the meatpacking district in Manhattan—just across the river from Jersey. Hygrade was opening the new location and Lou was going to run it. I didn't have to think twice about that. I had wanted to move to Manhattan, and working in the meatpacking district would mean a promotion and more money. That was an offer I happily accepted.

The meatpacking district was the hub of the meat trade in the Northeast for many, many years. Following the Civil War, the district was home to over 250 butcheries and slaughterhouses. It was just north of Greenwich Village on 14th Street, along the Hudson River, and was served by a spur of the New York Central Railroad. These trains brought animals directly into the slaughterhouses, along with produce and other cargo. It also took prepared sides of meat, poultry and other goods to distribution centers elsewhere. Gradually the slaughterhouses moved outside of the city, but the butchering and other activities remained.

Hygrade opening up on 14th Street was not just a new location, but also a new business for them. Up until then, they'd had a place in Brooklyn where they made the hot dogs for Coney Island, and had their big operation in Newark, where I'd just put in my three and a half years. On 14th Street they also opened a restaurant-and-hotel supply house. The operation was a bit more upscale, but the work was just as hard. Five days a week six of us commuted to work from Jersey to 14th Street. It was a big place, and the general manager was Henry Heisner. Lou Solomon was a manager, and they hired a foreman named Larry Fontana, who was very well known in the business.

I was glad to be away from Jersey, and enjoyed working in Manhattan, but the work was physically demanding. I worked most of the time, but I was also interested in having fun. Occasionally I would see the Graboski twins, who were working on a comedy routine that they were hoping to get on TV, or at least use to get a summer gig in the Catskills. They were also working in a deli on Second Avenue, and saving to go to Hollywood.

****

On Friday afternoons in the winter my friends and I would sometimes go to Madison Square Garden, where they gave free ice skating lessons. You had to pay a small entrance fee, pay to rent skates, and perhaps buy a cup of cocoa in the little canteen. At first I was pretty rickety on those skates, and so were Abe and Larry. They used to joke that we were "three Jews on blades," which they thought was hilarious. After a few weeks I got the hang of the skating and it began to be fun. It was certainly a nice change from my day-to-day life on Washington Street. Occasionally my Brooklyn relatives would introduce me to a Bessie or a Sadie from their neighborhood—hoping for a spark—but there was never a connection. Besides, being "fixed up" was not my style. I was too independent for that.

In those days, the Garden was very different from the Garden we know today. It was on 8th Avenue, between 49th and 50th Street. Still, it was then, as it is now, the home of the New York Rangers and the New York Knicks. Sports were never my thing, except for my Golden Gloves days in the DP camp, but I did enjoy the ice-skating.

One Friday, when the twins and I went skating I noticed an attractive young woman on the other side of the rink. She was petite and pretty with dark hair. She really caught my eye.

When I got out on the ice I skated around for a while, making circles on my blades, trying to look casual, and hoping the dark-haired girl would notice. I'd even learned to skate backwards—well, almost. I was showing off. She didn't seem to notice me. I saw she was holding onto the railing so I skated over and introduced myself.

"Hello," I said. "I am Sam." I was a bit embarrassed about my accent since you could just tell that this girl was American-born. There was definitely an unspoken social divide between the Jews who'd been here a generation or two and the post-war immigrant crowd, to which I clearly belonged. But still, I was hopeful.

"Hello, Sam. I'm Rose," the brunette said in a friendly tone.

"Can I take you for a spin on the ice," I joked. I could see she was a bit shaky on her skates.

She laughed, a nice sound. "I'm brand new to this," she admitted. Undeterred, I motioned to Abe to come over. Then we each took Rose by the arm, supporting her a bit, skated to the center, and kept moving as a unit until she felt more secure and could move better on her own. After a while of skating close to her I asked her if we could stop for coffee at the nearby Garden Cafeteria. She agreed and we skated right over there. Over coffee we continued our conversation, and I found her delightful. Then she let me know it was time for her to get home.

"I have to get home now," she said.

"Where do you live, Rose?" I asked.

"I live in Williamsburg, Brooklyn with my family," she told me.

"Can I drive you home?" I asked. I was proud of my new red and white Pontiac convertible, and figured it would impress her.

"Well, okay. Fine," she said. I found out later she had her own brand new car, but graciously let me show off a bit.

Before we turned in our skates I went over to my friends and invited them to take the drive with us. I figured Rose wouldn't mind, and she didn't. Before we walked over to get her the guys said, "You know she's not Jewish, right?"

"Why would you say that?" I was surprised. "She doesn't look Jewish," Abe and Larry said in unison. "Well, I don't look Jewish either, whatever that means, but I bet you she is." I replied. "Wanna bet? Put your money where your mouth is." Just like that the bet was on, and for big money—$200. So off we went. I wasn't worried. I just had a feeling about her.

We reached her house, and Rose invited us in to meet her mother. I immediately noticed that the Shabbat candles were already lit on their large dining room table. Later that night I let the guys off the hook and refused their bet money. I felt I had just won something much bigger.

I saw the girl I wanted, and didn't waste time. It took me a few weeks to win Rose over completely, and in January 1957 that was that. I know she had her reservations when this stranger with the funny accent proposed, but fortunately she saw some things in me she liked and overlooked a lot, I'm sure. Three months after we met I gave her a beautiful ring and we became engaged. The ring was nice enough, and somehow I even won her mother and father over, because we got along great. On June 29, 1957 Rose and I were married and began our life together. It has now been over 60 years.

****

In the summer of 1957, it was business as usual on 14th Street. I was a newlywed and looked forward to going home to Rose and to our new rental apartment in Rego Park, Queens each night, where I was happily settling in to married life.

Every Monday, Larry Fontana, the foreman, would hit me up for a loan of twenty dollars, and then would pay me back that Friday. I would take the repayment and deposit it into my bank. The loan saved him from paying a high rate of interest to some loan shark.

One Friday in August he had not returned the money as he usually did, so I asked him for the twenty dollars: "Hey, Fontana, I need that money to put in my account. I am a married man now, and my wife counts on it to buy groceries." In those days, twenty dollars would buy groceries for a week, and you'd have money left over. Of course Rose didn't really need the money, but I didn't want him to think I was a soft touch.

Suddenly Fontana jumped out from behind a side of beef that was hanging from the rail. His face is red and he began to yell: "You damned dirty kike," he screamed. "Are you trying to hustle me?"

I wondered if perhaps he'd been drinking. But I shrugged and tried for the high road. "You always give me the twenty back on Friday. It's Friday. Where is my money?"

"You people are all alike," he screamed. "A bunch of slimy Jews. Everybody knows you can't be trusted. You'd squeeze a nickel until the eagle screamed!"

Meanwhile, his boss, Lou Solomon, just stood there and said nothing while this anti-Semitic bastard attacked me—and all Jews. I was more horrified and shocked by Lou ignoring Larry's crazy behavior and not defending me. "Shut up, Fontana," I threatened. My English was getting much better and I understood everything he said. Still, I was trying to ignore his insulting slurs. But he didn't take my warning to stop there.

Fontana stepped toward me and began to threaten me physically, "It's too bad Hitler didn't snuff out every one of you mockies in Europe, and then come over here and finish the job."

That was it! He had gone too far. I grabbed the nearest knife and raised it over my head. "You *mamzer*, Fontana!" I swung the knife in the air and moved toward him. "You *should* know from Hitler, you bigot!" I yelled. By that time I was wielding the knife menacingly, and was more than ready to use it. Fontana ran out onto 14th Street. I raced after him with the knife in my hand, but he had ducked into a restaurant across the cobbled street.

Before I could cross the road, I was confronted by four members of the NYPD mounted patrol, seated high on their horses. I stopped short. One of the cops jumped off his horse. "Slow down, Buddy." He grabbed the knife out of my hand. "Okay, good. Now, what is going on?" By then the other three cops were also off their horses.

"Did you see that skinny little guy who dodged into the restaurant?" I sputtered, "I am going to kill him."

"Not today," said the biggest of the cops. The knife had blood on it from a carcass and I had blood on my apron. It didn't look good. "Why don't you tell us what's going on here?" he said calmly. "I wouldn't want to arrest you for carrying a deadly weapon." He whistled at the blood on the knife, to make his point. "That knife looks pretty deadly to me."

By then another cop had pulled Fontana out of the restaurant. They made us stand there like two little boys, while they admonished us both.

Thanks to the cops, I had cooled down a bit. I no longer had blood in my eyes and the intention to kill, but I was still blazing mad. I went back into Hygrade and raced up the stairs to the manager's office.

"Henry," my angry tone took him by surprise as I flung open the door. "Please have the bookkeeper draw up my final check."

"What's the matter, Sam?" *"Ask Lou."* I spat out the words.

Henry Heisner didn't know what to do. "Can't we talk about this? We don't want to lose you."

"You already have. I quit."

That was the day my life took a very different turn.

"I come from a people who gave the Ten Commandments to the world. Time has come to strengthen them by three additional ones, which we ought to adopt and commit ourselves to: thou shall not be a perpetrator; thou shall not be a victim; and thou shall never, but never, be a bystander."

— Yehuda Bauer (born April 6, 1926), Israeli historian and scholar of the Holocaust. He is a professor of Holocaust Studies at the Avraham Harman Institute of Contemporary Jewry at the Hebrew University of Jerusalem. Quote is from a speech to the German Bundestag, January 27, 1998.

16

The Rise of Master Purveyors

I was still hot under the collar when I stormed out of Hygrade, the final check Henry had reluctantly given me clutched in my hand. Thursday, August 16, 1957 was a blistering hot day. In my haste I ran smack dab into Nat Romanoff, who was standing on the corner. My thoughts were a bit muddled because I was so angry, but I had the presence of mind to stop when I saw Nat. It was a small area and everyone knew everyone. I quickly spotted an opportunity that I couldn't pass up.

"Hey, Red, what are you doing on the loose?" said Nat, a bit too cheerfully. "It ain't quitting time yet. S'matter, did Hygrade kick you out on your *tuches*?"

"No, in fact I walked out. Got the last paycheck I will ever get working for someone else." I waved the check in Nat's face, and told him what had happened at Hygrade. Then I slipped the check into my billfold. "From now on, I am going to be my own boss."

"Good on you, Sammy. That is the only way to go," said Nat. I could tell my story had won his sympathy. "How can I help?"

"You wouldn't happen to have a cooler I could rent?" I asked boldly. Nat, who was originally in the meat business, had come to New York from Russia in the 1930s. He'd gone on to invest in properties in the meatpacking district during the war, and by the 1950s Nat owned half of the properties in the district.

"Yeah, Red," Nat clinched a cigar between his teeth, "I think I can set you up. If you have a moment, come with me."

"I have all the time in the world," I replied, as I noticed the sunlight glinting off his bald head. It was so hot that day that steam was coming up from the old cobblestones. A really scorching New York day is not always so pleasant, especially when combined with the smells coming from the butcheries, but I felt liberated as I walked with Nat to a near-by location at 841 Washington Street. He pulled out a thick keyring heavy with assorted keys. After he fumbled a bit to find the right key, he opened the door to a small meat cooler. With a touch of pride, he pushed the door open and flipped on the light switch so I could get a good look. "Well, Red," he asked, "what do you think?"

"I think it looks far too big for me, Nat. I don't have any product right now. Or any customers."

"Ya' think so?" Nat spoke with his cigar between his teeth, which only further muffled his Russian accent. But when it came to accents I was no one to talk. "Here's the deal," he said. "I am willing to rent this cooler to you. It only has three rails, so it should be perfect for starting out. Are you interested? I can give it to you for $175 a month."

"I dunno, Nat," I replied, "it seems like a lot." I had some money put aside, but I wanted it to last while I started my new venture.

"Here's my best offer, kid. I know you just got married and all. I will give you this cooler and you don't pay me no rent for six months. Then, once you're up and running, you can pay me the back rent. It's a good offer."

It certainly is, I thought, but I was also wondering what Rose would say. Before, I only spoke for myself—now it was different. This was a new kind of thinking for me, since I'd been on my own for so long.

"All you have to do," said Nat, "is put up a hundred bucks as a deposit for the refrigeration. It's one of the rules of the market. And if you don't have it, I will put it up for you. I can't do better than that."

"Sounds good." I was at war with myself. "Can I think about it over the weekend?"

"Listen, I have five guys after me for this one cooler. It's hard to find one this size. You can't take no time to dither. And you can stick it in the eye of those schmucks at Hygrade."

"Okay, okay, I'm in!" I could feel my heart racing. This was happening so fast. An hour before I was a flunky working for somebody else. "Let's sign the paperwork tomorrow morning, and I can open up right away."

Nat's creased face broke out into a broad grin. "You're doing the right thing. We have to stick together. I came here with nothing, and now I am doing great. Just bought a three bedroom house on the island." I knew he meant Long Island.

"Sounds good," I said again, my excitement increasing, but still tinged with doubt. Could I pull this off? What would Rose think?

"Listen here, Red," Nat growled good-naturedly. "I wouldn't cut you such a swell deal if I didn't think you had the stuff. I have some idea of what you went through in the war. Many of my relatives suffered as well." He shook his head sympathetically, "Stick with me and you'll die a rich man."

"From your mouth to God's ears," I said, while I wrote out a check to put a deposit on the refrigeration and secure the small cooler. *At least*, I thought, *I don't have to worry about rent for the next six months.* Now all I had to worry about was buying stock and finding customers. But I already had a good idea of how I would accomplish both.

When I got home I began to explain my vision for the business to Rose. She could not have been more supportive and encouraging.

Rose knew I had some savings but she did not know the details. "Listen, Rosie," I informed her. "I have $12,500 put aside in the bank. I'm going to give you $6,500 to set up the house—go buy furniture, rugs, anything you want. I'm going to use the other $6,000 to get started on Washington Street. Is that fair?" She nodded, surprised and excited. She also offered to help me in any way necessary. Again I thought how lucky I was to have such a smart and supportive life partner.

****

The next morning I couldn't wait to get to the district. Nat kept a small office on West 13th Street and told me to meet him there. I was waiting on the curb before he opened. As soon as he unlocked the door he handed me a little stack of papers, which held my future. It was my lease to the cooler, and other documents that made it legal to do business in New York City. I was now the proprietor of a brand new business. Friday, August 16, 1957, as it turned out, was a pretty momentous day for me.

Nat, who was not a pushover by anybody's standards, seemed genuinely pleased that he could help me. He handed me a set of keys for the cooler, and also for a little office around the corner on West 12th Street that he said went with it—at no extra cost! The bare bones office did have a battered desk and a chair, but I didn't have a working telephone, or an order book. There was a lot to do, to say the least.

When I met Rose she was working at a publishing company, and still was. She did promise to come in and help me whenever she could, but I needed a right hand person right away to get me set up. Nat could see that I needed help, so he offered the services of his secretary, Judy, to help with some tasks. Judy's first job was to call Bell Telephone for me. An installer was there that same day. The efficient Judy also brought over some basic office supplies: pens, pencils, and notepads, plus an Order Book, "Now, I want to see that Order Book filled up in no time flat," Judy said, as she dropped off the stuff. She gave me a big smile and a wink. "Sam," she said quietly. "Nat wasn't fooling when he said that this cooler was in demand. He wouldn't do this for just everybody, I can tell you."

"Okay, thanks, Judy!" I said, deeply appreciative but still concerned. Now that I had actual rights to the cooler, it hit me hard what a massive commitment I had made. *But Sam*, I told myself, *you have always had confidence in yourself. Didn't you survive the horrors in Europe, against the odds? Why not take that same positive attitude into business?* Telling myself this made me feel a lot better about my prospects. Still, it was all ahead of me. Time would tell. No matter what, I was determined to control my own destiny and never again work for anyone else.

"Let me know if you need anything else, Sam!" Judy said brightly, as she left. "You know where to find me. And have a great weekend!"

I wasn't going to wait for the weekend. I had good relationships with some of the Hygrade customers, so I began making calls immediately. I told them there was a new wholesaler in business—me—who would make them better deals and offer better quality meat. Many of them were loyal to Hygrade and initially were annoyed that I called. But when I told them what happened, and explained that no one at Hygrade took my part, I quickly won over most of them. No one understood why the other Jews at Hygrade hadn't stood up for me, and further, why they hadn't kicked that anti-Semitic bastard out on his backside.

After making a list of possible clients, and calling those I thought seemed promising, I began knocking on doors of the best restaurants, hotels and clubs in town. I knew that calling on them in person could help me win them over.

I also had to find suppliers who had the stock I needed to build up a business. One thing I'd learned at Hygrade was that if a customer needed a certain cut and you didn't have it they would quickly move on to someone else. People in New York were, and still are, very picky, and the competition is always fierce. I had to be on my toes, for sure. I was good at that so I wasn't too worried. Once you've lost everything you have a high tolerance for risk. I'd been to the bottom so many times that I did not fear failure—or so I told myself. Compared to my previous life, I now had a new business, a new home and a new wife. I was living in luxury.

Later that day, a lawyer, Artie Schwartz, stopped by, also sent to me by my new guardian angel Nat. Artie said I needed to sign some more papers. While he was waiting he asked the BIG question: "Sam, you gotta have a name for this business. It's called a DBA, 'Doing Business As.' What are you gonna call this place?"

Given it some thought had not been on the top of my list but I had one idea. "I was thinking *Meister*," I said. "That's the German word for Master."

"I know what it means," said Artie, who could be a bit rough, "But, Pal, you're in America now. You've got to have an American name."

"How about Master?" I ventured, uncertainly. "Good." Artie scratched his head thoughtfully. "But not enough. You need something else. You sell stuff, right?"

"Yeah, Artie. So what else do we need?"

"How about adding the word purveyors?" Artie looked pleased with himself, using that fancy word.

"What does that mean, Purveyors?"

"It's just a jumped-up word that means you sell stuff, but it has a quality ring to it, don't you think?" Without waiting, he said, "From now on you're doing business as Master Purveyors, Inc. Okay, Sam?"

"Okay! I like it. Master Purveyors! Sure. It has class."

****

I was now officially the owner of Master Purveyors, and the very next day I went to pay calls on some of Hygrade's best customers. When they heard my story no one turned me down. Everyone gave me business right off the bat. Some gave me a piece of their business and others gave me *all* of their business. Having worked at Hygrade I knew how the company operated, which gave me an advantage. Since I had almost no overhead I was able to undercut their prices. Simple as that. When I went to see Bill Glickstein, who was the proprietor of McGinnis restaurant, Bill gave me all of his business right away because I gave him a better deal than Hygrade.

Bill was a great guy. He owned the popular, Irish sounding family-style restaurant on the bustling corner of 48th and Broadway, and also the building that housed it. McGinnis, which started in Sheepshead Bay, Brooklyn, was now located in the heart of the Times Square area, across from the famous Lindy's. It was patronized by plenty of tourists, and also by locals looking for inexpensive yet tasty meals. In short McGinnis was a very busy restaurant with a high turnover. Bill was known as The Roast Beef King, and sold sliced rare roast beef on a roll for 45 Cents. Can you believe it? That was good news for me because it meant that he bought lots of meat every week. Once I got that account going it amounted to six to seven thousand dollars in business each week. Getting the McGinnis account was a big break for me.

Now I had to have something to sell, and for that I had to find a supplier. To fill an empty cooler with three rails I needed about 40 sides of beef. Each of my three big rails held about 12 to 13 sides of beef. From my days in Newark I knew that Max Rosenberg ran the most efficient slaughterhouse in Jersey. Amazingly, both Max and his son Joel were survivors of Auschwitz. When they made it to America they went back into the business. I knew who Max was because he had been a good friend of my father's, and before the war ran the best slaughterhouse in Europe. Max was a master at the business. He could look at an animal and tell you how much it weighed within five pounds, and he was never wrong. He could also tell a quality animal, and predict which ones would produce the best cuts.

Naturally, right after I took the leap into my own business I contacted Max and Joel. They asked me to come to their slaughterhouse, where they processed about five hundred fifty head of cattle every day. They wanted to make a plan. When I told them what I intended to do, both of them laughed and clapped me on the back.

"My old friend Saul's little boy, becoming a wholesale meat dealer!" said Max, in a booming voice. "Sam, you have come far since you were smuggling supplies into the Bialystok Ghetto. Your father would be proud." He beamed with his own kind of pride. It was rare that this happened, and I was always overjoyed to connect with someone who knew my father or mother before the horrors. The fact that Max spoke for my father gave me a feeling of contentment.

Then and there we made a deal. Each day Max always gave me first pick of their animals, so I got the best animals that even their top customers couldn't get. Max didn't come right out and say it, but I knew that he felt we survivors of Nazi brutality should help each other in our new

213

lives. Max knew I was just starting out, so he also delivered the best car-casses without demanding payment, or even asking when I would send a check. In turn, I would help them out if they were a little short.

I could give you many instances where we survivors stuck togeth-er, to help bring success to each other. As they often say, it's not what you know, it's who you know, and connections have definitely made an enormous difference in the growth of my business.

Besides beef, I needed to find the best sources for veal, lamb and poultry, which were also always in high demand. In those days every-one ate meat at least two and sometimes even three times a day. In the early days I bought hot dogs and sausages that were ready made, and would mark them up and sell them to customers. I knew that if I carried a wider variety of products I was more likely to get business, because it made life simpler for my customers.

Once I had a business name and a couple of customers, Judy, who was still helping me out, ordered some business cards and business stationary. She even had someone design a little logo for me. I rented a truck from Olympia Trucking and hired one driver, Joe Carter. I cut the meat to fill the orders, and Joe made all the deliveries. Once he finished his deliveries for the day, I taught him to cut meat. That way he could also help me break down the carcasses, turning them into steaks, chops and ground steak.

One day, after I'd been in business for six months and had done well enough to pay Nat the back rent, Lou Solomon showed up at the cooler, and my jaw dropped. Hygrade was just around the corner, so everyone knew I was there. Still, I was very surprised that Lou had the chutzpah to show up at my place of business. He stood by the door looking very nervous. I was busy cutting up some steaks. When I heard him clear his throat I looked up with a combination of shock and anger on my face.

"Yeah, Mr. Solomon, can't you see I'm busy. What do you want?"

"Sam," he said almost in a whisper. "I don't know what to say."

Lou took off his cap and held it in his hands, looking rather pathetic. "I came to apologize, Sam. But I don't feel that there is anything I can say that will make it right."

"All I can say to you, Lou, is that low-life Larry is still at the company, and nobody did anything to stop him. I could have killed him that day. You're lucky I didn't."

"I have no power to fire that idiot. You know Hygrade's a big company. I don't have any say-so."

"Nobody gets why Jews like you didn't have my back. You're a turncoat to our people."

I could see that the blunt truth of my words upset him. "I have no excuse," he began. "What happened that day was very wrong. But I hear you're doing okay now."

"I'm not going to work for anybody else ever again. I am the boss here, and when I have kids one day they are also going to be part of my business."

"That's good, Sam. Every man should be his own boss," Lou looked careworn, and I was getting a bit less angry as our conversation wore on.

"Why aren't you at Hygrade now?" I asked, "It's still working hours, by my clock."

"They let me go, Sam. That bastard Henry just told me. They think I'm too old, but I am not too old."

"How old are you, anyway, Solomon?" I really had no idea.

"I'm seventy-two, Sam. But even at seventy-two, I gotta eat and keep a roof over my head. I don't have much savings."

"Sorry, Solomon. But what's that got to do with me?" I started to turn back to my butchering, clearly dismissing him.

After a long pause, Lou finally got to the point of his sudden visit. "I was thinking that perhaps we could partner up. I got a lot of contacts in the business, and I could bring new business in. Big new business!"

I didn't answer for a long time, making him twist in the wind. Finally I said curtly, "Sorry, Solomon, I can't afford you. I am a two-man operation here." I knew Lou was proud and he wouldn't beg, but I

215

also smelled desperation on him. He must have been desperate, or he wouldn't have swallowed his pride and come round to see me. After all, he waited over six months to make his big apology.

I had said my piece, but Lou would not give up. He began to spout a long list of top New York restaurants, steak houses, hotels and clubs where he had connections with the exact people responsible for ordering their provisions. I must say his list was tempting.

"Here's what I'm offering," Lou said, anxiously: "I bring in business and you pay me out of the profits from what I bring in. It's a straight-up business deal, not charity."

I put down my knife and wiped my hands on my apron. "Okay, Lou," I said. "We'll give it a try. What exactly do you need?"

"My rent is a thousand dollars a month. If I don't make my rent, I get kicked out of my apartment."

"Here's what I'll do. I'll pay you the thousand a week. You bring me business, and we'll see how it goes."

The following Monday Lou started to work for me. He was a model employee—on time and very efficient. He also made good on his boast. The first week he was on my payroll he brought in thirty thousand dollars in orders from gold star clients like the Plaza Hotel, the 21 Club, Luchow's and the Algonquin Hotel, to name a few. Needless to say I was impressed, and began to see that this was not a bad deal. I have to admit that I had initially taken a bit of pity on him. I was twenty-nine and he was many years my senior. I didn't really believe he could bring in what he did, or as fast as he did. Sometimes life offers you good surprises. They don't always make up for the bad ones, but they sure are welcome.

Once we got rolling, we had a good thing going. And we took turns: when I was making business calls, Lou was at the cooler cutting and filling orders. When he was calling on customers I was busy on Washington Street. For a year and a half it was smooth sailing. Then one night, to impress Rose on how well I was doing, I took her to one of the top hotels for dinner. The hotel was among my best customers and they were treating us like royalty. We were having a great time—until the chef, a French guy, suddenly came out of the kitchen and appeared at our table.

Rose and I were both startled when he demanded to know where his fifty dollars was—his "cigar money" as he called it. When I asked him what in the world he was talking about, he explained that each month when he put in his order Mr. Solomon gave him the cash to "buy cigars on me." He was making a scene, so I gave him the fifty dollars to quiet him. I was very angry that Lou was handing out bribes in return for business. I was also sure that he was not using his own funds but probably taking the money out of the business, which I later learned was correct. He had padded the petty cash so that the book-keeper wouldn't suspect anything and call it to my attention.

When Lou came in that Monday, I pulled him aside. "What do you mean, handing out money to customers? That's bribery," I whispered, and told him about the chef. "We don't do that here."

"I don't have to answer to you," Lou said in a belligerent tone, shocking me with his unexpected response.

"You do if you work for me. You are handing out money as kick-backs. It is my money you are using for an illegal purpose. So Mr. Lou Solomon, you *do* have to answer to me."

"Who the hell are you to question me? I could be your grandfa-ther," he said angrily.

"We do not do business that way, Solomon." I was blazing mad. I went over to the intercom and called to my bookkeeper, whose desk was around the corner from where we were standing. "Rudy," I said, so that everyone could hear. "Please make out a *final* check for Mr. Solomon. One thousand dollars, so that he can make his rent for this month."

That was the end of Mr. Solomon and me.

****

That's the way I run my business and that's the way I run my life. At the swanky hotel, the very moment I discovered what was going on,

217

I made up my mind that Lou Solomon had to go. But also, in fairness, I wanted to first hear what he had to say for himself. When he didn't have a good answer for me and, in fact got nasty and defensive, that was that. I could only assume he'd been playing games with *all* my customers, and none of that was okay with me.

Early on I established some rules, and I've lived by those rules ever since. First, I wouldn't put up with any shenanigans from employees. Lou was the first guy I fired for double-dealing, but unfortunately he wouldn't be the last. Nothing makes me madder than someone trying to cheat me, take me for a fool, or do anything that would make us look bad to customers, because reputation is everything.

The wholesale meat business is tough, competitive and certainly not for sissies. A predator could come from any direction at any time, so I always keep my eyes open. Like any business, it hasn't been all smooth sailing.

****

Master Purveyors has faced many challenges over the years. One of my biggest trials showed up in the late sixties. That was when the New York and New Jersey crime families tried to muscle in on the meat business by controlling access to livestock in New Jersey and other places. In those days I had taken in a partner, Harry Schragenheim, who came from a family of well-known German Jewish butchers. Harry and I were successful partners for ten years, but eventually I bought him out.

At that time, word was going around the market that some Mafia goons had been shaking down other industry dealers for money, claiming that we needed them. Most days I had lunch with some of the other owners at Frank's Steak House on West 14th Street. Frank's had been there forever, and it was a regular gossip mill. Over lunch I'd heard about the mob intimidation, but so far no one had bothered me or Harry. That is, until one afternoon, when this hood pushed his way into my cooler. He was carrying a valise stuffed with cash. He opened it to flash the contents. It clearly contained many thousands of dollars in hundred dollar bills.

"Who the hell are you?" I said, "And what are you doing in my shop? Take your dirty money and get out."

"Keep your shirt on, fella! As you can see, I got a lot of cash here. You can have it if you play ball with us. We want a piece of your business. We are in business together now."

"I don't need your dirty money. And I don't *play ball* with anyone. Get lost before I call the precinct!"

The guy looked furious and more than a little stupid, but he closed his valise and left. Very early the next day, however, when I tried to open up, my keys wouldn't work. I couldn't open my door. I called a locksmith. It turned out that one of our crime family "neighbors" had stuffed wooden matches in my lock. If they thought that a few matchsticks were going to deter me from doing business, they were badly mistaken.

I'd heard rumors that they had been messing with other meat dealers in the district. Vandalism and threats seemed to be the order of the day, so I wasn't entirely surprised when I arrived one morning to find that some arsonists had gone to my office and set fire to the front door. Even before I got to the office I could smell the smoky dampness of charred wood. At first I wasn't sure where it was coming from, but I was furious when I saw that my shop was the target. There were only a few fragments of blackened wood hanging from the old hinges.

It appeared that nobody had actually broken in, but this time I didn't waste a second. I called the cops of the 6th Precinct, on West 10th Street, which covers nearby Greenwich Village as well as the meatpacking district. The cops were on top of the mob, of course, because they were a scourge in lower Manhattan, and had tried to squeeze all sorts of businesses for protection money. To my shock, when Officer Murray and his partner showed up on Washington Street and looked around, they just kept shaking their heads.

"Sorry, Mr. Solasz, we can't do much here."

"But…but…" I said, at a loss for words. If the police couldn't do anything against the mob, who could?

The officer understood my chagrin, but he was adamant that the police were powerless. "I'd bet you a tenner that this is the work of 'Slippery' Louie D'Buono and his crew. They hang out at the Sons of Sicily Social Club on Mulberry Street. This has all the earmarks of Slippery, for sure. But, they're pros, Mr. Solasz, and cover their tracks well. Without more to go on, I'm sorry but there is nothing more we can do right now. I will call the Fire Department's arson squad, and maybe they can dig up more clues."

I was getting pretty aggravated, but Officer Murray calmed me down. "Look here. Mr. S. I know that they violated your property, and that stinks, but these bastards will stop at nothing. The next time they could go after you or your workers. They are murdering thugs. My best advice is keep your head down. Call your insurance company and get the door fixed ASAP. You need to get fireproof doors installed as a precaution."

"Okay, okay," I said, but I was certainly not satisfied that the police couldn't do anything more.

"Here's what you *can* do," the officer offered before they took off. "I've made a report of the vandalism, but it doesn't look like anything was taken. Keep your eyes and ears open. Canvas the other meat guys; see what you can learn. We'll 'beef' up our patrols," he chuckled at his terrible pun, "to let Slippery and the boys know that we're watching them."

As the cops promised, the arson investigators showed up later that day. All they could tell me was what I had already guessed. Someone had liberally sprinkled lighter fluid on my door, lit a match and ran for it. They told me that I was very very lucky that the fire wasn't worse, and repeated what the cop had told me. It was a live and learn situation, but those hoodlums were child's play compared to the Gestapo, so I wasn't too fazed.

Not long after that there was a general strike of the meatpackers and delivery drivers, who belonged to Local 342—the same union that controlled the market. When the strike hit, everything came to a complete standstill. No new meat was coming in, and we had no way to get existing orders out to our customers. One warm day, one of these mobsters stopped me on the street. "You gotta play ball with us now, huh?"

"No way, no how. Beat it before I get really mad," I said in my most menacing tone.

"Yeh? How you gonna get your meat delivered to all those fancy restaurants? We've got ways to deliver the goods for you—for a small percentage of the take, of course."

"Scram! I can manage."

Manage I did, but it was far from relaxing. For the next several days I loaded up my convertible and made the deliveries myself. On one of those runs, two highly suspicious cars followed me to my uptown customers. The way they were driving, they were clearly trying to run me off the road. So I put my pedal to the metal, and deliberately sped through three red lights, hoping a cop car might spot me. Unfortunately there were no cops around, but I lost the hoods that were following me anyway, and got the meat to my clients.

Another time, Harry took on the task—in the middle of the night—loading up a different vehicle and delivering our meat. We did have to go to some lengths to make our deliveries. At its peak in the fifties there were over two hundred meat packers in our district, employing 3,000 butchers, so the competition was fierce. But in my head I was still the Malach, and nothing was going to stop me from "getting through." Now, of course, it was no longer a matter of life and death. Outstanding service was one of the hallmarks that set Master Purveyors apart, and I wasn't about to disappoint any of my customers. Thankfully, after ten days the strike ended, and things went back to normal.

One day, sometime later, another Mafioso paid me an unexpected visit. Bold as brass, he came into my shop and said: "So, it's about time you changed your mind. We're not going to go away. You can't get rid of us that easily, and you need the protection. Otherwise, bad things can keep happening to you and your business, even your family out there in Queens."

That was a threat that pushed me too far. I went red in the face and grabbed the nearest weapon, which happened to be a machete, wielding it to cut through air. Then I ran at this guy, screaming: "Why should I kill myself, working so hard, and let you no-goodniks take it away from me? Get out of my face, and never come back."

The Mafia guy screamed: "You are a lunatic!" as he raced though the midday crowds on Washington Street trying to escape me. Unlike the time I ran after that louse Larry Fontana, this time I put down my machete and went back to filling an order. Interestingly, that was the last time anyone from Mulberry Street ever darkened the door of Master Purveyors.

****

I always made quick decisions. I learned that from the Holocaust days. There was never time to deliberate or think "Should I do this or should I do that" when a bayonet was pointed at me or a Gestapo guard in jackboots was running after me. I had to be quick to survive. When I made up my mind to go into business, even with some concerns, I still did it right away. Also, when hiring or firing, it was always an on-the-spot sort of thing. Even when I met Rose, as I said before, I knew right away she was for me.

I do business the way it was done in Europe, by a handshake. In America everyone has to have contracts and all sorts of paperwork. Hygrade was a big company. They did everything by the book. That wasn't for me. When I ordered meat from the slaughterhouses I never signed a thing. They sent me their products with the understanding that my word was good enough. I did that with my own customers too. There's an old expression: a gentleman's agreement. I paid on time and was paid on time. My no-system system worked. Everyone knew they could count on Sam. It sounds old fashioned today, but that's the way I did it. Also, I never break a promise. Once I make a commitment I stick with it. That way our customers know they can rely on me. With these ideas I built really strong relationships with my customers. I've been doing business with some of them for fifty, or even, with some, nearly sixty years now.

As I said, reputation is everything. Once someone starts to bad-mouth you, even if what they say isn't true, it poisons the well. Word travels fast, especially bad words, and other people start to doubt you, so I make sure my reputation is the best. I watch out for the quality of my products as well. From day one I knew that I had to deliver the best possible products to my customers. If you want to deal with top restaurants that have high reputations and charge high prices, you have to give them the best or you will fail. I have always made sure that my customers get the best product at fair prices. That is a winning formula, and I have never deviated from it.

When I opened on Washington Street, there were dozens of other meat wholesalers in one small area. Most of them were there years ahead of me. I knew that to rise above the others I would have to do something special. From the very beginning, I had the intention to create a very big business. As a kid I saw how hard my father worked to feed his large family. I knew I could work just as hard, but with the idea of becoming a major business one day. This wasn't Europe where you were locked into a certain position in life. If I'd wanted to have a small enterprise I would have opened a butcher shop in Brooklyn or Queens, where in those days there were dozens of small butcher shops. The minute I opened up on Washington Street I was playing for the big time. I knew I was a hustler. I'd learned that in Bialystok the hard way. *So*, I asked myself, *Why not hustle big time in New York? With no Nazis chasing me, I should do a lot better.*

"There is no answer to Auschwitz...To try to answer is to commit a supreme blasphemy. Israel enables us to bear the agony of Auschwitz without radical despair, to sense a ray of God's radiance in the jungles of history."

—Abraham Joshua Heschel (1907–1972), Polish-born American Rabbi and one of the leading Jewish theologians and Jewish philosophers of the 20th century. Quoted in An Echo of Eternity.

17

Poland: A Complicated Homecoming
Universal Truths Born of Unspeakable Horrors

Collecting a paycheck, no matter how hard you work for it, is very different from being the boss and trying to run a business. When you own a company you are responsible on every level. It really tests a person to have that responsibility. My first year was especially difficult.

When I worked for a big company, I was a butcher. That's it. Cutting meat day in and day out is difficult work. It takes a lot of strength. At the end of the week, when you're exhausted, you take your check and go home. In contrast, having your own business is a 24-hour, 7 days a week job. You are a salesman, purchaser, planner, deliveryman, a hirer and firer, and a thousand other things. No one at Hygrade trained me to be a business guy. I trained myself as a kid in the Bialystok Ghetto. I was always doing deals, satisfying my customers, swapping, trading, bargaining and negotiating. Back then of course, we were all just struggling for survival. It was a brutal training ground, but I did learn many lessons on which I have built my life, my family, and whatever success I have achieved in the world over the past 89 years. One thing that has helped me the most: I always had faith in my abilities. I did certainly learn that in the ghetto, where I was completely on my own at age 13.

By the end of first few weeks of owning Master Purveyors I was doing $25,000 a week in business. Within three or four months that amount of business had grown to $50,000 a week. By the end of the year I was grossing between $80,000 and $100,000 a week. Not a bad showing, considering that I started with an empty cooler, empty rails and no customers! In those days the average annual income for a family of four was $4,650. A typical tract house cost $30,000. A gallon of gas was 24 cents. A loaf of bread cost 19 cents, and I gave Uncle Sam 4 cents to send a letter. So grossing up to $100,000 a week was a lot of money in 1958.

At first I gave myself $50 a week to put into the bank. In time I made it $250 a week, and as the business grew what I put aside for myself became $500 a week. I held onto everything I could to invest in the future. I knew that if I wanted to grow my business I had to put money back in, and that meant saving every penny I could, after I made sure that I was providing for my family. Another reason for keeping the majority of the business money in my checking account was that I paid faster than my competitors. That was a large part of the reason I could get the very best meat to offer my customers. Nobody who did business with me ever had to worry about getting paid in a timely fashion. I will say that for the first six months I was in business we lived mainly on Rose's salary of $58 a week from the publishing house, where she was secretary to the boss. But when the business took off I said, "Enough. Quit your job." And she did.

When I opened on Washington Street, the minimum wage was $1.60 an hour, which seems unthinkable now. But I have always been good to my dependable employees. They put in a hard day for me and I paid them well. Trust me, it is no joke hoisting quarters of steer, which weigh between 220 and 250 pounds. As I said, when I started out, I had the one employee, Joe, who both delivered orders and cut meat. By 1960, after three years on my own, I had six employees, and was bringing in a solid $100,000 or more a week in business. When I find an employee who is really committed to the company, they can come to me if they need a loan—which they often do, and they always pay me back. I have paid for weddings and medical bills over the years. I have even posted bail for workers who were in a jam. There is something new happening every day.

After several years on Washington Street, our products were in such high demand, and we had so many prestige clients—Peter Luger, Smith & Wollensky, and the 21 Club among others—that we needed to expand. Luckily, by that time I was able to buy out another company, Old Bohemian, and we moved around the corner to 452 W. 13th Street, where we then had 20,000 sq. ft. of space.

However, by the late 1990s, the meatpacking district was fast becoming a "scene" for the trendy set. As the old meat companies faded away, bars, clubs, and boutiques began opening up. So in the spring of 2001, after 44 years in the Gansevoort market, we packed up and moved to Unit B14 in the Hunts Point Market, Bronx, New York, where we had double the space: 40,000 sq. ft. Today we have a total of 300 sides of beef hanging on numerous rails, 3 trailers, and 30 refrigerated trucks that fan out in every direction to deliver meat to our customers. Each day about 70,000 pounds of beef come into the shop, which adds up to about 500,000 pounds of beef every week. Needless to say, the operation is much bigger than I could ever have imagined when I first set up shop in 1957. But in truth I always thought big—and the bigger you dream, the better chance you have for your dream to come true.

Best of all, to me, is that what I told Lou all those years ago has come to pass. I blurted out that when I had kids they would come into the business one day. Of course I didn't have kids then. But then we had our first child, Diane, followed by sons Scott and Mark. Scott came into the business after one year in college and has been with me almost 40 years. Mark first went to law school, then successfully ran his own general practice law firm. I finally got him to join "the family business," and he has now been with me for 17 years.

The involvement of both my sons has enabled the business to continue to grow. These days we are even selling meat to Japan, as well as online. The boys do such a great job that they have made it possible for me to stay on top of things in areas where I can contribute the most, like dealing with customers, especially the long-time ones.

Diane chose medicine as a career and she's a wonderful optometrist with her own practice. About 18 years ago Diane's husband, Matt

Kudish, joined the company and quickly became an essential player, handling many key business matters. When I said my kids would come into the company, I didn't know how right I was. But they were born into the meat business, coming into the shop ever since they were little kids. In the old days, when Rose occasionally came in to help, she used to bring them in with her. Master Purveyors has always been a family enterprise.

****

For many years, I put my experiences in wartime Europe out of my mind. My life was settled, I was secure financially, my family was well raised. With the exceptional help of my wife Rose, my new life had grown into a mature and satisfying one. It embodied the American Dream of so many immigrants like myself who saw this country as a land of limitless possibilities and opportunities.

However, over time I began to think of the world I left behind—a world that was ripped away from me. As my kids were growing up they asked a lot of questions about my past. Sometimes their friends would be curious about my accent. Occasionally I would tell them a story, but I knew they did not really "get" it. My experiences were so far from their comfortable lives. Then my grandkids arrived, and eventually I was asked many more questions about our Jewishness, our roots, and the war. I didn't always want to address the pain, so I could be a bit indirect. However, I also felt, deep inside, that it was my duty to share at least *some* part of what I went through while I still could—at the least, with my extended family.

I had not been back to Poland since I left in 1945, and only back to Europe for a few months when I temporarily returned to the DP camp in Munich. For some reason I began to think more often about the night that the Bialystok temple burned, and all the death and desolation I had witnessed firsthand in that experience. On that singular night, the temple burned for hours and the stench of incinerated human flesh filled the air. How could I help my kids or grandkids to understand? I remembered the vow I made that night, so long ago, that if I could ever do anything to right those wrongs or bring any justice to those murdered souls, I would find a way. Over the years the day to day had absorbed my attention. Now might be the right time to resurrect my promise. But how?

The new world had been good to me, but Poland was my cradle. If it hadn't been for Hitler, I would most likely have lived there my whole life. I tried not to think about it. When you reflect on the toll one twisted man's drive for domination took in terms of human suffering, and, of course, the many followers who took up his bloody cause, the cost, all around, is beyond measure. When all is said and done, I'd made it out alive against tremendous odds. So I began to think about what I could do to pay tribute to my family, friends, neighbors, and other unfortunates who'd died that night. And not just that night, but also those who died throughout the course of World War Two. These souls were all part of the human family, while those who survived were all part of the great Jewish Diaspora.

****

Though I had not yet returned to Poland, still, from my first days in New York I never lost touch with my Bialystok roots. As it happens, there were and still are associations of Bialystoker *Landsleit* all over the world. In Yiddish, *Landsleit* means groups of Jews from the same city or town who stay connected even though they have spread out to many other places. Bialystok is a bond that keeps people glued together. Whether they are in England, Australia, Argentina or New York, they consider themselves "Bialystokers." To that end, they have created synagogues and Jewish aid societies that hold up the standard of Bialystoker values wherever they are in the world.

Long before I arrived on these shores, Bialystokers had settled on the Lower East Side of Manhattan. In 1826 some of them established a

Bialystoker Synagogue on Grand Street that is still active today. They also founded a wonderful Bialystoker Home for the Aged, which Rose and I supported for a long time. I was president of the Bialystoker Home for 16 years, did a lot of fundraising, and made personal contributions to maintain the home, which has since closed.

The Bialystok I thought about the most was my wretched, ugly experience of witnessing the Great Synagogue go up in flames. I knew I wanted to help call attention to what had happened there, and to honor those martyred souls who died such horrible deaths. Eventually, on a visit to Kiriat Yahud, Israel, I learned that there was an annual dedication at the site of the synagogue's burning. I also learned that there had never been any physical monument to those more than 2,000 plus souls who died there. I decided to travel to Poland from Israel to see for myself. One day, when we were back in New York, I said to Rose, "We are going to help fund a physical monument! I will set this in motion, and next summer you and I will go to Poland and attend the dedication of this memorial."

Rose was more than a little pleased. She knew I had not been back to Poland since I left there in 1945, and it was now 1994. Fifty years is a very long time. Rose herself had also never been to Poland. But she had often heard me swear that I would never go back to Poland. I still had nightmares. Was I sure? I had been through a lot, but so had all the many other Holocaust survivors. There is no shortage of amazing stories of survival. I don't feel all that special, only incredibly lucky. But, as I explained to Rose, besides going back for myself, I want to take our kids and grandkids. I felt they needed to know more about my story, and see for themselves the places that were myth to them and all too real to me.

When the Great Synagogue on Suraska Street had burned to the ground, the only fragments of the building that survived were the metal frames for the three cupolas of the wooden building. In a few hours, the rest of the building disintegrated into piles of ash and human remains. Much later, the street nearby became known as the "Street of the Ghetto Heroes." When I heard that the metal frames from the cupolas of the

Great Synagogue were its only surviving remnants, and that they apparently were still in or near Bialystok in various locations—damaged, but largely intact—I knew it was time to take action.

I'd heard that one metal frame was on a farm somewhere outside of the city, and I was determined to find it. I paid a local man in Bialystok to go from farm to farm in search of those cupola frames. Eventually he found the largest one on a farm not far from town, and I paid the farmer a thousand dollars to retrieve it and bring it back into the city. It had to be part of the memorial!

In August of 1995 Rose and I traveled to Bialystok and attended the dedication of the Memorial to the Great Synagogue. It was a big occasion, and I was greatly moved by the experience. Both priests and rabbis attended. Thousands of people came from all over the world, including grandchildren of those that were lost there. I had to fight back tears when I read the inscription on the newly installed memorial plaque. It reads: *"Our splendid sanctuary fell victim to the flames on June 27, 1941. 2,000 Jews were burnt alive in it by the German Nazi murderers."* Those words so perfectly evoked my terrifying memories that I had to step aside and compose myself.

Later we walked to the spot where five hundred men had been buried alive. Later still we went to the university, where we continued the memorials. I was even one of the speakers. After these dedications, so many people wanted to shake my hand and clap me on the back that I was a bit overwhelmed. It was deeply satisfying to participate in the dedication fifty-four years after I stood and watched the atrocity as a young teenager. That boy was long gone now, but his wounded heart still beats in my chest.

****

Once I found my way back to Poland, there were some other stops I felt compelled to make. One of them was to the Zaremba farmhouse, where I had masqueraded as a Christian to hide from the Nazis. The original farmer, Walter, Sr., and his wife, Yonka, were no longer alive, of course, and their son Walter, Jr. and his wife Regina had been running the place. Walter Jr. then died, and now his son Fronik—Frank in English—and his family were running it. It is still a working farm today, and a very successful one. At one point the old house had been in bad shape. It hadn't been the best quality to begin with and it was falling down from age. The son, Walter Jr., needed help rebuilding, so I had given him a nice contribution, since living with his family had saved my life. Today Walter Sr.'s grandson, Fronik, is living in a beautifully comfortable and remodeled modern farmhouse.

Before he died I did get to visit Walter Jr., the very same young man who hid in the barn with me and to whom I had gotten close—well, as close as I could, given my big secret. I told Walter Jr. my real story, that I was a young Jew from Knyszyn, hiding from the Nazis on his family farm, and not "Vonka," the kid who went to mass and took communion. I reported that his family always thought they were sheltering a Christian kid who didn't want to be sent to Germany to join the army or work in a factory. Walter Jr. said he and his parents never understood why I ran away without saying good-bye. I explained that the second the Russians liberated Bialystok I had desperately needed to get back to the city.

If I'd told them back in 1944 that I was a Jew, not just my life but all their lives would have been in grave danger. Walter understood. He joked that his parents said I was the best worker they ever had, and had been so sorry to lose me. Of course they had been curious about what happened to me, and whether I even survived the war. That I was alive after all this time came as a surprise to their surviving son and his family and friends, all of whom came around to meet me. It was wonderful to connect and close that loop. Interestingly, I think that, despite my explanation, on some level Walter Jr. still believed I was Christian. When I got up to leave he put his hand on my shoulder and said, "May Jesus Christ protect you and keep you safe always." Hey, it never hurts to be blessed. I know he meant well.

From that point on I have continued to visit the Zarembas whenever I return to Poland. I am always greeted warmly and invited to sit down to a huge meal. To this day I feel I owe that family a tremendous debt—one much greater than they ever knew, or I can ever repay.

Since I went back to Poland that first time in 1995 I have been going back every two years. On some occasions I have taken my entire family, other times the members of my family who are able to make it. By now they all have a better idea of where I came from and what their roots were, long before there was a Sam and Rose Solasz of Queens, New York. On one recent trip, in the summer of 2015, I went back to Knyszyn with several of my grandchildren. We stopped at City Hall to meet the Mayor, who told me that he knew a lot about me and my family. It was gratifying to know that my family was remembered after all this time. I was amazed to learn that the Mayor's father had told him stories about my father and grandfather. The Mayor told me that my father had been well liked and well respected by everyone in town. But then, when I told the Mayor that I needed to get a copy of my birth certificate—which I needed to apply for reparations, something I did not think it necessary to discuss with him—he looked surprised that I asked. "Don't you know, Mr. Solasz," he said, "that the Nazis destroyed all the papers of the Jews, and even of the Christians? The only documents that survived were the baptismal records from the Catholic Church."

"I came back to town to get proof of my birth," I told him, taking a deep breath to swallow my anger. "I was born Moishe Solasz here in Knyszyn on May 5, 1928, the youngest child of Saul and Esther Solasz. Do you need more than that to *create* a birth certificate for me?"

"Okay, okay! I have an idea," said the Mayor, "Please come with me." We moved to another room, and he called up two of the oldest people in the town and asked them to sign an affidavit stating that I was born in Knyszyn. These were people who had known my family. Frankly, I was surprised they were still alive. After they came in and did this, he called two people to sign as witnesses. *Ten* people showed up, all wanting to help. One woman, ninety-nine years-old, was especially eager to sign. It turned out that she had been an old girlfriend of my father's. I could hardly believe it.

Once we got the paperwork out of the way there was a lot of hugging and kissing. We even went to an apiary where they produce the most incredible honey, and the guy there said he knew me. In fact, he even remembered collecting pigeons with me when I was a boy. He gladly signed the affidavit. He didn't want me to leave, but finally we had to say good-bye. I left with a jar of honey.

When we went back to City Hall, I told the Mayor and other officials that I had something of interest to show them. Admittedly, they were curious. I asked my grandchildren to "hand me the list." It is a very valuable census, showing every Jewish-owned home in Knyszyn in 1929. The Mayor's eyes, and that of the other officials, nearly popped out of their heads when I showed them the list of all 1,300 houses owned by Jews, including the names of the owners, even listing all their children. All those houses had been taken from their rightful owners. At the time that I was liberated, a former Mayor thought I should have the Jewish census, so he gave it to me for safekeeping. I'd protected it all these years. My name was at the very bottom, because in 1929 I was only a few months old. When I pointed to my birth name, the Mayor was embarrassed, as he should have been.

The Mayor was shocked, and also bold enough to ask me if he could make a copy of the list for the city records, should any other Jews come to town looking for their birthright. The list was a valuable record and of course I let him copy it. But I did chastise him for giving me a hard time—questioning whether I was actually born in Knyszyn. Still, everything ended pleasantly enough. When I left they gave me gifts of baskets of fruit. I politely accepted, even though I didn't want them. As soon as I was in my car I tossed them out onto the side of the road.

One benefit of this visit is that it showed me I was still connected with people who knew me as a kid and knew my family. To have such ties—after so much upheaval, and after so many years—was really remarkable. It showed me that my life there was not just a blurred memory. Of course, these people were all Christians, since not a single Jew was left in Knyszyn. If it hadn't been for the Nazis, the Russians and all the rest I would most likely have lived out my entire life in that little town, like the people who signed the affidavit, and not have had the amazing life I've had. On the other hand, I would have had my parents and my large loving family. Today many young people get bored and restless in their small towns and emigrate to other parts of their country or the world. Perhaps I would have done that too. In any case I never had that choice.

****

I've now taken my children and grandchildren to Poland four times so that they could never forget the truth of my stories. I've explained the history and horrors I and millions of other Jews experienced during that time. We have also, as a family, made several trips to Treblinka and Auschwitz. I took them outside of Bialystok to see mass graves where 5,000 Bialystok women had been buried alive. When we were on that exact spot, I could see the expressions of shock and disbelief in their faces. I did not enjoy putting my loved ones through such pain, but I felt it was part of my mission to make these privileged American adults and kids understand, in a concrete way, what had happened to European Jewry.

Even now, the scope of such evil is difficult to comprehend. And, at the site of that mass grave, I was outraged to see that someone had erected a Christian cross instead of a Star of David to mark the place. If you didn't know the truth you'd think that all those women were Christians and not Jews. That was a lie, and I would not tolerate it. I hired a local attorney and sued the town to take down the symbol of Christianity and erect the Jewish Star. I was very happy to let the whole world know the real facts. It was Jewish women who were tortured and asphyxiated in a big hole in the ground. That was not the fate of Gentiles during the war. It took a year, but they made the change.

On a later trip, in 2011, I took fourteen family members to Poland. To take us around, I hired a local driver named Stefan. I told him what I needed and he got us a bus for 20 people. He told me it would cost $750 U.S. dollars a day. He took us anywhere we wanted to go for the full eleven days, even to Prague, the Czech Republic, in that beautiful state-of-the-art bus, owned by a Mr. Yukofski. On this trip I had become a regular tour guide. Unfortunately, the tour was not full of happy things.

When he took us into Knyszyn, Stefan pulled up in front of City Hall. "Why are you stopping here?" I asked, because I didn't want to waste time. In a couple of minutes, the Mayor came rushing out of the building to greet my family and me. The next thing I knew a hundred other people showed up, many of whom said they had known my family. Stefan's mother came and brought homemade ice cream because that was her business. She was excited to see us, hugged and kissed me, and didn't want to let go. The town was throwing a surprise party for the returning Solasz family. It was a great irony, I thought. Perhaps they were trying to assuage their collective guilt.

"How did they find out we were even here?" I asked Stefan, because I was puzzled. It turned out that he was related to someone we knew in New York, and that person tipped off the town that we were coming.

When it came time to pay the bill, I asked Stefan what I owed, and was surprised when he said his boss wanted him to only charge me $237 dollars per day. He said that because his boss's father and my father had been friends he only wanted to cover his costs. Later I met his boss. "You could charge me much more," I said, "and I would be happy to pay." "I am doing it for old time's sake," he insisted. "It is not every day that a local son returns, and the whole town is honored to meet you." He even gave us six bottles of vodka as a gift. Like the gift baskets I didn't really want their gifts, but no, I didn't throw the *vodka* out on the side of the road!

When we went to Bialystok, everyone made a fuss as well, including an ex-mayor named Rutkosky. He used to come to our hotel and hang out, just to be in our company. We have visited Bialystok several times now, and I can tell you that a beautiful city has risen from the rubble. Initially, when I was liberated and went back to Bialystok, the city was desolate, with nothing but piles of debris everywhere. Today it is a modern city with buildings that are sixteen stories high, which was unheard of before the war. They built a big beautiful opera house, and have six movie houses, plus lots of good restaurants and shops. It is a very different place today than it was in 1945, to say the least.

****

Of course I could not explain my life and roots to my family without also taking them to Israel. We have now been there many times, and I am so happy to see what Israel has become. When I first went there in 1948 as an illegal it was not much more than a few buildings in the desert. Boy has it changed! I owe allegiance to Israel because I believe in the nobility and justice of the cause. If it were not for the state of Israel Jews everywhere would be far more vulnerable than we are today. Every group must have a home base. Israel may be small in size, but not in accomplishment! And, vulnerable as she is, she is ours. I strongly believe that Israel, and what she stands for, offers a necessary refuge and protection for all Jews in this still deeply polarized world.

I was in the IDF, as I described earlier, and fought for the State of Israel. I am very proud of that. This little country in the heart of the Middle East is a bulwark protecting the rest of us, so I feel it is very important to show support for the Jewish state in every possible way. To me there is a direct link between Israel and the Jews who suffered in the Shoah. The persecution of the Jewish people in World War II greatly added to the impetus to establish Israel, with Judaism as the backbone of its value system. Even in 1948 this was actually not a new idea. A Jewish state had long been a dream of people like Theodor Herzl and Chaim Weizmann, who sought for many years to establish a

Zionist state. And of course there are thousands of connections to the Holocaust everywhere. There are now a great many European Jews who survived the Holocaust who emigrated to Israel. They helped to build the amazing country we know today.

An example is Dr. Sitron, the heart surgeon who was in the Treblinka-bound cattle car with me. He is the one who fixed the wound on my head. After I jumped out of the cattle car, I never saw him again. He wound up in Auschwitz, and survived. When he was liberated at the end of the war, he went to Israel and became a big heart surgeon there. He also wrote a book, published in Hebrew and Polish, in which he included a passage about my escape.

Dr. Sitron was one of the founders of Tel HaShomer, the biggest hospital in Israel. Tel HaShomer was founded as an Army hospital in 1948, and today it is part of Tel Aviv University and a wonderful teaching hospital for everyone. It is in the forefront of medical research and progress in Israel. The good doctor is gone now, but his son has taken over there. He is an esteemed cardiologist.

My family and I are very strong supporters of Israel. We do a lot of fundraising for various Israeli charities, as well as make personal donations. We have donated seven ambulances to Israel that now serve the needs of several hospitals. We also recently donated two three-wheel, high tech Ambucycles. Giving back is the least my wife, children and I feel that we can do.

I am proud to say that we are pretty well known in Israel. One thing I am especially proud of is that my name is in a video that keeps looping in a computer located in the basement of the Holocaust museum in Washington D.C. When I took my family there, I pointed out my name in the video, where I was described as an escapee. Part of the story is that after I jumped out of the cattle car bound for Treblinka—from which no one except me and the mother and child had ever successfully escaped before—Hitler's henchman, Adolph Eichmann, had gone looking for me and those two others, the woman, Itka and her small child, Asa. As I wrote, Itka was the one in the next car over who had

238

thrown her toddler out the window of the train, then she jumped, and a Nazi officer told her to grab her child and run.

****

Our daughter Diane had her bat mitzvah, and our sons Scott and Mark had their bar mitzvahs at the synagogue now called the Hollis Hills Bayside Jewish Center. When their children—my grandchildren—reached 13, they each also had bar or bat mitzvahs. Several times over the years Rose suggested that I might want to have one. As she jokingly said, "Sam, it is never too late to become a man." I thought I was man enough, but anyway I was always too busy, so I put it off.

One day, over our regular dinner at London Lennie's, in our old neighborhood of Rego Park, Rose put her foot down. "It is time, Sam. You're going to be eighty in a few months." That was how I found myself sitting in the Hollis Hills Jewish Center on a sunny Sabbath morning in May 2008, an 80 year old bar mitzvah boy, all dressed up in a new dark blue suit. The entire extended Solasz family was there to cheer Grandpa on. I squirmed a bit in my seat when the Rabbi introduced me to the congregation and announced that my bar mitzvah ceremony was about to take place. Everyone knew me, since we had been attending that synagogue for fifty years. I stood up, and the congregation started clapping.

During the ceremony my son Mark helped me out. He read my Haftorah and acted as "me" throughout, which we had gotten permission to do, since I had not been able to master the Hebrew prayers and verses of the Torah. Still, it certainly was a proud occasion for me, and made up quite a bit for something that had been lost in my young life.

As I sat in the quiet of the synagogue, I reflected on a beautiful Saturday on the 27th of June 1941 when I had reached my 13th birthday. On that day, instead of preparing for my bar mitzvah, I watched the grand and historic Great Synagogue of Bialystok go up in flames, heard the terrible screams, and witnessed how Nazi troops from Order

Police Battalion 309 threw firebombs into Jewish homes to force families out into the streets, so they could shoot them dead as they ran.

That day I was one of the fortunate ones. Not much later I would become "Malach"—the Angel of the Ghetto. Nazis would be looking for a red-headed kid named Moishe Solasz. He was lucky enough— and dare I say plucky enough—to become Sam Solasz.

I am glad they never found me, so I could tell you my story.

Author's Afterword

When I was young, I didn't believe that a bullet could rob you of your life, even though I witnessed death at the hands of Nazi guns almost every day. I think I just had the invincible attitude of youth. Plus, I was a listener. I listened to other people's experiences and watched the mistakes they made—then I put two and two together, to make sure I didn't make the same mistakes.

As painful as the Holocaust was, it taught me that I was a survivor. There were many times when I had nothing, yet I always found a way, and never gave up. In my life I am always optimistic about tomorrow. If you believe in tomorrow you keep going, keep enriching your life and your business. After my time in occupied Poland, I had nowhere to go but up.

There are many reasons why I am proud to be Jewish. Most of all I am proud of our culture of humanity and support for our friends, neighbors and strangers in need—despite all of the abuse and pain inflicted on us.

On my long-delayed Bar Mitzvah day, I thought of all the things I had to be thankful for. Now, with my 89th birthday just past, I have even more to celebrate. Life has taught me, in the hardest way, that every day matters; that every day gives us another opportunity to make life a little better for those we love, especially our children and children's children. Every day also gives us the privilege and obligation to remember and honor those who have fallen.

Every day gives us one thing more, and it's something priceless: another chance to be kinder to each other. The future of the most important family at large, the human family at large, depends on it.

Thank you for taking this journey with me.

"Now in the light of past and present events the bitter truth must be spoken. We feared too little and we hoped too much. We underestimated the bestiality of the enemy; we overestimated the humanity, the wisdom, the sense of justice of our friends."

—Chaim Weizmann (1874–1952), Zionist leader and Israeli statesman who served as President of the Zionist Organization and as first President of Israel from 1949 until his death. Quote is from his address to 22nd Zionist Congress, December 1946.

Acknowledgments

Thank you to our dear friend Sol Zim. He is a pioneer and an inspiration in the world of Jewish music and our beloved Cantor. As an outgrowth of his service as Cantor of the *Hollis Hills Jewish Center* (now *Hollis Hills Bayside Jewish Center*), and in recognition of his steadfast dedication to our community, Cantor Zim was awarded a lifetime contract as Cantor of our synagogue. In addition to Sol's passion for writing Jewish Music and his extraordinary contributions to Jewish music across the world, he is also dedicated to educating and teaching. Cantor Zim is Professor of Jewish Music at the *Academy For Jewish Religion* in Yonkers, N.Y. Sol Zim concertizes at Synagogues and Concert Halls throughout the world and also lectures extensively worldwide for other cantorial schools and is a frequent "Scholar/Composer in Residence" for many Jewish organizations and Synagogues, where he creates a lasting spark through his incredible energy and by spreading the love of Jewish music.

65729041R00140

Made in the USA
San Bernardino, CA
05 January 2018